CROSSING
&
CRUISING

CROSSING
&
CRUISING

*From the
Golden Era of Ocean
Liners to the
Luxury Cruise Ships
of Today*

JOHN MAXTONE-GRAHAM

CHARLES SCRIBNER'S SONS   NEW YORK

MAXWELL MACMILLAN CANADA   MAXWELL MACMILLAN INTERNATIONAL
TORONTO   NEW YORK OXFORD SINGAPORE SYDNEY

Charles Scribner's Sons
Macmillan Publishing Company
866 Third Avenue, New York, NY 10022

Maxwell Macmillan Canada, Inc.
1200 Eglinton Avenue East, Suite 200
Don Mills, Ontario M3C 3N1

Macmillan Publishing Company is part of the Maxwell Communication Group of Companies.

Library of Congress Cataloging-in-Publication Data
Maxtone-Graham, John.
    Crossing & cruising: from the golden era of ocean liners
to the luxury cruise ships of today / John Maxtone-Graham.
        p.   cm.
    Includes bibliographical references and index.
    ISBN 0-684-19154-7
    1. Ocean travel.   2. Ocean liners.   3. Cruise ships.
I. Title.   II. Title: Crossing and cruising.
G550.M219   1992
910.4'5—dc20   92-4131

Macmillan books are available at special discounts for bulk purchases for sales promotions, premiums, fund-raising, or educational use. For details, contact:

Special Sales Director
Macmillan Publishing Company
866 Third Avenue
New York, NY 10022

10 9 8 7 6 5 4 3 2

Printed in the United States of America

To the memory of a great
and good man,
Captain Alan Charles Bennell, RD*RNR, FBIM
late master of Queen Elizabeth 2,
this volume is respectfully
dedicated.

Contents

Preface

In two previous maritime books, I have delineated passenger ship-board from two separate seagoing eras. In 1972, *The Only Way to Cross* dealt with life on board North Atlantic liners, starting with the debut of Cunard's *Britannia* a century and a half ago. A dozen years later, I updated the subject with a companion volume about cruising's past and present called *Liners to the Sun*.

Loyal passenger-readers who enjoyed the original also embraced its sequel. I wrote *Liners to the Sun* because crusty North Atlantic devotees sometimes sneer at present-day cruising and I wanted to bring warm-water voyages into valid historical perspective. In both books, I purposely avoided numbers of rivets, numbers of eggs consumed, the weight of each anchor, and all that statistical trivia so dear to the ship-buff fraternity; rather, I did my best to answer the single, pervasive question that every satisfactory ship book must answer: What was it like on board?

Shipboard, in my experience, is shipboard, whether we endured the *Berengaria* heaving across an angry North Atlantic or glide peacefully on the *Sagafjord* over glittering seas off Bangkok. Present-day passengers are really no different from their predecessors, whatever their outward manifestation. Admittedly, we sometimes dress, talk, or amuse ourselves in ways that would doubtless have baffled or distressed our grandparents; but for the most part, at sea we behave just as they did.

In fact, the ships have changed far more than their cargo. Con-temporary profiles incorporate a relentless postmodernist look, and some of their interiors have metamorphosed from grand hotel to less grand mall. Service on a few might charitably be described as lacking finesse. Even management does its occasional best to sub-vert tradition: Upscale companies still insist on calling passengers "guests" and cabins "suites," and the president of Royal Caribbean Cruise Line (RCCL) recently announced that since passengers can enjoy so many activities on his vessels, he would henceforth eschew the word "cruise" altogether in favor of "vacation."

But regardless of this late-twentieth-century olla podrida, the way contemporary passengers acquit themselves at sea remains blessedly unchanged. The genus *Peregrinator americanus* flourishes. However the cruise lines have rewrought shipboard externals, traditional passenger dynamics exert their immutable sway. Whether embarked, as in the old days, to achieve the other side of an unsettled ocean or, like most contemporary passengers, dallying languidly around a bland island circuit, the tenor of shipboard life remains the same: on board ship, today is yesterday.

I hope that readers of *Crossing & Cruising* will be predisposed to share this conviction. My intention, as the title only too transparently suggests, is to bridge the gap between old and new, to link shipboard past with shipboard present within the covers of one volume—*The Only Way to Cross* and *Liners to the Sun*, if you will, conjoined.

Of course, mingling yesterday's purposeful crossings with today's indolent cruises may confuse or even antagonize adherents of one or the other. But that potential problem is easily solved. The chapters that follow have been systematically shuffled, like a deck of company playing cards on a smoking-room table. Crossing aficionados are advised to relish the odd-numbered chapters and skim (or skip) even-numbered ones. Conversely, cruise buffs should dwell on the evens while only perusing or ignoring the odds. Shipboard devotees like myself should feel free to enjoy both.

Hence, *Crossing & Cruising*: a look over the shoulder as well as a look over some of today's railings, remembrances from our North Atlantic past together with new thoughts on its warm-weather equivalent. Passenger shipboard is a richly diverse subject, and our preoccupation with yesterday's liners seems analogous to the current explosion—there is no other word—of cruise ships today. Over the past few years, I have sailed on several of them, especially the newer ones, and would like to share with my readers how companies are meeting—or evading—present-day passenger expectations.

The vast majority of their clients, incidentally, are American; Americans are pushovers for shipboard. Once immigration came to an end, Americans filled the liners between and after the wars as tourists. And when the liners stopped crossing in the mid-seventies, America went cruising instead. Americans continue to outnumber all other nationalities afloat.

Most of today's cruise ships are built, registered, and owned elsewhere—in Norway, France, Italy, Finland, Germany, and most recently, Japan. Regardless, their primary objective is the cruising American, *Peregrinator americanus*; millions embark annually.

Our most baffling technoindustrial irony is that American entrepreneurs and shipyards seem incapable of providing competitive tonnage to meet this inexhaustible demand, a task happily assumed by ubiquitous foreign-flag owners and builders. Though we suffer an eternal trade imbalance in everything from automobiles to television sets, we lead the world in exporting ships' passengers. Eighty percent of the world's cruise-ship clients are American.

But stay: *Crossing & Cruising* is intended as neither economic polemic nor nationalistic finger pointer. I care less about who builds or mans ships than, always, who books on them. Jan Morris, one of the world's great travel writers (a term she dislikes), once told me that she prefers not getting too involved with the places about which she writes so beautifully. Alas, I cannot agree, perhaps for a sound reason. The places about which I write are not fixed geographic entities but huge vehicles—mobile places, if you will—with which I have long been familiar and with which I seem to remain inextricably involved.

Rather than revisit cities, as Jan Morris does, my beloved ships revisit me, often unexpectedly; how captivating to be on board a vessel and sail by, anchor nearby, or berth alongside a vessel I knew intimately half a world away. My floating cities appear and disappear, either passing at sea or unveiled around promontory or pier shed. Mysteriously, they are there, and that evening, just as mysteriously, they are gone, leaving scarcely a trace. Once a vessel has sailed, no indication of her passage remains save a widening wake, a smudge of smoke, or an entrancing glitter of light along the horizon.

This volume, incidentally, though perfectly suitable for a library chair on a wet winter's night, is better suited to a deck chair, sheltered from subtropic glare or breeze of passage, to be dipped into at leisure after a good lunch, until the head nods and droops. *Crossing & Cruising* has been specially designed to collapse neatly at that moment onto a steamer-rugged lap, open at the page where it was relinquished, to be resumed after the arrival of the steward's tea tray. Bon voyage . . .

Acknowledgments

In preparing a book, there is always a host of people to thank for help and expertise.

For their assistance in preparation of the immigrant chapter, I am indebted to Arnold Kludas, colleague and director of Bremerhaven's Deutsches Schiffahrtsmuseum, David Williams of the Merseyside Museum in Liverpool, as well as fellow historians Edward de Groot and Robert Holdermans in Holland.

At Carnival Cruise Lines, Joe Farcus proved a patient as well as fascinating interviewee and Bob Dickinson a source of endless help. Special thanks, too, to Stephen Payne, Matthew Sams, Tim Gallagher, as well as Captains Lorenzo Calvillo and Giampaulo Casula.

Ann Davis Thomas, daughter of Arthur J. Davis of *Aquitania* fame, was most kind in providing details as well as photographs of her father's extraordinary career. Adding additional helpful input about the Cunarder were Norman Morse, final authority on all North Atlantic deck plans, Liverpudlian historian Kenneth Longbottom, Peggy Lovering, Richard Chafee, Everett E. Viez, and Peter Cowling of Mewès & Davis.

It was most kind of Bill Morris, Peter Spang, Cloty Hughes, Dr. Mary Jane Luke, and Hiroshi Anraku to share their *Stella Polaris* memories with me. Additionally, I am indebted to Walter Berg, now master of *Seabourn Pride*, as well as Captain Kjell Aasvik and Hotel Manager Volker Rollof of *Sea Goddess I* and Captain Tormod Hansen, First Officer Kaj Haagensen, and Chief Engineer Henry Staaeli of *Wind Spirit* for their unbounded enthusiasm. Special thanks are due Warren Titus for recalling early Royal Viking days.

In my *Normandie* quest, I am extremely grateful to Albert Rose for his keen and entertaining memory, to Jean-Pierre Mazeirat for sharing exhaustive details about his favorite vessel, to Wayne LaPoe, and also to Jean-Claude Hélary, president of Paris's L'Association des Amis des Paquebots.

In the chapter about delivery crossings, no one could have been more helpful than friends at St.-Nazaire, including Alain Grill and Jean Le Tutour. I am indebted to Captains Tor Stangeland and Svein Petterson as well as RCCL stalwarts Odd Martin Hallen,

Olav Eftedal, and Rich Steck. On board *Royal Viking Sun*, thanks are due Captain Ola Harsheim as well as Hotel Manager Peter Einfeld. Crystal Cruises was most helpful in arranging my presence on board *Crystal Harmony*'s delivery, and I would like to thank Arthur A. Sbarsky and Art Rodney as well as Darlene Pappalini. On the vessel itself, Captain Kai Julsen, Staff Captain Reidulf Maalen, Chief Engineer Erling Istefjord, Hotel Manager Dietmar Wertanzl, and crew purser Virginia West were extremely helpful; on board for the delivery, Erling Fredenberg was an invaluable fount of information.

Finally, help on the chapter about *Norway-ex-France* was made easier by a host of NCL friends, including Captains Tor Dyrdal, Geir Lokoen, and Arne Jorgensen; from ashore, I must thank Sven Dahl and Captain Kaare Bakke at operations and Fran Sevcek at public relations.

There were other staunch helpers as well, listed alphabetically as follows: Mickey Arison, Geoffrey Barraclough, M.D., Bryan Beaton, Peter van den Bemt, Julie Benson, Joseph Brandt, Phillipe P. Brebant, Captain Helge Brudvig, Rai Caluori, Natko Cincevic, Peter Compton, Dale Connelly, Jane Winslow Eliot, Richard Fain, Roger Fessaguet, Hiroshi Fujiwara, David Green, Peter Guldensupp, Neville Hawke, Willem Koopman, Wayne G. LaPoe, Walter Lord, Robert McCormick, Captain Carl Netherland-Brown, Captain Lennart Nilsson, Helmut Nootbar, Tiffany A. Riegel, Captain Kjell Smitterberg, Captain Nicola di Stefano, Peter Tonnishoff, Robert D. Turner, David Vietor, Captain Robin Woodall, and Karl Woraschk.

For the jacket, Stephen Card, the only marine painter I know who also boasts master's papers, has executed a most beautiful double portrait of the same vessel in contrasting liveries, crossing *France* and cruising *Norway*. From Oslo, the indefatigable Bård Kolltveit, marine historian/artist *sans pareil*, has once again put talented brush and pen to paper and produced another informative chart inside the dust jacket; we both hope it will remain useful as well as up-to-date for a long time.

In New York, my good friend and colleague Dolf Placzek was kind enough to take time out from his busy schedule to vet my manuscript; as always, his contributions have been invaluable. And finally, my dear wife, Mary, remains unfailingly helpful; always at my side at sea as well as the first to hear newly wrought chapters at home, she offers unflagging support, unflinching advice, and the best indexes in the business, and also remembers everything— names, faces, ports, and dates—uncommonly well. She remains, in every particular, indispensable and irreplaceable.

JOHN MAXTONE-GRAHAM
New York City, 1991

CROSSING
&
CRUISING

The simpler the bed, the better; it need be used only for about a fortnight. Where there are so many people crowded together, cleanliness should prevail, and everybody should take care to air his mattress, pillow and blanket on deck as often as possible. Moreover, each emigrant should take care to keep his place clean; the necessary cleaning materials will be available on board.
 —Handbook for Emigrants, *distributed by the Netherlands American Steamship Company*

It is a congestion so intense, so injurious to the health and morals that there is nothing on land to equal it. . . . Everything was dirty, sticky and disagreeable to the touch. . . . Evil and revolting conditions.
 —Extracts, *testimony of an undercover agent of the Immigration Commission on conditions in the steerage, circa 1908*

Streams of undersized, peculiar, alien people moving perpetually through consulates and steamship offices and delousing plants on their way from the slums of Europe to the slums of America . . .
 —Kenneth L. Roberts, Why Europe Leaves Home, 1922

Emigrating to New York

I n this nation of immigrants, many of our forebears first saw the New World from the decks of an inbound steamer in New York harbor at the end of a tumultuous, emotional immigration ordeal, their first and often only transatlantic crossing.

The image—indeed, the very dream—of that New York arrival is compelling. Emma Lazarus's "huddled masses," weeping and falling to their knees on the threshold of the promised land, remain among America's most firmly rooted historical icons. The recent rededication of the Statue of Liberty and restoration of Ellis Island as an immigrant museum serve only to burnish that image anew.

But what prefaced those arrivals? Every disembarkation in the United States had to be preceded by embarkation somewhere on the other side, and I can think of no better way to inaugurate our crossing chapters than by examining the neglected beginnings of those hallowed Edwardian crossings, before departing emigrant turned into arriving immigrant.

How, where, and under what contrasting conditions did the transatlantic polyglot embark for New York? Ocean liners crammed with immigrants did not just materialize out at sea beyond the Narrows; their arrival here was the culmination of passenger dreams no less than the fruit of aggressive steamship-company policy and manipulation. Yet most Americans know more about Ellis Island than Rotterdam's Wilhelminakade, Le Havre's Quai des Transatlantiques, or Liverpool's Landing Stage, more about admission of immigrants than recruitment of emigrants, more about joyous arrival than dogged departure. However familiar, almost cliché the triumphal finales, the debuts of those voyages are curiously neglected.

Although European shipping lines frequently incorporated the word "America" into their names—Holland America Line, Hamburg-American Line, Swedish-American Line, Norwegian America Line—significantly, the magical words "New York" appeared more prominently in their advertising copy. Early French Line publicity read *"La Ligne du Havre au New York." "Nach New York"* trumpeted the banner headline on German posters. Across the top of Holland America Line (HAL) broadsides ran the simple transatlantic equation "Rotterdam–New York." Swedish posters offering space on board vessels of the Hvide Stjerne-Linien (White Star Line) offered a tripartite option: *"New-York, Boston og Canada"*; America was not even mentioned. The linkage was firmly maritime, from port to port, from embarkation to disembarkation in New York, that exhilarating, mythic destination on the banks of the Hudson.

Of course, emigrants were not the only occupants of their vessels. Ocean liners welcomed a broad spectrum of travelers, each class accommodated along carefully segregated decks. The distinction of the ocean liner, as opposed to the land-based hotel, was its unique ability to cater to the rich, the not-so-rich, and the poor. First-class cabin passengers relaxed atop lavish upper decks, second cabin occupied less splendid quarters slightly aft, and steerage passengers were crowded deep within the hull.

Among those first- and second-cabin shipmates above were either Europeans whose business lay in the New World or, increasingly, Americans returning home, especially in early fall, from languid summers abroad. And although those contrasting upper-

and lower-deck occupants crossed as segregated shipmates in the same conveyance, their ways would part abruptly and finally upon arrival in New York.

Off Staten Island at Clifton was New York's Quarantine, the public health station just inside the Narrows. As the inbound steamer anchored, a flotilla of tenders came alongside. Immigration and public health officials boarded and passed quickly through first- and second-class public rooms for a cursory inspection of cabin passengers. Then, clutching mugs of coffee (often brandy-sweetened by pursers), they descended to the fetid berthing compartments for their most time-consuming task, examination of every immigrant passenger on board.

Mail tenders, meanwhile, tied up to the anchored steamer's hull while dozens of mail sacks—called portmanteaus by the postal workers—cascaded down canvas chutes onto the mail tenders' decks, sometimes so fast that the chutes caught fire. Reporters from New York's newspapers cooled their heels on the immigration cutter, smoking and yarning and, for those who hated it, trying to ignore the harbor's windy chop. They awaited the lowering of a cautionary yellow flag—pratique, or clearance—marking the end of quarantine. Only then were they permitted to clamber up the ladder to interview celebrated passengers.

As they boarded, the public health teams disembarked into their tenders, bound for the next waiting steamer. Then the anchors came up, and shepherded by smoky tugs, the vessel steamed slowly up New York's lower bay and obligatory passage past Bartholdi's immortal statue before finally docking at the North River piers, either Manhattan's or Hoboken's.

There, once their luggage had been unloaded, all cabin passengers disembarked, submitting to the ordeal of U.S. Customs examination. (Ordeal for whom? Recently, I asked a retired customs inspector how he felt about his years of duty on the piers. His reply was as surprising as it was heated: "There is *nothing* more—more *degrading* than pawing through other people's underwear!") Once cleared, cabin passengers surrendered their trunks to obliging Railway Express men and disappeared into teeming Manhattan.

But the immigrants' day had only begun. After an interminable wait on board, they trooped down their gangway last of all, staggering beneath the weight of their belongings. What a contrast to the cabin passengers, who had merely relinquished all impedimenta to porters: Returning home after only weeks abroad, they could ship bulky items home, whereas immigrants, relocating for life, brought with them everything they owned. Not only were there company limitations on luggage in the steerage; they had to be able to carry it all at once as well. Thus overencumbered, they were herded across the pier to waiting tenders, dispatched by the Immigration Service's Barge Office, for passage down-harbor to Ellis Island. There, beneath the echoing vaults of the Registry Hall, the immigrants would submit to a final ordeal.

Most were no longer the concern of the carrier, but any diseased or deranged unfortunates denied admission—"debarred" was the Immigration Service buzzword—could be handed back to the shipping company. Sharp-eyed immigration inspectors who spotted likely rejects disembarking from the tender would chalk the offending lapels with a coded stigma of medical ineligibility to alert doctors upstairs. Those hapless wretches had to be to returned to their port of embarkation *at company expense.* Small wonder that the steamship lines, in an effort to minimize the number of those forced repatriations, became increasingly selective about embarking none but the undeniably healthy in Europe. Only emigrant stowaways were more prohibitively expensive for the companies: Each one discovered and apprehended by the authorities meant a $1,000 fine for the line.

But regardless of those last-minute refusals, it would be safe to say that disinterest characterized the steamship companies' attitude at the western end of the run. We have its equivalent today at New York's airport terminals, glossily decorated for eastbound departure as opposed to the indifferent, utilitarian corridors through which westbound Americans trudge on arrival home.

In the same way, it was the sailings from European terminals, the start of the voyage, that preoccupied the steamship lines. That was the marketed end of the crossing, at what must be described as the wide end of the transatlantic funnel. For whereas nearly all transatlantic shiploads disembarked in New York, they might have embarked at a variety of European ports—Glasgow, Liverpool, Le Havre, Antwerp, Rotterdam, Bremen, Hamburg, Gothenburg, Genoa, Fiume, or Trieste. The emphasis of the emigrants' voyage was, curiously, the very antithesis of that which would obtain on board ships a century later. Whereas cruise clients are enticed with exotic destinations at the apogee of their voyage, yesterday's shipping men perceived their apogee—New York—as the drop-off point, the moment when they could relinquish their most numerous charges to Ellis Island authorities.

After 1900, westbound transatlantic traffic grew phenomenally. Throughout the 1840s, only 150,000 had crossed per annum; after 1905, over a million a year made the same journey. It has been estimated that during the century between 1820 and 1920, a staggering total of 34 million passengers crossed the Atlantic to America, preponderantly humble emigrants yearning for a new life in the New World.

Indeed, so numerous were those turn-of-the-century hordes that they were perceived less as individuals or even families than as elements of a tide. Throughout European emigration analyses, a liquid etymology prevails: extending the imagery, in 1892, a Continental Immigrant Pool was established. More than a pool, it seemed a brimming reservoir continually cresting over port margins and out into the sea. *"Il faut drainer les courants,"* recommended acquisitive officials of the French line.

After the turn of the century, it was not the Germans or Dutch or French who hemorrhaged from the Continent. Rather, it was the oppressed from a vast aquifer of misery to the east. Flushed from Eastern Europe's ghettos, a swollen current surged from steppe to port, sweeping Slavs, Armenians, Slovaks, Poles, and Estonians onto the waiting ships. Some would sail from Hamburg, Emden, or Bremen, closest and most convenient; others continued farther west to Rotterdam, Antwerp, and Le Havre. From Austro-Hungary and the Balkans, Bulgars, Bohemians, Moravians, Galicians, and Croats surged out to sea through Genoa, Naples, Trieste, or Fiume. Scandinavian emigrants faced a preliminary overseas passage from Gothenburg to Hull, thence onto trains that would carry them across the Pennines to Liverpool.

I have chosen, arbitrarily, to deal with the conditions of European embarkation and passage during 1905. It was the year marking the overlap between what the U.S. Immigration Commission of 1910 would characterize as "the old steerage," as opposed to the reforms of "the new steerage." The change from old to new had less to do with social conscience than increased competition as well as a remarkable escalation of tonnage. Then, too, that year of 1905 saw continued unrest and pogroms in Russia, precipitating additional floods of westbound Jews escaping the massacres. At Ellis Island, 1905 heralded the first million-passenger year.

On what vessels did those masses cross in 1905? There were no superliners yet: The *Lusitania*, the *Mauretania*, the *Olympic*, the *France*, and the *Imperator*-class vessels still lay over the horizon. From Britain's ports, Cunard's premier service was sustained by the *Lucania* and the *Campania*; before year's end, the pretty sisters, the *Caronia* and the *Carmania*, would appear, ushering in the modern towering hull. White Star service was maintained by the *Cedric*, the *Teutonic*, the *Oceanic*, and the *Baltic*, still steaming regularly out of Liverpool, two years before the company's competitive move to Southampton.

Waiting in the wings at Hamburg was Albert Ballin's newest liner, the *Amerika*, the world's largest, due out the following year. The *Deutschland* sustained his monthly express service to New York while vessels like the *Fürst Bismarck* and the *Blücher* served as slower fleetmates. Ballin's fleet, Hamburg American Line, often called by its German acronym, HAPAG, was overshadowed by his Hanseatic rival's: Three of Norddeutscher Lloyd's crack foursome of the *Kaiser Wilhelm der Grosse* class raced to New York, carrying the cream of the German traffic.

At 12,000 tons, the *Noordam* was Holland America Line's largest hull in 1905, although the first *Nieuw Amsterdam*, half again as large, was fitting out in a Rotterdam yard; the *Rotterdam*, the *Ryndam*, and the old *Potsdam* filled out the Dutch sailing schedules. Red Star Line's *Kroonland*, *Zeeland*, and *Finland* had Antwerp as their home port. From Le Havre, a quintet of seven-day steamers, each with a distinctive definite article on her nameboard, carried the tricolor across the Atlantic: *La Savoie*, *La Champagne*, *La Bretagne*, *La Gascogne*, and *La Touraine*.

At that time, only one line served Europe's far north: Scandinavian American Line vessels steamed west out of Gothenburg. Both Norwegian America and Swedish-American lines were a decade away. Similarly thin on the ground, two lines alone flew the stars and stripes: the Atlantic Transport Line's *Minnewaska*, *Mesaba*, and *Minnetonka* steamed between Tilbury and New York, while the American Line's quartet of municipal namesakes was the first transatlantic fleet to call at Southampton rather than Liverpool: the *St. Paul*, the *St. Louis*, the *Philadelphia*, and the *New York*.

According to an old saw, the first three rules of successful retailing are location, location, and location. Nowhere did this commercial watchword apply more cogently than to the transshipment of Europe's emigrants. By the luck of simple geography, Germany's "location" was a natural. With no major rival anywhere to the east, HAPAG and North German Lloyd were in prime position to embark the torrent of Russian and Polish traffic; Hamburg, Emden, and Bremen were ideally sited as first and easy embarkation points onto what company publicists had christened proprietarily "the German Ocean" for New York. Subsequent but less convenient stops along the North Sea coast were Rotterdam, Antwerp, and last on the continent, Le Havre. Liverpool lay slightly farther west but necessitated a cross-Channel link.

To offset their western disadvantage, agents of the Compagnie Générale Transatlantique (CGT) established recruiting points and railheads hundreds of miles from Le Havre. In fact, all transatlantic lines created central catch basins, even Hamburg American and North German Lloyd, which, one thought, might have been content with their easternmost geographic advantage. But in fact, North Sea and Channel ports served as deltas for the emigrant river.

Anxious to divert more passengers onto their vessels, the French established their primary inland railhead in the Swiss city of Basel. There, trainloads of prospective emigrant passengers from Austro-Hungary were funneled by rail to Le Havre. Indeed, once that Basel linkage had been inaugurated in 1876, almost every emigrant carried by the French Line began his or her voyage to New York in a country bereft of a coastline. The specially built emigrant rolling stock had open coaches (constructed *"d'après le système américain"*), which, twenty-four dusty, jolting hours later, would deposit hundreds of French Line clients at company hotels near the Havrois docks.

Ironically, years later, between the wars, the French Line boasted that it had the longest gangplank in the world; forgotten or ignored were those emigrant trains, snaking overland through Delle, Noisy-le-Sec, Aubervilliers, Les Batignolles, and Rouen toward the sea, the longest boat trains in the world. Once the route was fully operational, additional emigrant boat trains were fed into the system from Strasbourg, Belfort, and Modane. The company's efficient system extended overseas to Naples as well: Italian and Sicilian emigrants boarded special steamers for Marseilles, where they disembarked for yet another passage by rail north to Le Havre.

The French were not alone in this long-distance recruitment. To compensate for their disadvantageous Britannic isolation, Cunard established collection points miles from Liverpool in Fiume (the

present-day Yugoslavian port of Rijeka), siphoning off the eastern
Austro-Hungarian and Balkan traffic for passage via the company's
Mediterranean service to New York.

After its establishment in 1892, the Continental Immigrant Pool
functioned smoothly. Middle European governments were paid
annual stipends by steamship lines for the guaranteed delivery of
thousands of emigrants, either political or economic undesirables.
Interestingly, the emigrant trade was one of those rare economic
phenomena that profited everyone: Emigrants got a second chance,
steamship companies filled their holds, European nations cleaned
house, and expanding, limitless America welcomed a vast influx of
desperately willing and needed workers.

For the companies, the care and accommodation of their most
profitable human cargo predominated over every other embarkation preoccupation throughout Britain and the Continent. But before dealing with emigrant accommodation in the ports, we should
compare the flavor of a traditional turn-of-the-century passenger
port with the ambience through which most of us embark today.
Miami is currently the world's busiest passenger port, located at
the tip of Florida, which dangles on the threshold of the Caribbean.

For boarding cruise passengers, there is neither a crane nor a
shed in sight, only a long, handsome extrusion of white concrete
terminals, their spotless interiors more akin to airport than to sea-
port. Passengers move effortlessly from bus or taxi up escalators to
carpeted reception halls and thence on board via covered walkways
vaulting the piers below.

In fact, their feet never touch the pier. Only their suitcases do,
loaded on forklifts that thrust luggage containers directly through
port doors into the hull, together with the upcoming week's provisions and chandlery. There are neither trunks nor mail nor cargo
nor even gulls nor that unloved commodity, the bane of marine
superintendents throughout history, coal. Cruise ships' engines
gulp diesel oil instead, pumped from lighters moored on the vessel's sea side. So silent, discreet, and efficient is the process that
only a faint sulfurous reek betrays that bunkering has, in fact,
begun.

Indeed, Miami and Port Everglades just to the north seem dream
ports—futuristic, sun-dappled, and lapped by turquoise waters,
hosts to fleets of white dream castles. Throughout contemporary
cruising, custom and climate combine to insulate passengers from
any pungent realities; so in port and so on board. Cruise ships are

intentionally suffused with bland, sanitized unreality: embarkation from a Disneyland terminal, passage through a pristine channel past a smoke-free, noise-free, and apparently carefree waterfront and out into a perpetually calm, sunlit sea.

Come back a hundred years to grimy, gritty Liverpool, to the rumble of the iron-shod wagons rattling over cobbles and echoing down sloping steel bridges to the Landing Stage, to the imperious chuff and grating squeal of the boat train shunting inside Riverside Station, to the ceaseless, grinding whine of electric cranes, the raucous cries of stevedore and gull, the shrill wail of steam tug, lighter, and ferry, the clatter of anthracite hurtling down steel chute into bunker, and the blustery buffeting of northern ocean breezes. Inhale the pungent reek of coal smoke from engine and steamer funnel alike, the tang of tar, the rank stink of the Mersey's oily tide lapping worn, sea-slimed wharf. The palette was consistently dour—black rather than white hull, leaden piers 'neath leaden sky, gray Irish Sea mists, and beyond, the smoky, tiled, granite city.

That was the port constant of 1905, whether Liverpool or Le Havre, Antwerp or Rotterdam, Hamburg or Bremen. Until 1890, Liverpool was Europe's premier gateway to New York. All over Britain and the Continent, Liverpool's steamship posters offered tempting, lithographed promise of a new life in the New World, achieved via capacious steamers that would carry the starving, the oppressed, and the ambitious to New York. Continental emigrants in the thousands were ferried across Channel or North Sea to the giant, bustling port at the mouth of the Mersey. Initially, Cunard steamers sailing west from Liverpool went north about, as it was called, leaving Ireland to port as they steamed for America; later, when emigrants were carried, Queenstown, Cork's port at Ireland's southern tip, became an obligatory stop to siphon off Ireland's dispossessed.

Every emigrant journey to New York involved threefold expense: reaching the port from their village, lodgings in port against the oft-delayed day of sailing, and finally, passage across the ocean. Railway fare to the ports was cheap, often subsidized by the shipping line, the ocean-liner equivalent, if you will, of today's cruise lines' free airfare, from home to port and back again. As the traffic grew, housing in the ports was improved. Better and more pleasant accommodations supplemented or replaced the traditional boarding and lodging houses. Special emigrant hotels were built by the companies to house their humblest clients until the day of embarkation. The British government established a huge emigrant hostel at Birkenhead, across the Mersey from Liverpool.

Few cabin passengers were aware of these hostels for their less fortunate shipmates; they seldom slept overnight in Liverpool, arriving instead in the port on sailing day or, if they came down from the north, booking a room in the garish, convenient luxe of the Adelphi Hotel.

Creation of these exclusively emigrant establishments arose out of chronic abuse; between railhead and pierhead, the emigrants were fair game. Throughout history, wherever vulnerable traffic flows, the unscrupulous abound. When New York City served briefly as the abortion capital of the United States in the late 1960s, dishonest taxi drivers lay in wait at the airport for young girls bound for Manhattan clinics, overcharging outrageously for the ride.

So, too, at railway stations in every European steamship port. It was the custom for crooked runners, or touts—"crimps" was the Liverpudlian euphemism—to pass themselves off as representatives of shipping companies. They would meet every incoming train and, in fierce quest of a per-head commission, steer unsuspecting emigrant families to wretched, overpriced lodgings. Their victims were easy to spot—no one else on the platform was as hesitant or overburdened or, indeed, misinformed. En route to the lodgings, crimps often exchanged the emigrants' precious money for counterfeit American dollars. The only remote convenience these crimps offered was to steer their charges to lodgings accommodating the same nationality.

Liverpool's Great George's Square was famous for rows of shabby, often verminous tenements where families of over a dozen often slept, uncomplaining, in a crowded room with only four beds. And if sleeping conditions upstairs were intolerable, catering on the ground floor was little better. As late as 1906, the entire evening meal served to a family at a Dominion Line boarding house in Upper Frederick Street was corned beef, bread, and tea. Breakfast was sparser: bread, jam, and coffee, served on a stained table with no crockery whatsoever save chipped enamel mugs. In the evening after dinner, the emigrants' dining saloon became a smoking room of sorts as one of the cooks, playing a harmonica, would serenade his captive audience.

(Back in 1944, I sampled these mean commons in reverse, returning to wartime England after five years in America. Two dozen of us repatriated children disembarked from a Royal Navy carrier in the blackout and were put up overnight in the figurative descendants of those emigrant boardinghouses. The iron cots came complete with stiff blankets and harsh linen that, folded meagerly lengthwise, served as inadequate top and bottom sheet. Breakfast was bread only just anointed with margarine, dreadful jam, and transparent wartime coffee; we might well have been emigrants embarking third class to New York on the morrow.)

Adjacent to the dining room but forbidden entry were Polish and Russian emigrants housed in a long, drafty shed; their treatment was so abominable that they would sometimes riot against the abusive scoundrels hired to serve them as waiters. This calculated, nationalistic double standard obtained among every steerage class, both ashore and afloat: northern Europeans were kept apart and in far better surroundings than their ignorant, long-suffering shipmates from Eastern Europe.

Liverpool-bound emigrants from the Baltic came ashore on England's east coast. There was an Emigrants Home in Grimsby, down-Humber from Hull, where Scandinavian steerage passengers would disembark en route for New York. They were fed at long tables in what was called, shiplike, the third-class dining room, as though the hoteliers were conditioning their clients for the maritime nomenclature awaiting them during transatlantic passage. Both White Star and Cunard passengers were often housed in a halfway house in London called the Atlantic Passengers Hostel.

Marked improvement in Liverpool's emigrant housing occurred when steamship companies began providing their own accommodations in renovated row houses around St. George's Square. The White Star Oceanic Hotel, for instance, despite the cognomen "hotel," was composed of vast dormitories with double-decker iron bunks; admittedly, there were clean sheets, pillows, and blankets, but precious little else. Although crowded and plain, those linoleumed quarters were at least clean, and prices were cheap.

In Rotterdam, the Holland America Line built a spired and turreted emigrant hotel hard by the Wilhelminakade, the great Holland America pier. Instead of boat drills, there were daily fire drills. Accommodations were efficient but claustrophobic. Clients were literally stacked four high in vertical chambers made private by sliding doors; the rooms were scarcely larger than the bunks themselves and the stout ladder up which they clambered to bed. Cunard operated a hotel in Rotterdam as well, through which

TOP: *Steerage passengers for the* Lucania *are collected from St. George's Square by horse-drawn jitney, bound for the docks the day before sailing.* (The Board of Trustees of the National Museums and Galleries, Merseyside Maritime Museums)

BOTTOM: *After the turn of the century, the White Star Line managed its own emigrant hotels. Since the line's official name was Oceanic Steam Navigation Company, Oceanic made sense as a hotel name. To clinch matters, there is a white star over the fanlight of number 132.* (National Archives)

TOP: *Rotterdam's Emigrant Hotel: The letters NASM on the roof stand for Neder-landsch-Amerikaansche Stoomvaart Maatschappij, Dutch for the Holland America Steamship Company.* (National Archives)

BOTTOM: *One of the dormitories inside. Although emigrants slept three high before embarkation, they would find only double-decker bunks on board, thanks to American immigration laws.* (National Archives)

passed emigrant traffic destined for Liverpool and the company's hulls.

In fact, these hotels offered more than catering and accommodation; they also served an inevitable sanitary purpose, wherein every client had to submit to an essential ritual, delousing. This was an inescapable requirement for all emigrant families around the turn of the century: They and all their belongings had to pass through a ruthless disinfection process before admission.

Long before DDT, delousing of belongings involved exposure to steam pressure. All the emigrants' belongings—boots, suitcases, clothing, and bedding—were loaded into gaping horizontal tanks fitted with tracked wire-mesh conveyances. Once the loaded racks had been wheeled inside, the doors were swung shut and sealed, steam valves were opened, and the tanks and their contents underwent a prolonged high-pressure steaming.

It took half an hour. Then the doors at the opposite, or "clean," end of the tank opened, and the racks were wheeled out so that their poached contents could be redistributed. The distraught, naked owners, clad in large sheets or blankets, had been deloused as well. Rather than high-pressure steam, their purification had involved a harsh combination of a powerful green liquid soap and kerosene. In many cases, head and body hair were shaved as well. In the emigrant barracks at Naples, male emigrants were shorn in a mass barbering establishment whose staff boasted proudly they could process forty men per hour; in the adjacent female equivalent, the same hour disposed of only thirty females because there was less and probably gentler staff.

In fact, in every emigrant reception center, there were two successive delousing ordeals: one on arrival and another just prior to embarkation. After the first, families were still quartered on the "unclean" side of the establishment since they could still come and go along the streets of the port, where they might well become reinfested. But the day before they were to sail, a second fumigation served as final admission to the "clean side," where they were confined until they boarded the tenders.

In Liverpool, Cunard's delousing and reception center was called Sparrow Hall, a picturesquely quaint name for a single-story brick structure dominated, as was every emigrant facility, by the tall chimney of the adjacent steam plant. Indeed, the whole establishment offered a haunting foretaste of either boot camp or World

War II's infamous death camps. And though the chimneys were steam plants rather than crematoria, though the barbed wire merely separated the "clean" from the "unclean" section of the barracks, though no one starved, and though the end product was not death but life, the eerie symbolism of low barracks juxtaposed against tall brick chimney remains indelible and inescapable.

Perhaps not surprisingly, the Germans went several steps beyond the British, French, and Dutch. At Hamburg, on the banks of the Elbe, the Hamburg American Line laid out an extensive riverside facility. The original emigrant village, completed in 1901, was almost immediately expanded, five years later encompassing a total of more than sixty acres.

One entered beneath a clock tower; housed immediately behind it were delousing facilities, then an entire town that contained everything necessary for an indeterminate stay. Since the HAPAG planners did not intend to liberate their emigrant clients back into the slums of Hamburg, they provided every conceivable amusement within the village. There was a network of pleasant tree-shaded streets, two chapels and a synagogue, shops, a beer garden, and a music pavilion in which eighteen company musicians gave regular morning and afternoon concerts. It was an ambitious and eminently successful installation, probably the largest and most efficient facility anywhere in Europe. The company was especially proud of its sewage system, which did not permit any contaminated runoff from the steam tanks and bathhouses to foul the Elbe.

The reverse of New York, where immigrants disembarked last of all, Liverpool's emigrants boarded first. They had arrived in the port days before, and among their many agonizing financial pitfalls was the cumulative expense of lingering too long in lodgings. Early on the morning of embarkation, large open carriages—later succeeded by motor charabancs—with the appropriate steamer's name posted conspicuously across the front, would load up by curbs all around Great George's Square to carry the emigrants down to the pierhead and their vessel.

Liverpool lies at the mouth of the Mersey River. Its estuary has a curious geographic shape, a ventral or bagpipe silhouette, its narrow exit into the Irish Sea anticipated by a wider body of protected water, apparently ideal for docks. But ocean liners used the port at the mercy of fearsome tides. Tucked into the corner where England meets Wales, Liverpool rests at the apex of a giant sea

TOP: *The open door of a steam fumigation tank at Libau. All luggage, clothing, and shoes were steamed under pressure for half an hour while the owners, naked under company sheets, awaited their return.* (National Archives)

CENTER: *During World War I, HAPAG's Emigrant Village was used as a German army hospital. Posters of ships as well as the company's motto*—Mein Feld ist die Welt—*still adorn the walls.* (National Archives)

BOTTOM: *Liverpool's Landing Stage on a typical early morning: Nearest the camera is the Irish mail boat; beyond, the Maure-tania embarks passengers for New York. Note the taller gangways ordained for the taller Cunarder.* (Author's collection)

triangle, enduring in consequence an enormous tide differential. Twice each day, the waters of the estuary rise and fall thirty-five feet.

Over centuries of trade, such discrepancy in water levels had obliged Merseyside harbor engineers to find ingenious ways of berthing, loading, and unloading ships. Along either bank, all docks were protected behind embankment walls pierced by locks, creating an ancillary network of basins and docks immune from tidal fluctuation. Ships entered each inland system through what were called half-tide basins, watery foyers, if you will, permitting entrance or egress twice daily during the Mersey's high-water cycles.

What was known locally as "the top of the tide" heralded a chaotic period for navigation throughout the estuary. Steamers inbound from America would time their arrival for that moment. Additionally, on every flood, like school letting out for recess, all Liverpool docks and basins disgorged dozens of lighters and vessels that had been awaiting release from the interior locked systems.

But one, and only one, vital quay did lie out in the river proper. It was called the Landing Stage, an enormous floating dock connected to the riverbank by hinged booms and stout chains; seven road bridges (one for cattle) provided access from shore. Completed in its final form in the mid-1870s, Liverpool's Landing Stage was half a mile long, composed of a chain of contiguous steel pontoons, their top surfaces sealed with macadam. Along its length were waiting rooms, a ticket office, hairdressers, luggage counters, emigrant medical inspection halls, refreshment stalls, and customs sheds—all the inevitable clutter of conventional passenger steamer piers.

But as opposed to conventional piers mounted on fixed, immovable piles, Liverpool's unique Landing Stage was miraculously afloat, rising and falling with the Mersey. The Landing Stage served as the only convenient dock for inward or outbound vessels discharging or loading passengers. Present-day Liverpudlians are struggling to restore portions of their famous waterfront. Preservationists have, understandably, centered their efforts on renovating the Prince Albert Dock, an enclosed dock and warehouse complex, once the world's largest. But just downstream, now neglected, unknown and abandoned by even the Manx ferries, a remnant of the great Landing Stage is still in place, Liverpool's index of greatness, for decades the fulcrum of Europe's transatlantic passenger trade westward to New York.

Around the turn of the century, berthings at the Landing Stage were so heavily scheduled that masters embarked their passengers within a rigorously enforced two-hour span; inbound passengers from New York or Montreal surged off the vessel in only an hour. It was too precious a venue for coaling or any but last-minute mails; those essentials had been preloaded at the docks inland. Emigrants were preloaded as well, either in the docks or from lighters while their ship lay at anchor in midstream. Once they had boarded, tugs and docking pilots brought the ships alongside the Landing Stage for cabin passengers' embarkation. Cabin passengers, ran the Mersey Docks and Harbour Board's proud boast, always embarked from the Landing Stage; and if there was sufficient time, emigrants occasionally boarded from it as well.

Disembarkation at Le Havre was only slightly easier, direct from the steamers' main decks onto the Quai des Transatlantiques. This was the French Line's equivalent of the Landing Stage, although it was not afloat. Between ship and masonry pier, intermediate floating camels permitted passengers and mail alike to off-load on parallel gangway-ladders. Hence, at low tide, there was a steep vertical climb up and down.

Paris was only two hours away, and tracks for the boat train lay directly atop the pier. There were a few open-sided sheds; winter arrivals or departures in the port could be unpleasant on raw Channel mornings. In 1905, Le Havre's new Gare Maritime was a modest brick train shed surmounted by an equally modest clock-girt cupola. That apparent simplicity reflected the severe limitations of Le Havre's path to the sea for *les transatlantiques*. As late as 1890, it took a large French Line vessel thirty or forty minutes to reach the sea through a tortuous, twisting channel, during which time all other port traffic stopped. After maneuvering carefully through l'Ecluse des Transatlantiques into the deep water of the *avant-port*, they passed from port into Channel between the Batterie and Bastions de la Floride, where sightseers and fishermen always waved them off. Emigrants boarded, as in every steamer port, early in the day.

Up the coast in Belgium was the "Queen of the Scheldt," the port city of Antwerp, or to use its French rather than Flemish name, Anvers. Its piers, docks, and channels were vastly superior to Le Havre's, and Antwerp was home port of Belgian's Red Star Line. The docks lay upriver, sixty miles from the sea. Cabin passengers embarking at Antwerp would stay in the city's newest hotel, the Grand, from which the hotel would dispatch horse-drawn chara-bancs to meet incoming trains and subsequently dispatch them to ships. During 1905, in fact, the port's America dock was constructed, designed to load liners bound for New York with their human cargo.

Antwerp's distance from the sea typified the problems faced by sister ports farther up the coast. Rotterdam, Bremen, and Hamburg all shared the same navigational inconvenience, complicated as increasingly larger vessels were built by the turn of the century. The larger the vessel, the more complex and time-consuming the river ascent; the same ports that had accommodated sailing ships for centuries were suddenly, distressingly too far inland for large Atlantic steamers.

It would be safe to say that, in general, all passenger vessels turning around in European ports seldom remained at one quay. Vessels at the other end of the transatlantic run at New York's North River piers stayed put; once they had arrived and disembarked their passenger load, the only slight move they made before sailing day was a minimal shift within their slips to admit coaling barges between pier and hull.

At the eastern end of the run, in Liverpool, Le Havre, Antwerp, Rotterdam, Bremen, and Hamburg, the liners were forever changing venues within the port, discharging passengers here, coaling and victualing there, reboarding a new load of passengers here again several days later. Liverpool was typical: Ocean liners were parked within the fixed, tide-free basins alongside ancillary coaling quays against their day of loading and departure for New York.

Hamburg and Bremen lay too far inland and hence developed subsidiary passenger terminals closer to the sea. The Hamburg American Line boasted two embarkation and service locations down the river Elbe from Hamburg. The first was at Brunshausen on the west bank of the lower Elbe but still sixty kilometers inland. Until 1902, passengers would board tenders to embark on steamers anchored out in the river; once again, steerage first, cabin passengers last. Prior to the embarkation of any passengers, the ships were coaled and victualed in midstream.

Vessels continued to load coal and supplies upriver, but in 1902 the increasing draft of the hulls and the hope of avoiding extra hours of river navigation mandated construction of a handsome new cabin-passenger terminus at Cuxhaven, a little fishing port that lay on the eastern bank of the Elbe's estuary, 100 kilometers by rail

TOP: *An emigrant dining hall at Le Havre. Every piece of crockery was marked with the CGT* (Compagnie Générale Transatlantique) *cipher.* (National Archives)

BOTTOM: *Cuxhaven's famous Steubenhoft, the great ship/train passenger terminus downriver from Hamburg.* (Helmut Nootbar)

downstream from Hamburg. The new structure was called the Steubenhoft, and it would serve as the company's (and the world's) first great steamship terminal for cabin passengers.

Facing the North Sea, the Steubenhoft was an eclectic Victorian-Wilhelmian stone structure. Along the dunes at ground level spread a row of white-framed, neo-romanesque windows; high above them reared a campanile with a lighthouse perched atop it, rising out of a phalanx of four smaller turrets. Close by that tower was another prominent feature, a great dome surmounted by a glass lantern. Hard by it, a single, asymmetrical neo-gothic gable end faced the sea.

The whole complex boasted a festive, almost carnival air, dotted with flagpoles and combining the look of a fortress, seaside casino, railway station, and prosperous Nordic golf club. Passengers approaching the Steubenhoft from land or sea—either detraining from the hinterland or disembarking from a liner—were reassured by its exuberant architectural welcome. The railway platforms within its landward side disgorged cabin passengers, laden with hand luggage, from Hamburg; their trunks had gone on ahead and would be found on board the steamer. Directly beneath the great dome was a restaurant. (One wonders that HAPAG clients who had left Hamburg's Atlantic Hotel after breakfast for a noon sailing would need yet another meal before luncheon on board, but then as now, there is no limit to the prospective passenger appetite.) Under the same roof were housed additional passenger amenities— travel bureau, post office, reception hall, and within a single-story wing extending eastward to the piers, a long customhouse. There, beneath exposed rafters and the merciless glare of electric arcs, inbound HAPAG passengers submitted trunks and holdalls to the scrutiny of Germany's customs service.

The Steubenhoft is significant because it survives as HAPAG's most ambitious and pioneering ocean-liner terminal, combining under one decorative roof a useful compendium of passenger facilities. This was no jury-rigged waterfront expedient, as in Liverpool or Le Havre, half station and half piershed, but a true Passagier-Abfertigungshalle, literally a "passenger dispatching or processing hall."

But the Steubenhoft did not quite qualify as the "compleat" ocean-liner terminus, for back at the turn of the century, architects were apparently unprepared to bite the bullet and site the terminus directly adjacent to the vessels. In truth, the Steubenhoft was more wedded to railway than to pier. Two superior structures would appear later—Le Havre's Gare Maritime of 1935 and, yet even more advanced, Southampton's Ocean Terminal of 1950. The Ocean Terminal offered ultimate maritime ease: Passengers reaching Southampton's docks via the Waterloo boat train could descend from their train, complete formalities, and board their vessel entirely under cover; the passenger route, from railway compartment to ship's square, was enclosed within one commodious and convenient structure. I never disembark from a ship today—Lisbon in a downpour, for instance, or any number of exposed Caribbean piers—without longing for Southampton's archetypal convenience of paneled terminus and tubular gangway.

At the Steubenhoft, outbound passengers tramped through the plebeian customs shed and then emerged into the open air along unsheltered wooden catwalks to the ship's gangway. Things would not improve at Cuxhaven for half a century, until, in 1954, a proper hall was built parallel to the ship's berth so that embarking passengers remained under cover throughout, from platform to gangway.

It is extraordinary, in retrospect, that the perfect passenger terminal arrived so late, long after the fact. Throughout the heyday of ocean-liner travel before World War I, passengers of all classes in the millions endured archaic and primitive embarkations. In New York, for instance, not until the 1960s, when most ocean liners had already succumbed to the airplane, were belated improvements made. The most ironic function to take place in Manhattan's newly opened Passenger Ship Terminal in the summer of 1967 was Mayor John Lindsay's moving farewell to the *Queen Mary*, one of the ships for which the long-overdue Manhattan facility had been designed.

Only thirty miles south along the North Sea coast lay Germany's second great transatlantic port, Bremerhaven. As Cuxhaven is to Hamburg, so Bremerhaven is to Bremen. Located at the mouth of the river Weser, Bremerhaven served as the Norddeutscher Lloyd's threshold for New York. Its equivalent of HAPAG's Steubenhoft was the rustic, almost barnlike bulk of the Nord Halle. Suiting that sense of convenient abbreviation, adorning its half-timbered gable end facing the river appeared, in a graceful arc, the two-word semilogo "Nord Lloyd."

No brave tower reared overhead for North German Lloyd passengers, through a red-and-white lighthouse stood nearby. The Nord Halle passenger complex had been sited on an arrowhead of land bounded by water on two sides: on the Weser, a low pier for river ferries and tenders; on the other, the Vorhafen (lower harbor), which led, through a lock, into the Kaiserhafen, immune from North Sea tides. There inbound North German Lloyd steamers would tie up for week-long, home-port turnarounds at the Lloyd-pier.

Depending on the state of the tide, passenger embarkation would take place either inside the locks—at the Lloydpier—or outside the locks at the lone pier served by the Nord Halle. Along the inner docks, protective shelter was almost nonexistent. Boat trains arriving from Bremen deposited passengers onto open platforms gritted by coal dust blown over from open bunkers nearby. Clients in every class would clamber down from the carriages, pick their way across open tracks and then up onto a platform-pier, all the while exposed to North Sea damp and chill. Boarding the most luxurious conveyances in the world remained a logistic ordeal.

But passengers whose waiting steamers had berthed outside the lock could be brought via a rail spur to the land-side entrance at the Nord Halle, which boasted in its interior the same convenient refinements as the Steubenhoft. If the tide were wrong, though, then embarkation took place under open skies at the Lloydpier. Not until 1930 would a first-rate, lock-free facility be built, the Columbus Pier, a modern passenger terminal whose debut coincided with that of the *Bremen* and the *Europa* and would serve, postwar, as the easternmost terminus for the *United States*.

Once deloused, inoculated, and sprung from their port encampments, what would those embarking emigrants of 1905 find on board? It depended largely on the age and condition of their vessel. The newest ships always offered a higher standard of accommodation for all classes. Moreover, moored at either end of the North Atlantic run, the steerage compartments were cleanest, because steamship companies knew to anticipate government and public health inspections in port. Berthed at its terminals, in either Liverpool or New York, an ocean liner's lower decks boasted a conscientious, disinfected cleanliness that would deteriorate woefully after one sea day because of dense occupancy as well as the catastrophic results of seasickness.

The earliest congressional legislation that standardized berthing requirements on board transatlantic vessels dates from 1819: "The Act Regulating Passenger Ships and Vessels" was Congress's first attempt at improving shipboard conditions. Sixty-three (often miserable) sea years later, a more comprehensive law was required,

reflecting improved passenger living standards, increasing numbers of passengers, and huge increases in the size of ships as well.
The U.S. Passenger Act of 1882 was passed, once more "to regulate
the carriage of passengers by sea."

Theoretically, that federal legislation protected everyone on
board, but its most stringent safeguards really applied to those
down in steerage, passengers who, through ignorance, inexperi-
ence, and most of all, their apparently infinite numbers, were
most consistently abused. Take the matter of cubic allotment per
passenger, covered in Section I of the law. Each was to occupy
no less than 100 cubic feet, or if the passenger deck lay more than
two decks below main deck, 120 cubic feet. (Two children less
than eight years old constituted one passenger.) If that meager
cubic-footage minimum was found lacking, then the master of the
steamer could be fined fifty dollars for every inadequately berthed
passenger.

Nevertheless, as one observer reported, "persons carried are
looked upon as so much human freight," and indeed, 100 cubic
feet is very scant space; even the meanest second-class cabin
boasted several times that much. In the steerage, adhering grudgingly to the letter of all legislated minimums, the steamship companies observed the regulation with a ruthless nicety. Since only two
tiers of berths were allowed, steerage compartments were filled
with tight-packed row after row of wooden or iron double-decker
bunks. Each berth was exactly six feet long and two feet wide, with
only thirty inches of height between bunks, for a per-passenger
total of thirty cubic feet, about the dimension of two coffins. The
balance of each passenger's mandated "100 cubic feet" lay elsewhere in the compartment, either underneath both bunks or overhead near the ceiling. The 100-cubic-foot allotment was, in effect,
dispersed, rather as in New York skyscraper trade-offs, awarding
the emigrants unusable air rights.

As for the beds, they were not really bunks but, rather, meagerly
padded shelves. Mattresses were filled with either straw or sea-
weed, and if the emigrant had neglected to bring his or her own
feather pillow, the obligatory life jacket served instead. One gray
blanket was offered each passenger, so that on winter crossings
everyone slept in their clothes to stay warm and draped themselves
in shawls and overcoats piled, of necessity, on the bunk.

For that claustrophobic little double coffin had to suffice for
every shipboard hour, day and night, living, sleeping, resting, or

dressing. There was no chair or stool, no bureau or cupboard, no closet or locker, not even a row of hooks. All luggage, clothing, eating utensils, and belongings (remember, emigrants were relocating for life) had somehow to be stored within that narrow berth. Using floor space under the bunks was taboo. Although the compartment might be swept several times daily, steel decks were inevitably damp, while wooden ones, although sprinkled periodically with sand, still reeked. There were no wastebaskets or trash bins anywhere, and there was one woefully shortsighted omission: Astonishing as it seems, the company provided no receptacle into which those inevitably seasick passengers could throw up.

Privacy for female passengers was impossible. Section II of the 1882 law required the steamship companies to separate berths "as berths are ordinarily separated," vague legislative obfuscation at best. Single women, it went on, were to be separated by a "substantial and well-constructed bulkhead." This particular provision was seldom observed. One female agent of the Immigration Commission, traveling incognito as a Bohemian peasant in 1908, reported that the only "bulkhead" isolating the women's berths was a single horizontal iron pipe.

In an attempt at modesty, the women on that (unnamed) vessel hung clothes around their bunks to create at least a fabric bulkhead. They were less concerned about male fellow passengers (who were, in fact, berthed elsewhere) than about continual incursions by crew members. Section VII of the law laid down strict—and largely ignored—rules contravening that unconscionable practice of unauthorized crew visitation. Indeed, the wording of Section VII was, by law, posted prominently on steerage-compartment walls "in English as well as in the language of the crew"; but it was never posted in the language of the passengers and so remained incomprehensible to those it most cruelly affected. Inquisitive and arrogant harassment by ogling crewmen was inevitable for single women in the steerage. Another undercover female agent reported that crewmen passed through the women's compartments continually, especially before breakfast, when the occupants were trying to dress; "our protector," as she referred scathingly to an ineffectual factotum called the chief steerage steward, was the worst offender of all, taking unpardonable liberties with seasick female passengers. Although an interpreter was available—another provision of the law—he proved "indifferent and remote." Steerage women traveling alone were badgered night and day by persistent, rapacious crewmen, unhindered and often joined by their supervisors. While, traditionally, sailors have always boasted a girl in every port, those on emigrant-carrying steamers had their pick of defenseless young women throughout westbound crossings as well. Provision of stewardesses might have made a difference, but the only stewardesses in the old steerage were on duty in the hospital.

Section III of the 1882 law dealt with required ventilation, mandating that every fifty passengers should have the advantage of two 12-inch ventilators. Under conditions in normal living quarters, this might have been adequate; but nothing in a steerage compartment was ever normal. Ventilators gaping atop wet decks often admitted green seawater, and during winter gales especially, cold and wet steerage passengers preferred to close ventilators rather than admit icy mid-ocean drafts. So ventilation, save in calm summer weather, was problematic, and a continual reek of stale air, unwashed bodies, litter, cooking smells, and vomit made steerage compartments almost uninhabitable. Rough weather reduced many passengers to a kind of bunk-ridden, listless torpor that had as much to do with lack of oxygen as with seasickness or debilitation. Cabin-class passengers looking over their after railings commented regularly how early their steerage shipmates sought the open decks, regardless of the weather. The immigrants were there, quite simply, because ventilation belowdecks was so inadequate as to be intolerable.

There were regulations about the provision of bathrooms as well, "more honour'd," to quote Shakespeare, "in the breach than the observance." Bathrooms, or to use the steamship vernacular, washhouses, were sometimes separated from the compartments by stretches of windswept decks. The same facility catered to males and females alike. They were, customarily, steel-walled chambers about seven feet by nine feet, with either a four-foot trough for washing dishes or double rows of laundry tubs down either side, with no soap, no towel, and more cold salt water than hot. The sole hot faucet was used not only to wash hands, faces, and hair but also for rinsing eating utensils and chamber pots. The floor was constantly awash, mopped dry and disinfected harshly only on the last morning of the voyage, once again in anticipation of a public health inspection. Some passengers occasionally found inviting doors marked "Baths" but, on application, were advised that these were old second-class signs no longer applicable.

The U.S. law of 1882 mandated a daily medical inspection during every crossing for which immigrants would queue up and pass by one of the ship's surgeons. He largely ignored them, remaining deep in conversation with a colleague as his ostensible patients shuffled by; thanks to the vigor of the companies' sanitary regime ashore, he knew they were vermin-free, and apart from the inevitable, incurable seasickness, little warranted his attention. Passenger attendance at those daily inspections was enforced by cards that were supposed to be punched by the supervising medico. More often than not, the cards were punched, six holes at a time, by an obliging steward "to spare you from waiting in line every day"; convenient, doubtless, for both passengers and doctor, but not what the framers of the Passenger Act had in mind. One steerage woman worried that her inoculation had not taken and lack of a scar might prevent her from landing. The doctor admonished her through the interpreter: "Don't worry about that hole in your arm, it's the hole in your card that counts." He was quite right.

Present-day cruise passengers are fed handsomely and almost continually. Not so down in the old steerage. Each passenger was issued a spoon, a fork, and a workingman's tin lunch pail. When the breakfast bell sounded at five minutes to seven, they raced to the adjacent dining area. This admittedly contemporary household word must suffice, for there was no dining saloon per se, as in second or first cabin up above, only a section of compartment with very few tables and benches, customarily reserved for women and children; the younger passengers were given milk. Male passengers would pass by the serving stewards with tin plates held out and then try and find space to eat, sometimes carrying their rapidly cooling pannikins out on deck. Female passengers who had seized the moment to dress when the compartment emptied before breakfast and were consequently late had no breakfast at all.

One wonders how much those latecomers were deprived. Steerage meals in general were described as wholesome in the original but so abused in the cooking as to be nearly inedible. One passenger estimated that half the food prepared for steerage passengers ended up hurled over the side. On British vessels, breakfast invariably began with porridge (alien to most European peasants), bread, and prune jam. Prunes were, indeed, the great generic comestible of the steerage at Ellis Island as well. Cheap and nourishing, prunes entailed only one logistic disadvantage: Despite special barrels provided for discarded pits, immigrants spat them onto the floor instead, in such sticky profusion that infuriated authorities periodically banned them.

Even breakfast coffee was unrewarding, since, like all steerage catering, it was prepared indifferently: Lukewarm water, sugar, milk, and coffee grounds were merely stirred together in a galvanized iron pot. During every midday meal, a junior ship's officer circulated among the steerage passengers, inquiring repeatedly, "Does the food taste good?" "It has to, we must eat something" was the predictable, aggrieved response.

In fact, passengers in the steerage could buy supplementary rations from a steward-run canteen, although too often the only luxuries available were drink for the men and fruit for wives and children. Worse, the very existence of that profit-making canteen diminished the quality of normal steerage catering; inferior or indifferent meals meant more trade at the canteen counter. (The same opportunity fell to entrepreneurial stewards on World War II troopships; many of them sold between-meal sandwiches to famished GIs.)

The only exception to the voyage's dreary commissariat appeared on the last night: a spread of eggs, onions, and fried potatoes. This relatively festive supper was not a steerage version of the gala dinner but had been calculated to foster an aura of contentment against the morrow's arrival and inspection. "Look happy," lied the chief steerage steward solemnly to his charges, "or you won't be permitted to land."

Of course, they would land in any event, and the unpleasant memories of their crossing, no less than their confinement in the port prior to embarkation, would fade. New and confusing sights and sounds would replace them, a heady synthesis of Bartholdi's welcoming sculpture in the harbor, the distant, incredible spires of Manhattan (which more than one impressionable immigrant perceived as mountains), the last hurdle and possible reconfinement at Ellis Island, and finally, the incomprehensible babble of Manhattan or a train journey west and south into the heart of this overwhelming new land.

It was inevitable, of course, that "old steerage," the norm of 1905, would be superseded by "new steerage" in the years to follow. Radical improvements were prompted simply by market forces. Emigrant numbers in excess of a million a year after the turn of the century triggered the construction and launch of bigger vessels. Larger hulls meant increased pretension and refinement on the upper decks, which, in turn, spawned improved conditions below. Inevitably, whenever first and second class were radically upgraded, the same renovative urge spilled over into steerage quarters as well. Indeed, many companies would follow the example of Hamburg American Line president Albert Ballin, who banished the term "steerage" and substituted "third class" in its stead. A phrase from *The Shipbuilder*, referring to the new *Olympic*-class vessels of 1911, is apropos: "Third class passengers today have greater comforts provided than had first class passengers before the great modern developments in passenger carrying."

Additionally—and perhaps this typified the sound business logic that created the new steerage—the old penny-pinching attitude was outmoded. For too long, steamship companies had insisted that emigrants would not appreciate improvements in shipboard conditions; moreover, it was stoutly maintained that if such upgrading occurred, the company's profit margin would suffer. But it became clear that enlightened shipping owners who made it their business to improve accommodation and catering were still able to operate in the black.

Before we arrive at the end of our transatlantic crossing, it is worth examining briefly the flavor of the new steerage to come. Gone were interminable stays in port, gone on board the berthing compartments: Passengers were housed in cabins holding anywhere from two to eight berths, berths made up with perhaps ancient linen—castoffs from cabin accommodations above—but plenty of blankets. The white-painted floorboards were kept spotless, and space on the floor for baggage, hooks on which to hang things, and even the simple, civilizing convenience of a mirror had been provided. Walls between cabins had openings top and bottom for the circulation of air but otherwise guaranteed absolute privacy for families, who, for the first time, could cross bunked together rather than segregated by sex in different compartments. Section VII was scrupulously observed, and no crewmen save assigned stewards were permitted in cabin country. Baths and showers were available for a supplementary but modest fee, and every washhouse was equipped with roller towels, soap, and more and cleaner basins.

Stewardesses were conscientious and concerned, although, it must be noted, more so when tipped. As on present-day shipboard, everyone performed better when tipped, especially that third-class fixture, the interpreter, invariably lazy and indifferent until bribed to perform the most rudimentary service.

There were, for the first time, public rooms for the third class. Portions of the lower deck were divided along the keel line, with a smoke room for men only on one side and a proper dining saloon for all along the other. Modest amenities included a piano, a clock, and a navigational chart. Before each meal, the long dining tables were set with pickles, apples, oranges, and an array of condiments in cruets. No longer would steerage children beg for fruit from the cabin passengers overlooking the after well deck. On cheerful red tablecloths, stewards deposited heaping china platters and, at the end of the meal, cleared them for washing in the pantry. Out on deck, there was more space for the third class, no longer a wasteland of winch and hatch cover but room for a promenade or seat in the sun. And, hallmark of their cabin shipmates above, bouillon was dispensed to the new third class on deck at eleven. At midmorning, everyone had congregated there, anyway, because stewards were scrubbing third-class cabins and public rooms in anticipation of the captain's daily inspection.

New steerage would, indeed, be a welcome improvement over old steerage conditions, and 1905 was the watershed year. By and large, the most insidious abuse in the old steerage compartments had been indifference. Lackadaisical supervision, hand in hand with only a grudging compliance with the law, had tarnished shipboard concern for the companies' humblest but most profitable clients.

And predictably, in 1905, the year of that great surge, the first ominous mutterings about the suitability of the latest immigrant flood—the watery symbolism had crossed the Atlantic intact—were heard. The year previous, 812,870 had come ashore at Ellis Island; in 1905, 1,027,421 would disembark. The September 1905 totals alone—90,772—were the highest in the history of the Bureau.

In early December, a Conference on Immigration convened in Madison Square Garden Concert Hall under the auspices of the National Civic Foundation. On hand as host was August Belmont, president of the foundation, and in attendance were Frank Sargent, U.S. commissioner of immigration, and significantly, Samuel Gompers, president of the American Federation of Labor.

Before their first meeting, the conferees rode a private subway train to Manhattan's South Ferry, then steamed by special ferry to

Ellis Island. After being ushered throughout the complex, they gathered on a balcony over the Registry Hall, watching fascinated as queues of immigrants from the *Kaiser Wilhelm der Grosse* snaked through the railed pens. For a lark, some of the distinguished visitors consented to a superficial medical examination, cheered on by their colleagues from above.

But that good-natured preamble would be eclipsed by inflammatory oratory back at Madison Square Garden. Archbishop John Ireland set the tone, thundering from the podium: "America has room for 100 million good immigrants but not room for one bad immigrant." Samuel Gompers, frequently interrupted by cheers, demanded federal intervention, warning the delegates that his constituents (most of them, incidentally, immigrants from earlier shiploads) wanted immigration curtailed.

Moderate voices were ignored. Harvard's president, Charles Eliot, had no sooner urged fairness to the new arrivals than a burly delegate from Ohio jumped to his feet. "We don't want worms and riffraff from southern Europe," he bellowed from the floor, "people who can live on two beers and a biscuit all day!"

It was clear that by 1905, in America's popular conscience, there were good immigrants and bad immigrants. The conference revealed a mood of angry mistrust, a consensus that whereas earlier immigrants had been honest, hardworking, and hence desirable, recent shiploads deluging East Coast ports carried only undesirables, *Luftmenschen* (devious types who seemed to live on air) and "the defeated, the incompetent, and the unsuccessful."

Predictably, the most vociferous were the newly established, those who feared displacement by others teeming in their wake. The classic survivors' syndrome was at work: "I'm on board, pull up the ladder." That ugly, isolationist mood would lead, ultimately, to the Dillingham Immigration Restriction Act of 1921, which dammed the tidal surge forever; though rigorously screened quotas continued to trickle in, the days of more than a million new Americans a year were over.

After World War I, North Atlantic vessels catered to a new breed of passenger, the tourist. And though most tourists would desert liners for jets by the late sixties, shipboard of another kind thrives elsewhere. Mass sailings from the Old World have given way to mass sailings from the New. Passenger numbers today dwarf yesterday's: The million immigrants of 1905 were as nothing to the nearly 4 million cruise passengers of 1990.

But a significant psychoemotional gulf separates present-day passengers from their steerage forebears. To use army administrative lingo, contemporary cruise passengers are casuals; rather than relocating for life, they board for the fun of it and, having completed an essentially pleasurable if fruitless voyage, disembark at the same pier from which they had embarked a week earlier. In stern Ellis Island terminology, they might almost qualify as rejects, "returned to their ports of origin at company expense."

Chapter 2

We don't give away anything anymore. In fact, we haven't for about four years now.
  —Joy Cadieu, Carnival marketing promotions specialist, July 1989

The downside is that cruise ships are a preview of all expensive retirement homes. We're overpampered but patronized. We're treated as if we had all lost our intellect. We're supposed to scream with joy over childish games. And there are all sorts of traps out there to separate us from our money.
  —Ashley Cooper

Nobody ever retires a ship—it's too damned profitable.
  —Robert Dickinson, senior vice-president, Marketing and Sales, Carnival Cruise Line

Carnival, Carnival, Carnival!

How better to bring yesterday's teeming shipboard hordes up-to-date than by examining the cruise carrier that embarks more passengers today than any other?

I must be honest. When friends were advised that I planned not only a cruise but also a chapter about Carnival, eyebrows—indeed, eyeballs!—rose heavenward. "You'll hate it," they scoffed. In response, I pointed out that one cannot ignore Carnival any more than one can sensibly ignore Red China.

Moreover, I did not hate my *Jubilee* cruise. Some aspects of the Fun Ship experience were, admittedly, not to my taste, but then, life on board several far more elegant ships is not, either; a more detailed critique will come later. I came home from Miami with the overwhelming realization that Carnival is here to stay, Carnival is an efficient and voracious money machine that dominates the cruise industry, and Carnival is, overwhelmingly, the future. One of every four cruise passengers today boards vessels owned by this extraordinarily successful line. Indeed, Carnival, Carnival, Carnival!

The company came into being two decades ago with a very modest debut in early 1972. The first flagship was a ten-year-old recycled liner from Canadian Pacific Railway, the *Empress of Canada*, a midsized maritime casualty done in by transatlantic jets. She had been withdrawn from Liverpool–Montreal service in November 1971 and laid up.

Almost at once, she was bought for Florida cruising by a Boston firm called American International Travel Service, Inc. (AITS). In charge of operations was Ted Arison, a shrewd and experienced Israeli engineer, heir to a shipping business, whose invaluable prior Miami experience had been as North American manager for Knut Kloster's Norwegian Caribbean Line.

Carnival's first vessel was scheduled to sail on her inaugural cruise in March 1972; at the time, that 25,780-ton liner would be the largest vessel based in the port. Her transformation for Caribbean service was, in fact, only superficial, because *Empress of Canada* had originally been built with part-time cruising in mind: An open-air pool was already sited on her afterdecks, and the vessel was fully air-conditioned. Public rooms and cabins remained largely as they had been on the North Atlantic. To this day, entwined within decorative brass railings on board, you can still find more than one cipher "CP" for Canadian Pacific.

Exterior changes were largely cosmetic. The hull was painted white, and the single midship stack was emblazoned with Carnival's new logo, a design achieved by expeditious and economic default. During their twilight years, Canadian Pacific had replaced its traditional red-and-white checkerboard funnel patch with a crescent-shaped livery; to save time, paint, and reconstruction, Carnival adapted that CPR symbol into a red, white, and blue funnel crescent of their own, a reverse "C" for Carnival.

The final metamorphosis was a new name. In a symbolic crossing-cruising rechristening, *Empress of Canada* became *Mardi Gras*, a maritime Ekaterinburg, if you will, Atlantic Empress displaced by a populist Caribbean regime. The name, the spirit it conveyed, and the hastily refurbished vessel it adorned were the first hesitant steps of what would become Carnival's gaudy and incredibly successful Fun Ship fandango.

The *Mardi Gras*'s first cruise, in March 1972, began disconcertingly. En route to sea, she ran aground. In those days, Miami's channel, Government Cut, was dredged to a depth of thirty feet; the *Mardi Gras* had entered the port light, but by the time she sailed, her draft at the stern was twenty-nine feet six inches. Although the pilot recommended retrimming and the master waited until the flood tide, a stiff northeast gale turned the vessel's nose as she passed beyond the breakwater. An either misunderstood or inaccurate rudder command from pilot to helmsman resulted in a sharp turn to starboard instead of port, and the ship grounded gently but firmly on the limestone and coral bottom south of Government Cut.

There she remained for twenty-four hours, finally removed by a flotilla of tugs. Divers inspecting the hull found that the *Mardi Gras* had hung up directly beneath the keel, where, in fact, plating and framing were strongest; the hull was dented but otherwise undamaged. The cruise continued. Compounding the embarrassment, 300 travel agents were on board as guests of the line. An amusing episode survives from that stranding: One unnerved passenger-couple accidentally conceived their first child that night and, nine months later, sent Ted Arison a birth announcement, advising him that they had christened the babe Sandy to commemorate the grounding. Delighted, Arison gave the family a free cruise.

For two years, the company limped from pillar to post, flirting with bankruptcy. Although passenger loads on board the *Mardi Gras* were respectable, the parent company in Boston kept all profits, leaving Miami ship operations in dire financial straits. Additionally, in the words of Carnival's public relations director, Tim Gallagher, AITS "bypassed travel agents, selling directly to the public. Needless to say, this alienated the travel-agent community, leaving Carnival Cruise Lines with virtually no support from the trade." (That early disaffection of travel agents would change, as we shall see.)

In 1974, Arison bought the *Mardi Gras* outright for a token dollar, together with $5 million in debts. He revamped the company's service on board and, within a miraculous month, had managed to turn a voyage profit. Success grew with the fleet. The following year, Arison bought a second superannuated Canadian Pacific liner: The *Empress of Britain* became the *Carnivale*.

In 1978, the former *Transvaal Castle* of the Union Castle Line and, subsequently, the *S.A. Vaal* of Safmarine joined Carnival's fleet as *Festivale*. Arison's largest purchase to date, the former

South African liner was gutted. Many of her accommodations were revamped into (more) smaller ones, and to increase capacity further, additional cabins were wrought within redundant, cavernous cargo-and-mail holds.

Renovations on this third vessel were completed in Japan, and the company's transition team, Technical Marine Planning of London (which still oversees all Carnival newbuilding) ran afoul of that country's adamantine import restrictions. Still frozen solid on board when the ship tied up in Kobe were seven tons of Argentinean beef, remnants of the vessel's North Atlantic commissariat. Since the ship's service electricity would shut down and refrigeration would cease, the owners wished to dispose of the superfluous meat and offered it as a donation to the poor of Kobe. But stringent Japanese beef import quotas forbade landing so much as an entrecote. A second possible alternative—throwing the meat over the side—would have polluted Japanese waters.

After the transition team had gorged on beefsteak for breakfast, lunch, and dinner, the remaining meat was, of necessity, packed into steel drums. These were welded shut and lined up on the fo'c'sle head. There they sat for several months, sometimes in the blazing sun. Near the end, every drum swelled ominously; had one actually burst and wafted a carrion reek throughout the Kawasaki yard, the Japanese might have thought twice. But none did, and the putrid remains were finally dumped into the Pacific en route to the United States.

Another local difficulty involved disposal of the S.A. *Vaal's* almost-new carpeting. Carnival wanted to replace it with carpeting keyed to their own color scheme. As with beef, so with carpeting: Offloading was forbidden. The final solution was less noisome than the beef catch-22 but just as cumbersome. Every scrap of carpet was cut into one-foot squares. Then, to ensure that these would *never* find use ashore, each square had to be painted. Only then were stacks of daubed Axminster swatches consigned to dumpsters at the yard. As later generations of American trade officials have discovered, Japan does not suffer imports easily.

Arison completed the 1970s with a three-ship fleet, economically converted and immensely profitable. Similar to numbers of transatlantic predecessors, Arison would, with a single exception—one-of-a-kind *Tropicale*—generally deal with trios of ships, save for the last: *Imagination* is scheduled as a fifth for the *Fantasy* class. The *Mardi Gras*, the *Carnivale*, and the *Festivale* shared in common a

TOP: *Carnival's ingenious and economical adaptation of Canadian Pacific's final crescent-shaped logo.* (Author's collection)

BOTTOM: *Joseph and Jeanne Farcus on board the brand-new* Fantasy *in 1990. Their output is prodigious, their sense of what will work unerring.* (Author's collection)

sturdy transatlantic heritage. Several other vessels of that vintage are still steaming elsewhere, among them ex-Sitmar tonnage now absorbed within Princess Cruises: the *Star Princess*, the *Sky Princess*, and the *Sea Princess*.

Those British-built vessels were designed with a stern proviso in mind, able to cross with impunity during "Winter North Atlantic," terse shorthand for a kind of maritime hell. This was the significance of the legend "W.N.A.," the lowest (hence, lightest) indicator of the Plimsoll Line, a round symbol found at the waterline of every ship's flank, indicating safe loading levels. The ships' pronounced sheer and camber, combined with stout scantling and plate, give their hulls a doughty, almost indestructible strength, of a kind markedly absent in cruise-ship newbuilding. They will, presumably, survive forever. Beneath domed casings in their engine spaces, Parsons steam turbines whir effortlessly, reliable and essentially maintenance-free. Since they do not run to bow or stern thrusters, tugs sometimes shepherd them in and out of port.

What splendid thoroughbreds they are! Their evocative profiles, long fo'c'sles, centered deckhouses, and single stacks betray dignified breeding from the past, crossing Percherons put contentedly out to cruising pasture. It is interesting that the 1990 edition of Carnival's brochure indiscriminately lists new and old ships: The *Festivale* comes first; the new *Fantasy*, last. Neither seniority nor size nor pretension is given priority, only the length of cruise each vessel offers.

In the summer of 1981, I visited several European shipyards, among them Denmark's Aalborg Werft A/S, where Carnival's fourth vessel, the *Tropicale*, hull number 234, was fitting out. This was the first newbuilding that Carnival had ever undertaken, and it represented a radical departure from any of their existing vessels. Not only was the *Tropicale* one of the first box-shaped hulls filled with (surprisingly large) modular cabins; she also boasted first installation of the company's distinctive funnel.

Mention of that fixture, Carnival Cruise Line's technodecorative shipboard crown, seems an appropriate moment to introduce its creator. Joseph Farcus is a young architect-designer, short, cheerful, unassuming, and engagingly uncomplicated, who was born in Pennsylvania, moved to Florida at the age of ten, and never left. After training in architecture at the University of Florida, Farcus was first employed by the firm of renowned architect Morris Lapidus, who, in 1954, had completed his chef d'oeuvre, that monument to beachfront architecture, Miami Beach's Fontainebleau Hotel.

In fact, while still employed by Lapidus, Farcus paid his first professional visit to a Carnival cruise ship. Lapidus's firm had been retained by Arison to do some interior work on board *Carnivale*, and Farcus, the new young associate, reported on board to oversee implementation of his superior's design. His first professional shipboard visit seemed final realization of a long-cherished childhood dream: One of ten-year-old Joe Farcus's most prized books had been *How to Draw Merchant Ships*.

Within a year and a half, Farcus had opened his own office, and Carnival Cruise Lines had become his client. He has remained their designer of choice ever since. The *Tropicale*'s interior design was his first full contract. Farcus was anxious to improve cabin dimensions; too often, he felt, they were cramped, the bathrooms especially so, "where the entire bathroom becomes the shower." On board the *Tropicale*, he would establish a remarkably generous cabin standard for a seven-day ship, in excess of 169 square feet, including bathroom, well above the industry norm.

Of course, Farcus did not achieve this by himself. Most owners undertake newbuilding with what is called a steering committee: a team of owners, naval architect, designer, and corporate as well as ship's officers who oversee every step of the labyrinthian process. I asked Farcus who served on Carnival's steering committees; his response was that Carnival's steering committee was really Ted Arison.

With his enviable shipping and engineering background, Arison is frighteningly competent and can, after only a brief visit to any corner of a vessel under construction, divine potential trouble spots no less than their solution. Shipyard personnel are always astonished at finding an owner who can speak their language, read a drawing intelligently, and remain articulately knowledgeable about their arcane world.

In fact, Carnival does boast an ad hoc steering committee, composed of Ted Arison, now chairman of the board; his son Micky, president since 1979; Meshulam "Mike" Zonas, operations and sales; hotel boss Everett Philips; and designer Joe Farcus. Nevertheless, it is Arison *père* who remains the company's unquestioned final arbiter.

A case in point? Resolution of the open-or-enclosed-bridge controversy for the *Holiday-* and *Fantasy*-class vessels, also scheduled for a Holland America trio to come. Carnival masters, entering or leaving port, dislike enclosed bridges because they are insulated, literally, from feeling the wind on their cheeks; and a crosswind acting on those vast Carnival flanks makes Caribbean harbor entrances—Nassau and Freeport, for example—a worrisome maneuvering challenge.

Indeed, so prone are Carnival's boxy hulls to wind pressure that bollards have been plucked like molars from Miami piers by strong offshore breezes. The remedy, incidentally, is installation of thrusters fore and aft, propellers within transverse tunnels athwart the hull that can impel the vessel sideways. (Unfortunately, thrusters overheat easily: The *Tropicale*'s bow thruster was once burned out from overuse. So on *Fantasy*-class hulls, each of six thrusters is water cooled so that they can be used *in extenso* during wind-plagued dockings.)

But back to the open-or-enclosed-bridge debate. Though masters like the wind on their cheek, enclosed bridges protect delicate navigational equipment from destructive humidity and salt air. When, in the early 1990s, general arrangements (G.A.) for the new HAL trio were being discussed, Arison polled every Carnival master: Should the bridges for the new class be opened or enclosed? Without exception, every captain recommended they be open. But Arison's final decision was unequivocally to keep them enclosed.

Arison, his son Micky, and corporate subordinates have successfully entered into service four consecutive classes of Carnival tonnage: the earliest trio of converted liners, the single interim vessel *Tropicale*, three *Holiday*-class ships, then four *Fantasy*-class giants and an impressive Holland America trio in train. That newbuilding track record represents a continuum of mutual collaboration and achievement unique to the industry.

Although he is quick to point out that Carnival is merely one of his clients, Farcus remains an indispensable member of the company's team. With only the collaboration of his wife, Jeanne, he designed a formidable work load of seven vessels as well as the Crystal Palace, Carnival's giant hotel-casino in the Bahamas, all within one demanding decade, a daunting task for any husband-and-wife team.

Solo implementation on this scale is unique. On board Royal Caribbean Cruise Line's *Sovereign of the Seas*, for example, decorative chores above and below deck were parceled out to several Scandinavians: Njål Eide conceived the vast Centrum, Mogens

Hammer was responsible for the theater, and Robert Tillberg designed the double-decker indoor-outdoor restaurant. Similarly, when the *Queen Elizabeth 2* was fitting out during the late sixties, Dennis Lennon completed one or two public rooms but, in addition, integrated various subordinate designers' work into a tranquil whole.

One has to search back as far as the 1890s, to either Johannes Poppe, Norddeutscher Lloyd's resident architect, or Charles Mewès's celebrated work for the Hamburg American Line, to find role models for Farcus's extraordinary solo effort. Yet both of those nineteenth-century predecessors had ateliers of draftsmen assisting them; Joe and Jeanne Farcus turn out everything themselves.

I first met Joe on board the company's second vessel, the *Carnivale*, in January 1990. She was tied up downstream from Carnival's Miami terminus for six weeks of what is known in the trade as wet dock, as opposed to more ambitious hull work undertaken of necessity in a dry dock. *Carnivale* was undergoing a $12 million renovation before repositioning to Port Canaveral. The first of several hundred marble tiles had been cemented to the dining-room floor, and throughout the vessel, Farcus was updating cabin decor and plumbing.

He showed me through some of the upper-deck suites whose vintage paneling and furniture were being restored or replaced. Seen in brilliant Miami sunlight, those scarred wooden walls, heavy wardrobes, and institutional sofas seemed cumbersome, relics of the days when interiors served as snug retreats from North Atlantic chill rather than for cool breathers between swimming and sunning, a look dating from the *Empress of Britain*'s maiden voyage of 1956. That almost quaintly substantial paneling and furniture underscored the dramatic shipboard changes that have occurred within three oceangoing decades. Dour northern palette has succumbed to vibrant Caribbean hues.

But back to Carnival's funnel. At an Aalborg shipyard conference in late 1980, during the *Tropicale*'s early construction, there was discussion about what shape the newbuilding's single funnel should take. (The descriptive "single," relating to contemporary cruise-ship funnels, seems redundant: The only multistacked passenger vessels built since the *Rotterdam* of 1959 are the *France*, the last *Kungsholm*, and the Seabourn ships.) While shipyard personnel racked their brains, Farcus sketched on the back of an envelope. What emerged was a single futuristic structure with a raked, tapering trunk that divided in half at the summit, directing smoke to either side through elegant, branching wings. Although reminiscent of the *France*'s distinctive *cheminée à ailerons*, Farcus's funnel had no cap and boasted the addition of a forward wind scoop that increased its efficiency.

The young Floridian was pleased that though the Danes were initially skeptical, his funnel has since proved its worth seven times over. By the time it was installed on board the *Fantasy*, its original form had been refined, the angle softened, and its branches given a leaner and more graceful upward flare. Farcus's distinctive stack remains unique and serves to identify, as any good funnel should, every Carnival vessel.

Creating a funnel and having it adorn most ships of a fleet may be a gratifying design imprimatur; but Joseph Farcus's work below-decks for Carnival remains even more memorable. During our lunch on board the *Carnivale*, Farcus characterized his design intent, afloat as well as ashore at Nassau's Crystal Palace, as "leisure-time design . . . a playful, fun feeling." His architectural credo, he has written, is simplicity itself, derived from Vitruvius, the great Roman architect of the first century B.C. The Vitruvian triad? *Commoditas, Firmitas, Venustas* ("Fitness, Firmness, Delight"). Quite simply, Farcus wants passengers "to have a good time, whether"—and this is important—"participants or observers." He tries to create interiors that serve as "entertainments, the type of entertainment where you are not sitting in the cinema watching the entertainment on the screen, you are totally involved. You're at the same time part of the show and part of the audience."

Several times before actually sailing on the *Jubilee*, I had toured Carnival vessels and been struck by the novel vibrancy of Farcus's work no less than his extraordinary range of antic invention. Overscale graphics heralded one fanciful public room after another, all extravagant, Formicoco creations. Farcus insists that he never designs down, does not pander to Carnival's unsophisticated clientele, and characterizes himself as a traditionalist. And whatever the sum total of architectural effect, Farcus insists that his approach is deadly serious, that he is *not* in the business of "shock."

One detail that caught my eye on board *Jubilee* typifies his touch: The grout between the black tiles of a lobby planter was bright magenta, an affectation I found duplicated throughout the Crystal Palace's men's room. Magenta grout: Prescribing that giddy color

ABOVE: *The upper course of Carnival's first winged funnel, seen on the pier before installation at Aalborg's Yard in Denmark. Designed off the cuff by* wunderkinder *Farcus, it graced* Tropicale, *the company's first newbuilding.* (Author's collection)

LEFT: Fantasy's *funnel has been refined over the years into a leaner, more fluid shape.* (Author's collection)

for such a mundane joint seems pure Farcus: vivid, unconventional, and with a gleam of manic whimsy.

In effect, I think he has capitalized on late-twentieth-century America's obsession with pop fantastical recreation: Postmodernist shopping mall, casino, and park have proliferated into total-immersion escapism. The stereotypical sourcebook is inevitable: colonial raj, Victorian riverboat, Wild West, enchanted castle, Broadway musical, or cult film. Whereas Disney invented the genre, his Hollywood confreres have since gone one better, enticing tourists to parks wherein they may relive, vicariously, past television and movie experiences, transferred from screen to fiberglass reality. Similarly, Fun Ship interiors slide out to sea as giant, floating theme parks.

Joe Farcus is of the verismo school of design—his interiors are not derived from an original; they are originals. He begins within steel limitations: The configuration of his interiors is established by what is called the G.A., or general arrangement, the naval architect's allotment of public rooms of predetermined capacity, worked out according to the owner's specific needs. Once the G.A. has been finalized, then Farcus is free to embark on his thematic invention. Theoretically, he could, for every trio of Carnival vessels, merely design in triplicate, especially for a company that tends, as we shall see, to shun the passenger recidivist. Regardless, each vessel of a Carnival threesome has been adorned with different treatments for identical areas, each making its own distinctive decorative point.

Let us examine, for example, the libraries he created for the *Holiday*-class threesome. I like Farcus's libraries, large, quiet spaces, unoccupied for most of the day, the abode, one must assume, of his "observers" rather than "participants." One of Carnival Cruise Line's unhappier characteristics, I discovered, is a noisy ship; hence, that library peace seems doubly attractive, blessed oasis of quiet amid the jungle turmoil. The *Holiday* has the Carnegie Library, sheathed in a variety of exotic paneling; on the *Jubilee*, the library is called Churchill's, with a baronial stone (alas, unworking) fireplace as well as several suits of armor posed around the room; the *Celebration*'s is called simply Admiral's, its bookcases interspersed with authentic ocean-liner models and memorabilia; adorning a huge light fixture overhead are backlit broadsides of *Normandie* and *Queen Mary*. Though all the libraries' names strive for a kind of spurious "clubman" grandiosity, they convey precisely the ambience that Farcus intended. (I am reminded, on the same subject, of a glorious signage howler on board the *Royal Viking Sun*: DICKEN'S LIBRARY.)

Up on the *Jubilee*'s Lido Deck I found a splendid Farcus tribute to ocean-liner history. The Funnel Bar and Grill is the informal breakfast/lunch/tea restaurant serving both pools; its name deserves memorializing if for no other reason than it is *not* yet another "Windjammer," as sorely overused on board today's cruise ship as "gourmet dining." In fact, the *Jubilee*'s real funnel pierces the forward end of the room, but its anonymous casing is flanked by two round, rivet-studded, funnellike walls concealing cafeteria lines; scattered aft among the tables are historically accurate miniature stacks interspersed with clusters of nonworking ventilators. The thematic thrust continues atop every table: Embedded therein like flies in amber is a collector's dream of steamship brochures, posters, postcards, and luggage tags. Signal flags adorn the ceiling, and immaculately scrubbed teak stretches underfoot. Primary funnel and ventilator colors pleasingly reflect table and chair accents.

Indeed, Farcus tends, on board all Carnival vessels, to concentrate heavily on the primaries, extending from the unabashed red, white, and blue funnel logo above throughout many interiors. To me, this seems entirely apropos, for primaries serve as the color idiom of man and sea—the unmistakable, reassuring, cheerful polychromy of lighthouse, buoy, flag, and funnel.

More recently, Farcus has expanded his horizons. When boarding the first of the *Fantasy*-class hulls in early 1990, I was intrigued to see how, within the five years since *Holiday*'s debut, Farcus had come of age. Overall, the innovative flame burns as brightly as ever, yet amid the glittering extravagance and sometimes garish excess were signs of a new sophistication and maturity.

Of course, evaluation of the *Fantasy*'s decorative bent is partially skewed by the visual impact of its central atrium, which Farcus has christened the Grand Spectrum. Atria began appearing on a variety of rival cruise lines during the 1980s and reached a crescendo of sorts on board the *Fantasy*. Princess Cruises started the stampede in 1984 with the *Royal Princess*'s two-deck atrium. Royal Caribbean Cruise Line upped the ante with the *Sovereign of the Seas*' five-deck Centrum; Norwegian Cruise Line (NCL) followed suit with the *Seaward*'s pallid two-decker, to be overtaken by the *Fantasy*'s seven-deck Grand Spectrum, which in turn was outranked by RCCL's *Nordic Empress*'s nine-deck extravaganza, also called the Centrum.

The upshot is that atria have flooded the maritime design market, extending from megaship to miniship. Both Seabourn vessels have an atrium of sorts, as does the more recent *Radisson Diamond*, although both are small vessels catering to only a few hundred passengers. Are these small-ship atria merely glamorized open stairwells? No, according to Vincent Kwok, the Radisson ship's designer; he insists his is a legitimate six-deck atrium complete with glass elevator and open staircases, just like the larger prototypes. So atria, it appears, have become entrenched as cruise-design dogma and will remain as inevitable an on-board fixture as bingo or midnight buffet.

Whereas the *Sovereign*'s Centrum gleams with brass, Farcus lined the levels of the *Fantasy*'s Grand Spectrum with miles of concealed neon tubing, creating a formidable illuminative orchestra. Throughout the atrium as well as Promenade Deck and theater, three contrasting neon circuits snake within white plastic soffits. By day, the white plastic seems opaque, all of a piece with the ship's gray-white Fantastico marble. But late in the day, as Grand Spectrum's skylight dims, Farcus's neon concerto begins.

Neon comes in four shades of red, blue, green, and yellow; Farcus has embraced all but the yellow. Thanks to a gradual computerized cross-fading of all three colors, an infinite spectrum—a Grand Spectrum, in fact—should theoretically be possible. But because fire regulations require each neon tube to remain at least two inches from its neighbor, the blend is less efficacious than it should be. The long segue, for example, from Mobil red dwells only fleetingly in the haunting indigo-lavender bands before surrendering unequivocally to Sunoco blue.

What the eye no less than the spirit absorbs is less a color spectacle than the sensation of being trapped within an Artkraft-Strauss neon spectacular high above Times Square: "You're at the same time part of the audience and part of the show." Farcus's words came back to me as I stood uneasily on one of Grand Spectrum's balconies after dinner. Such is the cumulative intensity of those glowing neon lumens that one becomes transfixed. Grand Spectrum's pyrotechnics have neither the benevolent twinkle of Tivoli lights nor the comforting gleam of conventional incandescence. The delicate pencil lines of unadorned neon, encased within semiopaque plastic, have been amplified into crayon smears, an effect that is, at the same time, startling, stupendous, and yet somehow menacing.

LEFT: *Farcus's neon concerto be-gins with bands of green neon.* (Author's collection)

BELOW: *Along the Promenade Deck, the same color-keyed glow outlines the windows.* (Author's collection)

Preprogrammed light changes embody one of Farcus's design watchwords: the need in architecture for recurring surprise, an allowance for some hitherto unperceived aspect of a structure or space to emerge subsequent to one's first impression. In fact, Farcus hopes one day to design a complex of buildings ashore that will, in apparent defiance of the natural order of things, gradually change shape and interrelation. Grand Spectrum's nocturnal color baths obviously anticipate that dream.

Manipulating public-room lighting on board ship is scarcely new. Years before Joe Farcus was born, Doris Zinkeisen implemented the same effect in the *Queen Mary's* Veranda Grill, an almost imperceptible blush from peach to rose. But that discreet shift was nothing compared with Farcus's surging polychromy. Though Carnival's *Fantasy* brochure merely hints at "subtly changing light environments," Farcus's neon effect overpowers with the impact of a particularly lurid display of northern lights.

One wonders: Will honeymoon couples booked on board *Fantasy*-class vessels eschew sunset on deck for Farcus's sunset in the Grand Spectrum? Perhaps Farcus has passed a milestone, aping indoors scenic phenomena previously restricted to the horizon. I occasionally worry about the cumulative sensationalization of ship-board interiors, special effects that turn passenger heads inboard and, paradoxically, away from sea, sky, and island.

Before leaving Grand Spectrum, it is worth noting that only its two lowest levels are connected by stairs. Passengers may ascend via a ceremonial dividing staircase from Empress Deck to Atlantic, but from there on up, they must either ride neon-encrusted glass elevators or walk forward—temporarily leaving the atrium—to the main staircase. I think this absence of vertical passenger access hurts the space; the *Sovereign's* Centrum, as we shall see, is enriched—nay, justified!—in that passengers can negotiate its various levels on foot. Whereas Centrum is functional, Grand Spectrum is not; Royal Caribbean's passengers actually use their atrium, whereas Carnival's can do little more than gape over its railings.

One day at sea, I toured *Fantasy* with Joe Farcus, strolling along the Century Promenade. As on every Carnival Promenade Deck since *Holiday*, this traditional shipboard fixture occupies only one side of the vessel, yet another refinement from Ted Arison. Rather than flanking centrally located public rooms with symmetrical narrow promenades to either side, Arison suggested that a wide promenade should occupy the vessel's starboard side only; adjacent public rooms, no longer confined amidships, have a portside view directly over the sea.

One *salon fantastique* especially impressed me: Indeed, apart from a sole disruptive element, I thought it Farcus at his very best. Cleopatra's Bar overlooks one of Grand Spectrum's railings, a convincing facsimile of an Egyptian tomb. (If one questions, even momentarily, why, on board a late-twentieth-century cruise ship, one should order drinks in an Egyptian tomb, then one is clearly not attuned to Farcus's third Vitruvian principle.) The walls are covered, Farcus assured me, with authentic hieroglyphics that, together with handsome "bronze" (fiberglass) doors, painted sarcophagi, brooding statuary, and random-paved granite floor, combine to stunning effect. Tables are imprinted with Egyptian motifs, and Farcus found just the right chairs in Holland, with sinuous, asymmetrical burled maple backs and black lacquered legs, that add a splendid art deco look. To me, they seem perfectly at home in Luxor: the movie connection again, straight out of an Agatha Christie Nile thriller from the thirties.

In fact, the small triangular area of Cleopatra's Bar is clearly inadequate as a setting for Farcus's selection of heroic, funerary statuary. Conversely, however, those overscale figures impart an intriguing, necrological mood. We seem to have stumbled unawares into a vault beneath the Cairo Museum. Almond-shaped granite eyes keep watch, staring in haunted, sightless proximity through dust-moted amber light. In sum, a decorative tour de force.

Alas, the only aberrance is a major one: Cleopatra's Bar is also a piano bar. A circular black bar containing a revolving piano dominates the space. Patrons lean on an encircling faux keyboard while an overmiked pianist prevents conversation in that otherwise pleasant room save during welcome breaks. The dread sobriquet "piano bar" reduces Cleopatra's Bar from retreat to roadhouse and, in the process, sabotages its inspired design.

(Do passengers, I wonder, really crave the vulgar camaraderie of the piano bar? Presumably they do, for piano bars on board cruise ships are as inescapable as atria; perhaps shy or lonely passengers find solace therein. Yet for every half-dozen devotees clustered boozily around the Yamaha, dozens more are anxious for quiet. I collect insufferable cruise-ship piano bars: among the worst,

TOP: *Cleopatra's, Farcus's whimsical bar on board the* Fantasy. *But for the deafening singer/pianist, one might spend all night.* (Author's collection)

BOTTOM: *Two utterly contented Carnival passengers reboard the* Jubilee *after a day's shopping and swimming ashore in St. Thomas.* (Author's collection)

the Schooner Bar on board the *Sovereign of the Seas*, complete with leather-lunged, amplified singer/pianist. But we shall discuss cruising's electronic abuse elsewhere.)

Aft of that Egyptian chamber, our next destination was the Cats Lounge. Farcus has immortalized not only Andrew Lloyd Webber's musical *Cats* but its trash-can scenery as well. At his local supermarket, he told me, he filled a shopping cart with familiar logos, and, at the register, challenged the baffled cashier to guess what he was going to do with his purchases.

Clearly, he put them to novel use. We entered Cats through a shiny, ridged tunnel—in effect, through an open-ended salmon can lying on its side. Once inside, we were engulfed in a wasteland of monstrous pop detritus: bar surmounted Ronzoni spaghetti box, Kiwi polish cans served as tabletops, and a Ritz cracker box of gargantuan scale accommodated a full-sized fire-station door in its facade.

But whereas Cleopatra's Bar offered enchantment, the Cats Lounge's kitchen-sink kitsch did not. I found it a decorative one-liner, a disposable, instantly biodegradable conceit. Perhaps Warhol's notorious Campbell's soup cans have spoiled me, but as far as the *Fantasy* is concerned, I am certain that Cats Lounge will remain a solid Farcusian winner, delighting, as both Farcus and Vitruvius intended, thousands of passengers to come.

Who embarks on the Fun Ships? Answer: Everyman from Everywhere, U.S.A. From the beginning, Carnival has cast its unique marketing net over virgin waters. "We began selling cruises," explains Tim Gallagher, Carnival's director of public relations, "where no one had ever thought of selling cruises before. In the middle of the country, far from the sea."

As a result, teeming schools of passenger plankton, the tiniest fish at the bottom of cruising's food chain, were—and still are—netted as Carnival clients: the most malleable, most susceptible, and most easily pleased clientele of all—unsophisticated, inexperienced, and significantly, devoid of cruising preconceptions. Week in, week out, thousands of neophyte passengers embrace their Fun Ship experience with naive delight, realizing a bountiful return on their Carnival investment. Every aspect of their week afloat is engineered to please, from vivid colors to plentiful, uncomplicated food, from breezy daytime indolence to a glitzy, Las Vegan regime after dark.

When Mary and I sailed on the *Jubilee*, we had just disembarked from the *Norway* and, having been warned about the Carnival passengers' high jinks by naysayers in New York, tried to construct a typical Carnival passenger profile. During our meals, we discreetly scrutinized fellow diners in the Bordeaux dining room. Directly behind us were two large, round tables of company-incentive winners, star salesmen and their wives from a Pennsylvania firm of equine suppliers. First-time passengers all, they were pleasant, well-mannered, and only occasionally but good-naturedly ribald.

At another neighboring table, the passenger makeup seemed the nadir of inappropriate seating: Five middle-aged single women had, as dining companions, a trio of hirsute youths who sported, for lunches at least, singlets and beer cans. Yet, to our astonishment, that unlikely mélange coalesced: The boys' occasional shock tactics were neutralized by a barrage of solicitous mothering, never more overwhelming than when one of the lads appeared on crutches in mid-cruise.

Yet despite largely benevolent table manners, I must report that the *Jubilee's* second-sitting passengers did flunk a subtle but unerring litmus test, the trial of the dropped tray. Inevitably, as happens in every ship's dining room at least once each cruise, during the frenetic dinner rush, a hard-pressed steward accidentally upends his tray, producing a monumental spill. The *Jubilee's* crash interested me less than the response: Whereas experienced passengers will try to ignore both the event and the poor steward's distress, Carnival's broke into a burst of shouting applause; some even rushed over to videotape the wreckage.

But that episode proved, thankfully, only an aberration. After our week with Carnival, Mary and I were left with the unshakable conviction that, behaviorally, their passengers are identical to passengers on any seven-day Caribbean vessels. However, passenger noise levels are significantly higher. A coterie of young men whose ringleader was accommodated in the cabin next to ours congregated boisterously in the corridor prior to every meal.

But, to my mind, they and too many of their fellow passengers were noisy because the *Jubilee* itself was noisy. Loudspeakers brayed relentlessly all week long, whether pitches for personalized cruise videotapes or songs howled by the Gazebo's guitarist, whether the shrieks for shapeliest leg competition out on deck or the hysterics of a drag competition among beefy male passengers in the Universe Lounge. Obtrusive noise seems to generate additional noise; perhaps Carnival's Legion Hall hugger-mugger is no more than a Pavlovian response to the company's relentless loudspeaker levels.

The man responsible for bringing those passenger hordes flocking on board the company's hulls is Robert Dickinson, Carnival's marketing—there is no other word—genius. A slim, bespectacled figure, Dickinson worked originally as a financial planner at the Ford Motor Company's Dearborn office. He joined Carnival in August 1973, hired by AITS, the original Boston owners. After December 1974, he recalls, "I began working for Ted Arison rather than with Ted Arison"; at this pivotal moment, Arison assumed complete control of the company.

One of Dickinson's first marketing chores was to overhaul the line's slogan, a pallid bromide characterizing the *Mardi Gras* as "flagship of the golden fleet." Since the flagship was patently not golden and since there was no fleet anyway, Dickinson changed marketing course onto a less pretentious tack, convincing potential clients that the ports were secondary to the ship. The *Mardi Gras* was jazzed up with more music, more casino, and more—more *fun!* In fact, the *Mardi Gras* became, under Dickinson's guidance, the first Fun Ship—a concept and a campaign that has withstood the test of time and remained a hallowed cornerstone of Carnival's image ever since.

Bob Dickinson also dreamed up another marketing ploy that has successfully dragooned every travel agent in America firmly into Carnival's camp. Throughout the hinterland, unsuspecting travel agents are visited by anonymous shills called "mystery clients," similar to Michelin's celebrated "mystery diners," who rate thousands of French hotel and restaurant menus each year. But whereas the Michelin men are evaluating, Carnival's men (or women) are rewarding—rewarding, that is, for specific, correct answers.

The travel agency scenario plays as follows:

> *Mystery Client*: I want to go on a vacation. What do you recommend?
> *Travel Agent*: What about a cruise?

At this point, the mystery client hands over a crisp ten-dollar bill. But had the travel agent responded instead: "What about a *Carnival* cruise?" he or she would have pocketed a thousand dollars in cash on the spot.

Inevitably, Dickinson's "mystery clients" are eagerly anticipated by every travel agency in the land; also inevitably, travel agents blurt out "Carnival Cruise" in response to every blind inquiry. It is a marketing scheme of Machiavellian ingenuity, one that has been in effect for nearly a decade at a modest cost of half a million dollars.

On nearly every other cruise line, passengers are courted assiduously to return; special parties and premiums await them when they reembark. But Carnival sales reps have been imbued with a different marketing slant. Dickinson's theory is that if there are too many repeaters, the sales force is not doing its job properly in attracting new clients. "If the repeats rate creeps beyond 30 percent," he suggests, "by definition, we are not expanding the cruise industry as fast as we desire."

This paradoxical recidivist philosophy is the linchpin of Dickinson's marketing thrust. Indeed, the rest of the industry remains eternally in Carnival's debt for having spread the cruising word so assiduously. Television's banal *Love Boat*, first broadcast in 1977, has been credited with popularizing mass-market cruising, but I tend to differ. Whereas they may have glorified it, Carnival had beaten them to the punch with the *Mardi Gras* half a decade earlier.

It used to be said that only 5 percent of America has ever booked a cruise. During a recent conversation, Jim Godsman, peripatetic chief of the Cruise Line International Association, updated that figure; among household members over the age of twenty-five with an income of over $20,000, only 10.7 percent have taken a cruise. This target market is ripe for infinite expansion; safe to say that Carnival has recruited and continues to recruit more neophyte passengers than any other company.

Behind Dickinson's boyish, bespectacled face lurks a steel-trap mind. He knows his ships, their particulars, and their markets frighteningly well, and he has a phenomenal capacity for remembering names and faces. On *Fantasy*'s press cruise, I watched in awe as he summoned onto the stage well over a hundred Carnival sales representatives who were on board, never using notes to match names, faces, or often as not, some anecdote about a promotion, a new baby, or a recent hometown event. At a subsequent press conference—a nonordeal both he and Micky Arison seemed to relish—Dickinson was smooth, knowledgeable, and glib in the best sense of the word, bandying answers and, occasionally, wisecracks with the maritime press. Yet all is not glibness: I have seen Dickinson listen, unflinching and genuinely concerned, to a babblative travel agent's half-hour lament.

As of 1984, in pursuit of more flocks of Newpassengers, Carnival entered the three- and four-day cruise market, a Miami staple dating back to the days of the Eastern Steamship Company in the early sixties. Dickinson sees the short cruise as a magnet for Newpassengers—a chance for them "to get their feet wet" while at the same time reducing their investment of time and money.

A glance at Carnival's brochure prices indicates that short cruises are money-makers. During 1990, for example, a category 7 cabin on board the *Mardi Gras* in high season generated $745 for a three-day cruise and $885 for a four-day, a total of $1,630; for a week aboard the *Festivale*, the same-category cabin generates $1,575, a revenue differential of $55 in favor of the split week. And certainly fuel costs for shorter itineraries are lower. But port stops and docking fees are doubled: The *Mardi Gras*, during two consecutive shorter cruises, sailed in and out of Fort Lauderdale twice and into three other ports as well. *Festivale* sailed in and out of San Juan only once but called at four intervening ports. But the three- and four-day market's offsetting drain—and it is a significant one—is free airfare, the substantial cost of flying twice as many short-time passengers into and out of the home port.

For my taste, four days is simply unsatisfactory. A minimum of a week seems an optimum stay on board, time to know the vessel, the steward, and the regime. Those flying in from the Midwest have scarcely adjusted to the new time zone before disembarking. Then, too, Carnival's inescapable three- and four-day ports are Nassau and Freeport, scarcely prize-winning Caribbean way stations. But by the same token, Nassau is the location of Carnival's Crystal Palace resort, and most passengers' day ashore will include a visit there.

(I achieved Crystal Palace on foot, something that I doubt anyone, islander or passenger, has ever done before. I made it into a pilgrimage, walking from Nassau's Prince George Dock along a busy coast road to the Crystal Palace, a distance of several enervating miles. I had convinced myself that Farcus's dream palace by the sea might best, like Chartres, be approached on foot. I don't think I was right, but a visit to Farcus's largest nonfloating commission did prove rewarding. Although the hotel towers' exterior colors are ingeniously refreshing, the interior floor tiles are problematic. It amused me that he had disguised the swimming pool's towel chute as a ship's cowled ventilator! But Crystal Palace, since then, has proved a disappointment and Carnival is seeking a buyer.)

The Bahamas are close to Florida, although in the case of *Holiday*-class vessels, that remains a technological disadvantage. Running medium-speed diesels at consistently low speed—no more than seven or eight knots—raises maintenance costs sharply. Diesels are most efficient turning over at or near top speed; idling snaillike between Florida and the Bahamas does them no good whatsoever.

Small wonder, then, that the *Fantasy*, Carnival's largest and newest class of vessel, has diesel-electric drive, efficient at any speed. She was launched immediately into the three- and four-day market, which gives some indication of Carnival's commitment to those lucrative split weeks, free air notwithstanding. It costs passengers slightly more to board the *Fantasy*—"to pay for all that neon," deadpanned one company employee—but it did not hurt business. Carnival was not alone in assigning its latest and glitziest tonnage to a short itinerary. In mid-1990, a rival vessel, Royal Caribbean Cruise Line's brand-new *Nordic Empress*, was sent out on a similarly languid schedule.

By the late eighties, having packed its existing hulls to capacity, cash-rich Carnival became aggressively acquisitive. But its first proposed expansion was generated in-house. The company planned a new, upscale dream, identified throughout the industry as the Tiffany Project, a rich and radical departure from the company's regular bread and butter. Envisioned was construction of a fleet of six Royal Viking–sized hulls, built and manned by Swedes. The vessels were rumored to have lavish deck plans, offering all-suite accommodation, worldwide itineraries, and a hefty per diem— everything, in sum, that Carnival's conventional product was not.

Details of the Tiffany Project's profiles and/or interior designs have never been released. Even now, with the project shelved, perhaps indefinitely, neither Farcus nor Dickinson is prepared to reveal sketches or hint at general arrangements.

In fact, the Tiffany Project was dislodged by two successive acquisitions, one aborted, the other successful. First, against all odds, two of the three owners of Royal Caribbean Cruise Line—Norwegian shipping companies I. M. Skaugen and Gotaas-Larsen— announced in the fall of 1988 their intention of selling their two-thirds of the company to Arison. Oslo's ship-owning fraternity buzzed like a hornet's nest. The whole affair was reminiscent of the

Royal Viking flap of 1975, when one of three owners of that line decided arbitrarily to put his third—in fact, the *Royal Viking Sea*— on the block. (The other two partners finally bought him out.) It was to avoid precisely that kind of unilateral deacquisitioning that the RCCL partners' contract stipulated that each partner owned *a third of each hull*. Moreover, no third could be sold without giving right of first refusal to the remaining partner or partners.

Royal Caribbean's third partner was another Oslo-based shipping company called Anders Wilhelmsen; the company is now run by two sons of founder Anders, Arne and Gjert. The Wilhelmsen brothers retained ownership and, after a period of intense, frantic, and always suspenseful international dealing, raised the $600 million that would keep RCCL out of Carnival's ownership, bravura financial survival at its best.

The entire cliff-hanging procedure was watched with a kind of fascinated horror throughout the industry. Carnival's proposed absorption of Royal Caribbean would have created a Caribbean megalith; perhaps the most heartfelt sighs of relief were heard at Kloster Cruises, whose NCL division would have faced a formidable Miami adversary.

But Arison had another coup up his sleeve. In January 1990, with the cooperation of Nico van der Vorm, Carnival bought out Holland America Cruise Line, a gigantic leisure conglomerate that included not only the *Rotterdam*, the *Noordam*, the *Nieuw Amsterdam*, the *Westerdam*, and their sizable Westour holdings in Alaska but recently acquired Wind Star Sail Cruises as well. Although barred by a mid-seventies labor dispute from an actual Rotterdam base, the line's vessels had, in terms of spirit and decor, remained flawessly and unequivocally Dutch. Now, suddenly, the company had been swallowed by an upstart American cruise line.

On the eve of the company's Carnival transfer, a Dutch officer wrote me:

> Holland-America Line and Carnival of January 15th, the deal is signed and HAL is over after 116 years. Another line is history. Well, words can never say what I and many others feel on this moment.

But his initial, nostalgic dismay notwithstanding, that same Holland America veteran later characterized Carnival's takeover as inevitably desirable. Perhaps his change of mind arose out of a change of expectation. Certainly, Carnival's expectations postmerger were startling: Micky Arison and Bob Dickinson alike confessed that Holland America's greatest surprise dividend was its upscale quality, so high that their Tiffany Project was summarily shelved.

Though Dickinson is prone to contrast Carnival's Chevrolet with HAL's Cadillac, I find it hard to agree. Harder yet is a means of determining the various cruise lines' snob pecking order. Basic opposites are easy: The *Seabourn Pride*, for example, offers superior accommodation, food, and service to the *Costa Riviera*, just as the *Sea Goddess I* outperforms the *Caribe*. But can one differentiate between Carnival, Norwegian Caribbean, and Royal Caribbean, the three Miami titans dominating the seven-day market? And where does the *Rotterdam* rank compared with the *Royal Viking Sun* or the *Crown Odyssey*? In that mid-competitive range, distinctions blur, and comparative evaluations are difficult. But it is fair to suggest that Holland America fell between stools, patently superior to the Caribbean's seven-day fleets but less patrician than Royal Viking or Cunard, on a mid-market par with Sun Line, Princess, and Royal cruises. So I respectfully differ with Messrs. Dickinson and Arison: However impressively upscale their Dutch purchase may seem to them, it does not approach the obvious pretension of their moribund Tiffany Project.

Moreover, the Dutch had withdrawn from upscale competition. From the mid-eighties on, Holland America seemed determined to renounce every vestige of its former elegance. The *Rotterdam* no longer offered world cruises or long voyages of any kind; neither N-ship—as the *Nieuw Amsterdam* and the *Noordam* are called for convenience—rarely embarked passengers for longer than a week.

But the company's outlook immediately improved. Like any proud new father, Carnival lavished parental care on its latest offspring. A vigorous program of renovation and expansion began. The thirty-year-old *Rotterdam*, perceived as a nostalgic company treasure, underwent a $15 million overhaul and was dispatched on a South American circumnavigation, ironic and heartening resumption of the long voyages that Holland America had recently eschewed. Renovated and restored, the cherished Dutch flagship steams confidently into her fourth, unparalleled decade of service. Additionally, two projected newbuildings that, pretakeover, HAL had tentatively ordered at a German yard were canceled; but they were replaced by a Carnival-inspired three-ship order at Italy's

Fincantieri yard. They will be called *Statendam, Maasdam*, and *Ryndam*, a fitting renascence of evocative names from the company's past. Thanks to Carnival's impressive cash infusion, Holland America's future has never looked brighter.

At *Ecstasy*'s christening in New York, I chatted with a Holland America executive. He suggested to me that one advantage of their absorption by Carnival was "that they leave us completely alone." However, certain autocratic Dutch ways are subject to Carnival kibitzing. A hotel manager on an HAL vessel in the Caribbean recently canceled a 300-passenger shore excursion because of a downpour and possible inconvenience to the ship. Ashore, the aggrieved island tour operators complained to Carnival headquarters in Miami. Within moments, a shore-to-ship call reached the vessel, inquiring icily not only about the tour operator's loss but, even more pointedly, Carnival's loss as well. The upshot? The excursionists went ashore, rain notwithstanding. The episode underscored for Holland America crews and shore staff that the new owners will not countenance preventable revenue loss anywhere.

Throughout its invincible ascendancy, Carnival continually irritated its rivals. Jean-Claude Potier, formerly North American head of the French Line and founder of Wind Star Cruises, once suggested to me that Carnival "turned their passengers upside down by the heels, then shook them until their pockets emptied." Carnival ships moored at Dodge Island between cruises in Miami hang a provocative banner over their outboard railings, taunting passengers on board incoming rival tonnage: "WE HAVE THE FUN." This used to infuriate Potier. "Why should *they* have all the fun? What about the fun on *my* ships?" he demanded. (The ironic conclusion, of course, was that his Windstar ships were ultimately absorbed by Carnival; Carnival had all the fun, after all.) Officers on the inbound *Norway* have a common pejorative for what they perceive as Carnival's boxlike, gaudy *Holiday*, referring to her only as *Holiday Inn*.

Among all that success, only one jarring disappointment nags: the sudden, catastrophic failure of Helsinki's legendary Wärtsilä shipyard in 1989. Wärtsilä Marine had been a highly respected, venerable Finnish establishment that seemed a bedrock of shipbuilding reliability and skill, famous as birthplace of both Royal Viking's and Royal Caribbean's fleets.

In the aftermath, it is hard to know exactly what went wrong. A retired Wärtsilä hand of long experience wrote to me:

It somehow seems as if many years of service have gone down the drain. Many of my old yard friends feel the same. . . . I think the whole thing was the combined effect of heavy subsidies for years in other countries (government competing, not yards), the absence of Soviet orders lately, perhaps too optimistic visions of market prospects and bad handling of the whole thing by politicians.

As we shall discuss elsewhere, I was surprised at several curious design and finish shortcomings on board one of the yard's predecessor hulls, the *Royal Viking Sun*. And I had heard tales, as well, about skilled Finnish shipwrights defecting from bleak Helsinki winters to take better-paying jobs in warmer climates to the south.

Another revealing clue came from a conversation I had with Joseph Farcus on board the *Fantasy*. Farcus had specified on his original drawings that the main staircase walls were to be covered with large blue-bordered panels of white galvanized steel, crisp and maintenance-free. But during *Fantasy*'s fitting-out, shipyard workers installed sheets of Formica instead, a cheaper and often-used substitute. Farcus blew the whistle and referred the yard foremen back to his original specifications; reluctantly, the galvanized steel was put into work. Perhaps endemic to that and/or previous shipyard failures as a whole, the builders had not read all of Carnival's fine print before accepting the contract.

In candid retrospect, I think Wärtsilä's glory days were in the seventies and early eighties, when ships were smaller and specifications less demanding. Compare the classic simplicity, for instance, of 1970's *Song of Norway* with the towering complexity of 1990's *Fantasy*. Over those two shipbuilding decades, the cruise ship has burgeoned into a multitiered, technological colossus, and I suspect that somehow Wärtsilä Marine did not, or could not, rise to the challenge. Then, too, perhaps no-nonsense Scandinavians prefer straightforward cruising basics—suitcase, cabin, pool, and no frills. Is the move of cruising's newbuilding south—to St.-Nazaire, Pappenberg, Fincantieri, or even faraway Nagasaki—inevitable? Are those southern (or Far Eastern) yard managements more attuned to the owners' quest for luxe that seems somehow alien to conservative Finns?

Whatever actually prompted the Wärtsilä Marine failure, no client was more horrifically affected than Carnival Cruise Lines. In 1987, Arison had placed a huge order at the Finnish yard for all three *Fantasy*-class vessels, and the financial collapse occurred before delivery of the first. The *Ecstasy*, the second, existed only as an assemblage of cut steel and would be delivered in the spring of 1991 from a reorganized yard called MASA-Yards, the new corporate name that a group of creditors—Carnival among them—had given to resurrect defunct Wärtsilä Marine. Though the name "MASA" is in reality an abbreviation of managing director Martin Sarakangis's name, wags throughout the industry suggest that the acronym really stands for "Mickey Arison Strikes Again."

The joke is not without a historic basis in fact. Wärtsilä was the third yard to go belly-up in connection with a Carnival contract. First was Denmark's Aalborg Werft, which, having completed the *Tropicale* in 1982, was then awarded the contract to build the *Holiday*. She was finished in 1985, identified by the company proudly as a "SuperLiner," although in truth she has completed only one line voyage ever, delivery from Denmark to Miami.

Among other teething problems, she had poor stability and, as a result, sports a supplementary pontoon welded across the bottom of her transom stern, its purpose to improve stability by extending the hull's waterline. *Holiday*'s "fins," as the appendages are known, bear witness to an inadequate initial design, not uncommon with the first vessel of a new class. Shortly after *Holiday*'s delivery, Aalborg Werft A/S went out of business.

Next was Malmö's Kockums yard in Sweden, which built the second and third *Holiday*-class ships side by side, the *Jubilee* and the *Celebration*. Lessons learned from the *Holiday*'s construction and trials were applied to the two sisters, and no stern appendage was necessary. But, once again, after delivering the vessels in 1986 and 1987, respectively, that yard, too, went under.

Then came the appalling default at Wärtsilä. The *Fantasy* arrived on Miami station several months late, and the *Ecstasy*, the second of the class, was completed at a markedly increased price—$250 million as opposed to the *Fantasy*'s $200 million price tag. The third of the class, the *Sensation*, will be built at MASA, as will a fourth and fifth *Fantasy*-class monster, identified as the *Fascination* and *Imagination*. Carnival is amplifying this trio into a quintet. Norwegian shipping interests have bought into the yard, renaming it Kvaerner-MASA Yards. At the same time, Carnival sold its 11 percent share at a profit. Within a month, as though to live up to their "Carnivore" pejorative, the company made an offer for Premier Cruises' red fleet out of Port Canaveral but backed off when

ABOVE: *Smiles of success: At the New York naming ceremony for the Ecstasy, Micky Arison poses in front of Carnival's latest.* (Author's collection)

LEFT: *Bob Dickinson atop the dining-room staircase; behind him is Joe Farcus's peopled dome.* (Author's collection)

no agreement could be reached. But a subsequent move to invest in a half share of upscale Seabourn Cruises was finalized in early 1992. Odd bedfellows, Carnival and Seabourn: Perhaps the ghost of the Arisons' Tiffany yearning lingers on.

So, despite that Wärtsilä glitch, Carnival continues to grow. Whether rival lines scorn it or not, the company's formula works: Every weekend, one Fun Ship after another eases down Government Cut, brimming with a tank-topped, polyestered, gold-chained clientele for a scrupulously orchestrated week—wet-T-shirt competitions, beer busts, knobbly-knee contests, and male-nightgown beauty pageant, the lot. They disembark at a selection of travel-worn islands in a mood of strident satisfaction, and although none are actually encouraged to return—thanks to Dickinson's expansionist marketing philosophy—many do.

Indeed, Carnival presents an awesome threat to their biggest rivals. Norwegian Cruise Line and Royal Caribbean Cruise Line eye the Fun Ships with uneasy dread; although its weekly prices are among the lowest in the industry, Carnival does not always necessarily undercut the competition. In fact, the inexpensiveness of a Carnival cruise tells only half the tale: To my mind, its epic appeal is the vessels' nonthreatening, exuberant informality.

I have twice sailed with Carnival and look forward to seeing more of their ships over the years to come. One recurring, unmistakable characteristic pervades all Carnival tonnage, instantly recognized each time I board: their palpable aura of success, a reflection of the Arison dynasty's unassailable Midas touch, a consistent adherence to formula, the persuasively long tenure of top management, and overall, a two-decade achievement of unparalleled maritime growth. In sum, Carnival runs eighteen taut ships.

I saw Joe Farcus briefly on board *Ecstasy* during her New York christening reception. Her interior neon effect—*Fantasy*'s "crayon smear"—has been masked behind decoratively pierced screens, both to convey the vessel's jazzy, urban/metropolis theme and to create a different look from the prototype. I asked him how the *Sensation* was proceeding. "I'm working on it," he answered, smiling wearily. Joe is also working, at Ted Arison's request, on main lounges and discotheques for all three Holland America newbuildings at Fincantieri. Adding the Farcus touch to the restrained Dutch palettes is jarring or, at the very least, incongruous; jazzing up historic Dutch interiors, customarily designed in Holland by Freek de Vlaming, seems ill-advised. Perhaps Carnival's Holland

America stance is not as "hands off" as I was led to believe; this seems to me the thick end of the wedge.

As long as cruising's demand sustains, Carnival's future seems boundless. I asked Bob Dickinson what the next vessel might be. Nothing larger than the *Fantasy* class, he assured me. As for Carnival's aspirations about a huge *Phoenix* type of hull, he dismissed it out of hand: "Too large and too inflexible" was his immediate response.

The company's giddy momentum will surely spawn gigantic new additions to the fleet; I am convinced that, around the millennium, another red, white, and blue trio will glide consecutively up Government Cut into Miami—yet another Arison triple play: Carnival, Carnival, Carnival!

Chapter 3

Dear Celine:
> *How do you like this big boat? It's so big I think you'd get lost on it. There are lots of children about your age on board. One little girl has both a governess and a nurse with her. Lots of love, Esther.*
> —Aquitania *postcard written to Celine Schiott, aged eight, by her sister, July 4, 1928*

Overrule this motion, please!
> —*Justice Benjamin Cardozo, seasick at the* Aquitania *railing, when asked if he wanted anything*

Then in June, 1927, came the great voyage of my life in the Cunarder Aquitania, *for it was on her boat deck in a deck tennis game that I was introduced to a tall beautiful girl who needed a partner. That was the beginning of a partnership that was to last with unbelievable happiness for over half a century. Needless to say, the* Aquitania *stands all by herself at the top of the list of my favorite ocean liners.*
> —*Edward Pulling*

Aquitania, Cunard's White Star Liner

R egress with me now through eight decades of maritime history, from Cleopatra's Bar to Palladian Lounge, from Fun Ship to fine ship, from Joseph Farcus's late-twentieth-century postmodernism to the refined, Beaux-Arts sensibilities of Arthur Joseph Davis.

It occurs to me that ship buffs seeing this chapter's title may well fear for the author's sanity. But the apparent error is quite conscious, reference to either a curious Cunardian anomaly or, more likely, a shrewd Edwardian marketing decision.

I am persuaded that the *Aquitania*, enshrined as one of Cunard's most hallowed creations, was almost totally defined within White Star parameters, a near carbon copy, if you will, of the *Olympic* rather than a larger extension of the *Lusitania* class. The finished vessel reflects too many White Star characteristics: an inflated hull, an enlarged passenger capacity, and dimensions strikingly similar to the *Olympic*'s. Belowdecks, she boasted a swimming bath, a gymnasium, lavish interior decoration, and even a planned extra-tariff restaurant, about which more later. Indeed, the only *Olympian* fixture overlooked was a squash rackets court.

Responsive shipbuilding was the hallmark of turn-of-the-century competition. White Star had built the *Olympic*-class vessels in response to Cunard's wildly successful *Lusitania* and *Mauretania*, which, in turn, had served to counter *Kaiser Wilhelm der Grosse* and *Deutschland*. The only difference, of course, was speed: White Star had never been interested in fast passage for its own sake, eschewing the prestige as well as preoccupation of the Blue Riband in favor of a more placid ride and more luxurious surroundings. Since 1871, founder Thomas Ismay had succeeded with passenger-pleasing comfort, and if the *Olympic* crossed in six rather than five days, the expanse of space and cumulative luxe on board presumably outweighed the perceived inconvenience of an extra day at sea.

Let us examine Cunard's and White Star's building chronologies; how did their respective design phases overlap? The *Olympic*'s general arrangements were promulgated at Harland & Wolff's yard on July 31, 1908, the summer following the successful debut of the *Lusitania* and the *Mauretania*. Cunard's board of directors met in their Liverpool boardroom to discuss the *Aquitania* formally for the first time in December 1909, a full year and a half after the *Olympic*'s general arrangement was common knowledge. A specific letter of instruction did not reach their builder of choice, John Brown's Yard on the Clyde, before September 1910. This meant that a nine-month period of gestation passed before Cunard settled final criteria governing displacement, speed, and general arrangement of their new Cunarder. A month after that letter was received, the *Olympic* was launched. The *Aquitania*'s building order was placed in December 1911, although the actual keelson—"as high as a man"—was not laid until June 1912.

Alas, no documentation exists to prove that the *Olympic* served as Cunard's inspiration; neither John Brown's archives at the University of Glasgow nor Cunard's at the University of Liverpool offer any evidence. Indeed, this kind of material seldom finds its way into company archives. But it remains clear that the *Aquitania*, though ostensibly the third of Cunard's huge triumvirate, was cut out of different cloth from her consorts. Though she could steam dependably and keep pace with *Lusitania*'s and *Mauretania*'s express service, *Aquitania* would offer Cunard passengers a taste of the paneled majesty they might otherwise seek on board White Star or Hamburg American Line.

To the layman, the new Cunarder seemed to match her earlier prototypes, sporting the same quartet of pumpkin-and-black funnels, all of them working, incidentally, in contrast to the fourth dummy funnel bringing up the rear of the *Olympic*-class profile. But at 46,000 tons, *Aquitania* displaced half again as much as *Lusitania* and *Mauretania*; her beam was a hefty 97 feet as opposed to the earlier ships' 87½ feet. Additionally, she would carry 4,000 as opposed to 3,000 passengers while still making the required sixteen-day voyage to New York and back to sustain Cunard Line's weekly service.

Her profile was denser, her hull bulkier but at the same time steadier, to use a favorite company comparative. More significantly, the dimensions of the *Aquitania* and the *Olympic* were remarkably similar. The Cunarder was slightly longer, 865 feet overall as opposed to White Star's 850 feet; a 97-foot beam for *Aquitania*, only 92 feet for *Olympic*; a displacement of 46,150 tons for the Cunarder versus 45,000 tons for the White Star vessel. A comparison of gross register between the two vessels is interesting: *Aquitania*'s 45,647 was slightly less than *Olympic*'s 46,359. Overall, however, the two hulls seemed nearly identical.

That the *Aquitania* slightly exceeded the *Olympic* in every respect is not surprising, for it was always the prerogative of the imitator to inflate, to make its vessel unequivocally the largest, if not in the world, at least within the United Kingdom. The world record would be achieved a month prior to the new Cunarder's maiden voyage by HAPAG with the second of the *Imperator*-class, 53,000-ton *Vaterland*. In fact, the *Vaterland*'s maiden voyage was moved up to mid-May of 1914: Albert Ballin, head of the Hamburg American Line, was anxious for his vessel to reach New York in advance of Cunard's. Hence, on May 14, the day *Aquitania* first steamed into Liverpool, *Vaterland* sailed from Cuxhaven en route to pick up her Southampton passengers before continuing on to New York.

But in contrast to the graceful *Olympic*-class profile, Cunard woefully overstacked the decks, giving the *Aquitania* a boxy top-hamper. (It might have been worse: One early option, entertained but rejected by Cunard, was to incorporate an additional superstructure deck.) And although the *Aquitania*'s forward bridge screen curved gently, it was concealed from view by two layers of squared-off promenade crossovers. Although these crossovers remained boldly open to the seas, it is revealing that, save for the bridge, sturdy protective portholes comprised all bridge-screen fenestration below. The *Lusitania* and the *Mauretania* did betray their bridge-screen curve, as would, of course, both the *Mary* and the *Elizabeth*; that great bulge of forward deckhouse was such a pleasing and majestic feature of the *Queens*-class ships.

The *Aquitania's* first funnel stood extremely far forward, tight against the back of the bridge. Behind it, the length of the *Aquitania's* Boat Deck, clusters of bell-mouth ventilators reared up around each funnel base. Indeed, this marked naval architect Leonard Peskett's most noticeable departure from the clean-swept upper-deck profile with which Alexander Carlyle had graced his *Olympic* class: Whereas the White Star boat deck was almost antiseptically spare, the *Aquitania's* had a cluttered, overbusy look. Moreover, though the funnel quartet was also graced with the *Lusitania* nine-degree rake, the profile lacked both the *Lusitania's* vigor and the *Olympic's* powerful grace. Further defining her four-square presence, the *Aquitania's* poop railing rose to the same height as her fo'c'sle head, establishing a pronounced fore-and-aft balance rather than the *Mauretania's* racy, down-at-the-stern crouch. By no stretch of the imagination did the *Aquitania* fit the popular Cunard sobriquet "flyer"; she looked—and was—too staid and, from certain angles, only just avoided the ponderous. Steaming into heavy seas, she would, according to her crew, plunge just as the *Mauretania* did, but with a weary dignity rather than savage glee. It is not surprising that the *Aquitania's* two best views are both from astern—Maurice Rosenfeld's stirring photograph, taken during a stiff breeze off Ambrose Light, and Charles Turner's canvas of a New York arrival, funnels and Woolworth Building alike bathed in early-morning sunlight. Always, the *Aquitania* exhibited a beamy, patrician disdain, with none of the dashing rake of her earlier consorts.

And, in truth, "dash" was not the image the company wished to project; the first huge vessel built in the United Kingdom since *Titanic*, she was purposely suffused with an aura of safety and security. "Even the timidest voyager," suggested E. Keble Chatterton, "cannot but feel safe and not less comfortable than in his home or hotel." Double-banked boats encircled the Boat Deck, prudence that her original design had not included; she was festooned with more than eighty lifeboats, including two wireless-equipped motorboats. "Recent events have once more grimly shown the importance of efficient means of intercommunication between vessels at sea," commented the *Shipbuilder*. "From the inception of the design," *Engineering* reminded its readers about the *Aquitania*, "the Cunard Company made provision to take off every soul on board."

Other snippets from contemporary journals reveal both the company's as well as the yard's preoccupation with post-*Titanic* reassurance. Lifeboat capacity, noted the *Shipbuilder*, is "for 4584, or 382 in excess of the total complement of the vessel." "G Deck," the same journal continued elsewhere, "has been made watertight for the full length of the ship." An inner skin eighteen feet inside the hull—in truth, the inner wall of the flanking coal bunkers—served as potent reassurance in the event of sideswiping an iceberg. Moreover, John Brown's Yard went to considerable lengths to publicize flotation reserves even though as many as five of the *Aquitania's* forward or after compartments might be flooded. All these specifications represented additional White Star linkage: Although never articulated, *Titanic* and its haunting legacy permeated *Aquitania's* design philosophy.

The vessel was launched at John Brown's Yard by the Countess of Derby on April 21, 1913, a date at odds with customary northern practice; launches of experimentally large new steamers usually took place during warm months to profit from the slipperiness of lubricant tallow and soap atop the fixed ways; both *Queens* and *Mauretania* entered the water for the first time in September, *Lusitania* in early summer. The ways had been extended, and over the previous winter, the clatter of Clyde dredges never ceased. Everything had to be deepened: the waters off Greenock, along the north side of Newshot Isle, the fitting-out basin, and especially at the very foot of the ways so that, as the Cunarder's bow "dipped," it would not strike the bottom. But the launch—the largest to date from that Scottish yard—proceeded without difficulty, and the *Aquitania's* knifelike stem was eased into one of the two landward notches of John Brown's fitting-out berth by sunset of the same day.

It would remain there for just over a year. One unique structural feature bracketed that prow, provision of additional mooring hawsepipes forward of the regular ones. These had doubtless been provided specifically for mooring the vessel in the Sloyne, that treacherous body of water upriver from Liverpool's Landing Stage, but these fail-safes were never put to use, at least in the Mersey. A second distinctive aspect of the *Aquitania*'s fo'c'sle head was the presence of ungainly twin ventilators rearing up twenty-eight feet high forward of the mast, between numbers 1 and 2 cargo hatches. There to provide fresh air for crew and third-class forward compartments, they needed their height to keep out green water that could deluge the bow in rough weather.

On Sunday, May 10, the new Cunarder negotiated the trip down the Clyde without incident. Local Presbyterian ministers relinquished their customarily interminable sermons to allow parishioners a glimpse of the monster's progression to the sea. The vessel spent the next three days on trials, worked up slowly from twelve to twenty-four knots off the Skelmorlie Mile. In fact, the company's definitive speed tests would have to take place during service on the Atlantic. The *Aquitania* had been in the water for thirteen months, and her hull would need cleaning to evaluate her potential accurately. Moreover, unlike the *Lusitania*'s and the *Mauretania*'s debuts seven years earlier, no Blue Ribband, no parliamentary subsidy, and no admiralty angst was at stake; no German upstart required humbling, only that this larger, beamier "White Star" Cunarder prove she could keep pace. In fact, the *Aquitania*'s turbines were more advanced than the earlier Cunarders': Whereas, of the *Mauretania*'s quadruple screws, only two could go astern, on the new vessel all four propellers could operate in reverse if required.

Liverpool would greet *Aquitania*'s maiden arrival with an impressive new facility called the Gladstone Dock. In fact, the Mersey Docks and Harbour Board had rushed construction of this essential dock specifically to please Cunard. The company was understandably unhappy with Liverpool as a home port for their increasingly larger steamships.

To appreciate their concern, we should reexamine, momentarily, Liverpool's limitations for docking liners. Britain's "port of empire," as we have seen, endures an enormous tidal differential. Waters in the Mersey estuary fall thirty-five feet between flood and ebb. So precipitous was that fall that, throughout history, Liverpool's harbor engineers had arranged along either bank of the Mersey an ancillary locking system containing perpetual high water. Only at the top of the Mersey's flood were the lock gates opened to admit or discharge ships arriving or departing the port. The tides ruled Liverpool.

With the 1907 debut of *Lusitania* and *Mauretania*, Cunard, worried that its vessels might well be either damaged or imprisoned by docking regularly inside, arranged an anchorage in the open river farther upstream, in an area of the river known locally as the Sloyne, where they were secured to one of two substantial buoys, Cunard A or B. There they could be bunkered and provisioned and, additionally, embark their steerage passengers.

Just prior to sailing time, these giant new Cunarders would leave the Sloyne and tie up downstream to take on cabin-class passengers and mails. They did so at that ingenious Liverpool fixture known as the Landing Stage. Year-round, day and night, Liverpool's Landing Stage was such a hive of activity that berthing times were rigorously scheduled to accommodate an unending succession of traffic. Two hours were permitted to load ships but only one hour to discharge them. Once inbound vessels left the Landing Stage, tugs maneuvered them within Liverpool's protected interior docks. The *Lusitania* and the *Mauretania* either moved upstream to moor in the Sloyne or entered Liverpool's interior docks as well.

Whereas New York harbor's primary nuisance was nicked or broken propeller blades, what required constant repair in Liverpool were hull plates dented or crumpled while negotiating narrow lock gates separating interior docks from the Mersey. In September 1908, the *Mauretania* scraped badly against a dock wall, and the following month, the *Lusitania* struck the dock entrance at Tranmere, across the river at Birkenhead. The following February, the *Mauretania*'s starboard flank brushed noisily along the wall entering the Huskisson Dock: "Starboard side bunker in way of # 1 stokehold had its coal trimmed away from the damage," read the marine superintendent's bleak report. "Web plate frame and knee # 205 were bent in. Plate had to be removed in dry dock since it was below waterline." Unscheduled dry dockings were expensive and disruptive; almost without exception, all were traced to difficulties resulting from the Mersey's notorious tidal fall.

Cunard was extremely anxious to avoid the same pitfall with the forthcoming *Aquitania*: Squeezing her wind-catching bulk in or out of narrow lock gates when notorious Mersey gales blew would be asking for trouble, as would mooring in the Sloyne, an anchorage susceptible to fractious winds and tides. In 1911, *Mauretania* had broken loose from Cunard A in a gale.

So, well before *Aquitania*'s launch, the Cunard Line made clear to the Mersey Docks and Harbour Board that they would not tolerate current Liverpool conditions—a piece of calculated maritime blackmail with a predictable outcome. Having already lost White Star's express service to Southampton, Liverpool was not about to let first-string Cunarders go as well.

In 1910, work was begun on a new Gladstone Dock named, incidentally, not after the famous prime minister but after Robert Gladstone, chairman of the Mersey Docks and Harbour Board until 1911. It was opened by Their Majesties on July 11, 1913. Although, like every Liverpool dock, it had to be protected from the Mersey, entry into the Gladstone was easier, directly east from the river; sensibly, the 120-foot-wide, quarter-mile approach chamber was lined with resilient wooden staging rather than unforgiving stone.

At its landward end, the Gladstone Dock served either as a coaling or maintenance pier and as the world's largest dry dock. Once a ship had entered the dock proper, a sliding gate would be moved across the opening, enclosing the new facility and its occupying vessel entirely; then the dock would be drained.

Due to silt around the dock sill as well as a malfunctioning diesel pump, the Gladstone Dock was not put into full use until October of the same year, two months after the royal opening. The *Mauretania*, in fact, became the first Cunarder to use it as a fully operational dry dock.

The following spring, the same dock easily accommodated the *Aquitania*'s ninety-seven-foot beam. Fresh from her trials, the Cunard Line's largest vessel passed without incident along the wood-lined approach channel and came to rest within the dock. The once-recalcitrant gate slid shut beneath her counter, and after five hours of pumping, Mersey water was drained completely from the dock, leaving the vast new ship settled down onto her prearranged keel blocks.

Her underwater plating was scoured and painted, and a fortnight later, rainbowed with flags, the RMS *Aquitania* departed the Gladstone Dock—astern, it must be noted sadly, an inelegant Mersey entry—and repaired upriver to the Landing Stage, ready to embark her maiden-voyage passengers. She was moored, in fact, within a stone's throw of the great Liverpudlian architectural troika dominating the Pierhead: to the north, the Royal Liver Building; to the south, the turreted Mersey Docks and Harbour Board Building; and under construction in between, slightly lower but no less imposing, Cunard's brooding Italianate headquarters, not occupied until 1916. I cannot resist quoting from John Hampton Chadwick's effusive poem that greeted its completion:

> *Tower up! Tower up! Majestic pile, above ye old Dock-sill*
> *In classic form, Renaissance style, product of sanguine*
> *will . . .*
>
> *. . . Superb the edifice now stands as monumental sign—*
> *Symbolism of the brains and hands*
> *That forged the Cunard Line!*

As the *Aquitania* moors at the Landing Stage in the summer of 1914 on her first commercial voyage, a final observation about this archetypal Edwardian liner's exterior. Conditioned as we are today to laboriously styled cruise ships, we should remember that almost no aesthetic manipulation distorted her profile. *Aquitania's* imposing puissance arose simply and unequivocally from a no-nonsense minimalist principle: Form followed function. Save for the dashing rake of her funnels, nothing about the vessel condescended to style: What was there—a proven arrangement of mast, funnel, ventilator, superstructure, stem, and counter stern—had been wrought solely to expedite the *Aquitania* and her human cargo comfortably and reliably across a dangerous Atlantic in all weathers. Edwardian naval architects and shipbuilders shaped these wondrous vessels as was, without aesthetic flourish or gratuitous design folderol.

Is this why, perhaps, traditional ocean-liner profiles remain so pleasing, *because* their designers, builders, and owners eschewed stylistic adornment? Without question, the most evocative passenger vessels—those haunting four-stackers—were wrought with only practicality in mind. Contemporary designers go to extravagant lengths to foment profile drama. On board *Aquitania*, though stylistic proliferation ran rampant belowdecks, her profile was all business.

The vessel's interiors were the work of Arthur Joseph Davis, a cosmopolitan English architect who emerged from his thorough and fruitful French training a dedicated graduate of the Ecole des Beaux-Arts. Born in 1878, Davis had studied on the Continent from the age of sixteen, educated in both Brussels and Paris. From an early age, he seemed to transcend nationality: His French was flawless, and he moved effortlessly from atelier to salon without linguistic or cultural hindrance.

During his apprenticeship in Paris, Davis came to the attention of the great Alsatian architect Charles Mewès. Mewès, twenty years senior and vastly more experienced, was fresh from his 1898 triumph of the Paris Ritz. He was sufficiently impressed by this talented young Englishman to propose a London partnership, a practical no less than artistic expedient: Mewès spoke no English and felt alienated and ill at ease in the British capital. Moreover, his wife had died in 1896, and widower Mewès had to raise his three daughters alone.

Furthermore, he evidently perceived in Arthur Davis the kind of assured elegance he lacked. Charles Mewès was all benevolent rusticity, a round Rabelaisian figure, a man who had arrived and cared little for appearances; in fact, sketched into the foreground of one of Arthur Davis's elevations for the London Ritz is the unmistakable, eccentrically hatted and caped figure of his Alsatian partner. Small wonder that in young Davis, Mewès cherished the kind of impeccably tailored bon vivant who would serve as point man for Beaux-Arts in London.

Just after the turn of the century, eighteen-year-old Arthur Davis returned from Paris to his native London. The partnership with Mewès would not be formally established until 1903, by which time the two men had already completed their pioneering Palm Court and Grill for the Carlton House Hotel on the corner of Haymarket and Pall Mall. It was an instant success, characterized some years later by the *Journal of the Royal Institute of British Architects* as having introduced "French standards of elegance into modern English Architecture."

What exactly was it about that Carlton House renovation that so captivated London? To begin with, the timing of the new Franco-British partnership was just right. Hotels in England were blossoming, with the same lavish comforts achieved by their American and French counterparts, and London's fashionable were on the qui vive for a new elegance. The renovated Carlton House offered a Beaux-Arts refreshment: rather than late-Victorian fustiness, all feathers and fern, here was a return to decorous eighteenth-century calm.

One entered a lower Palm Court, half of which was surrounded by a balconied terrace railed in bronze, at the top of a gentle seven-step staircase. ("All his stairs have treads which grow broader as they reach ground level," Sir John Betjeman would write approvingly about Arthur Davis years later.) A vast skylight admitted a pale wash of light by day, a necessity, since most of the fenestration surrounding the balcony's level revealed only the exquisitely chandeliered Grill beyond, forerunner of the partners' *coup de théâtre* to follow at London's Ritz.

But it is the Palm Court especially that merits our attention. Civilized grace reigns, as well as that elusive but essential ingredient of every successful public interior, an almost palpable invitation to *linger*. Congenial groups of chairs and the occasional sofa beckoned, serving as gathering place before a ritual ascent to dine. Significantly, it was precisely the kind of elegant surround in which dapper, well-tailored Arthur Davis belonged; one sensed that the Carlton Grill fitted him as comfortably as his glowing, elastic-sided Lobb boots. All London shared his predilection: The Carlton Grill became a popular and welcome oasis from the city's bustle.

Looking today at pictures of its vanished luxe, one is reminded, inescapably, of a lounge on board a great Edwardian steamer, oasis from the turbulent Atlantic. The Carlton's Palm Court seems an archetypal Promenade Deck public room that might well have been found on board, say, the *Aquitania*.

That Carlton commission served as the first distinguished achievement in a Beaux-Arts cavalcade of London successes for Mewès & Davis. Next came the domed corner building for the *Morning Post* in the Strand (later to be fatally amended) and, uniting Green Park and Piccadilly, the restrained, ingenious elegance of Europe's second Ritz Hotel, completed in the summer of 1906. London's Ritz, now beautifully restored and renovated, is a jewel of a hotel, graceful, serene, and luxurious, with a dining room overlooking Green Park that brought to lavish perfection its Carlton prototype.

No other London architectural firm better exemplified the great Beaux-Arts spirit, transferring that distinctive and monumental eclecticism intact from Paris into the rich fabric of Edwardian London. Queen Victoria was dead, and at long last, an almost elderly Prince of Wales had ascended the throne. Following "King Teddy's" singular example, England entered an era of unparalleled

TOP: *Morris Rosenfeld's classic portrait of the* Aquitania *inbound toward Ambrose Lightship in the early 1920s, perhaps the most evocative ocean-liner photograph ever taken.* (Everett E. Viez collection)

CENTER: *Charles Mewès at the desk of his Cologne office.* (Ann Davis Thomas collection)

BOTTOM: *Arthur Joseph Davis at the age of thirty-four. The photograph was taken in 1912, the year Davis tackled the* Aquitania. (Ann Davis Thomas collection)

°S.S. AQUITANIA".
First Class Smoking Lounge.

TOP: *Out in the field: Unusually dapper with cane and homburg, Mewès checks progress on the roof of London's Ritz.* (Ann Davis Thomas collection)

BOTTOM: *One of Arthur Davis's few surviving architectural drawings for* Aquitania. *It is, in fact, a preliminary treatment that illustrates to perfection the room's spirit if not precisely its final disposition.* (Mewès & Davis)

indulgence; Mewès & Davis's exacting, refined elegance suited that extravagant decade to perfection.

Once the Ritz had opened for business, the partners produced Pall Mall's unsurpassed paean to clubdom, the Royal Automobile Club, complete with a Pompeian swimming bath in its basement that would find its way, essentially undiminished, into the basement of every *Imperator*-class trio to follow. Indeed, it was the press of those Hamburg shipping commissions that recalled Charles Mewès back to his Continental practice, in Cologne with his German partner, Alphonse Bischoff. Albert Ballin, head of the Hamburg American Line, was preoccupied with launching the vast *Imperator*-class vessels and bound his architect of choice's contract with an ironclad proviso: Until the three HAPAG vessels were complete, Mewès was forbidden to undertake any outside (for which read "British") steamship work or even to share his renderings or decorative intent with his British partner.

In fact, the wily Ballin had acted with Machiavellian prescience. Cunard, treading the path the fashionable were beating to Mewès & Davis's door, offered the firm the design commission for their new *Aquitania*. But whereas Mewès himself was contractually obliged to refuse, Davis was under no such constraint. He alone was hired to undertake the new Cunarder's interior decoration. For a thirty-four-year-old architect, it was a prestigious assignment; the giant vessel would be his first ocean liner.

The offer was made in late 1912, long after *Aquitania*'s general arrangements had been established with the yard, too late for Arthur Davis to request of his client that the vessel's four uptakes—those troublesome central chimneys rising from furnace to funnel, piercing every deck en route—should be divided and directed toward the vessel's sides instead. Mewès had made the identical suggestion to HAPAG during construction of the *Amerika* in 1904; shrugged off then, he prevailed for the design of the *Vaterland*, second of the *Imperator*-class trio building at Hamburg's Blohm & Voss works. Only the *Aquitania*'s engine casings, aft of number 4 funnel, were divided and rose up as intruding buttresses on either side of the first-class smoking room.

Beaux-Arts design philosophy thrives on symmetry, flourishing best along a fixed axis, a succession of public rooms opening one into the other. Within the restrictive confines of ocean-liner architecture, uptakes amidships became stumbling blocks at odds with this ideal, and it is a measure of Arthur Davis's wisdom and skill that he rose above those nagging maritime necessities to create a formidable, if asymmetrical, triumph along *Aquitania's* Promenade Deck.

Having surveyed the vessel from afar, I am always at a loss to know where to begin, on what deck of a new steamer to inaugurate examination of her interiors. The old shipping journals always started unrealistically at the top, describing new vessels from the Boat Deck down, the very reverse, curiously, of the order in which they were constructed. Then again, to do Arthur Davis full and immediate justice, one is tempted to alight immediately along the Promenade Deck, high in the vessel, adjacent to his most exquisite succession of public rooms.

But for our purpose, permit me an indulgence as I masquerade as a maiden-voyage passenger embarking at Liverpool. My crossing to New York and back will be one of three achieved during that last peaceful summer of 1914; in early August, Europe would be engulfed in hostilities, and the beautiful new *Aquitania* would undergo a bewildering variety of structural and decorative changes undreamed of that peaceful spring.

On board our comfortable boat train, known as an American Special, I lunch in the restaurant car as we tear through the spring Midlands fields. Once in Liverpool, we remain in our carriage as the fast London locomotive is replaced by a smaller tank engine. It chuffs us off the main line at Edge Hill and drags us through the interminable mile-long tunnel known as the Victoria and Waterloo. In daylight again, our train snakes along what seem like tramlines embedded in cobbles, wheels squealing around tortuous dockland curves. Since we encounter vehicular traffic now as well as pedestrians, we are literally led by a flag-bearing LMS employee who walks in front of the engine; he carries with him the keys to locked train gates en route, in particular the Prince's Dock swing bridge.

Finally, the train stops beneath the glazed roof of Riverside Station, hard by the Landing Stage. We are urged into haste by respectful, if impatient, station personnel, pocket watches in hand; a second American Special is due momentarily. Two vans disgorge a mountain of trunks. We transatlantic passengers—especially the Americans—are encumbered with last-minute parcels of London loot, retrieved from overhead racks. Out on the platform, I collar a willing porter whose rumbling, iron-shod barrow I follow out the station entrance, across Prince's Parade and down an iron foot-bridge that slopes gently—the tide is flood—onto the Prince's Landing Stage itself.

Though the *Aquitania* awaits, I can see only portions of our vessel. It was the same for embarking Liverpool and Manhattan passenger alike: The ship was never seen complete in either port, only in parts—a segment of black hull here, a gleam of white superstructure there, or towering overhead, an orange black-topped funnel wreathed in smoke. On postwar crossings, after Cunard's move to Southampton, one's best—and only—view of the entire vessel would be at Cherbourg. There, until the Gare Maritime was completed in the late thirties, approaching or de-parting by tender, one could see anchored *Aquitania in* (glorious) *toto* rather than fragmented.

In Liverpool, each *Aquitania* class had its own embarkation point on three adjacent decks. Third class had boarded by tender earlier that morning, or even the day previous, swarming through side ports down on Main Deck. Alongside the Landing Stage, second-cabin passengers clambered up aft onto Shelter Deck, two decks higher, the same relative level by which the *Mauretania's* first-class passengers used to reach their vessel's "Grand Entrance."

But the *Aquitania* was a taller vessel, and her first-class passen-gers would enter through ports in the shell plating into the first-class Foyer on D, or Upper, Deck, which, despite its name, was low down in the hull. No longer would Cunard first-class passengers ascend a sloping gangway, cross an open deck, and enter the deck-house; they would be absorbed, as today, through the hull plating, directly into the vessel's belly.

As I enter, French names for familiar fixtures confront me, thanks to Arthur Davis's pervasive Gallicism: Just as the Grand Entrance or ship's square is now Foyer, so Purser's Desk has become Bureau. Similarly, Cunard's traditional dining saloon has been renamed, grandiosely, Restaurant Louis XVI.

Upper Deck is the lowest first-class passenger deck (save for swimmers or gymnasts) and lies at the bottom of *Aquitania's* main staircase. Even though laden with hand baggage and anxious to reach my cabin, I cannot resist a glimpse inside the nearest dining-room entrance, one on either side of the foyer's afterwall. It is an imposing and novel Cunard space because *Aquitania* is the first Cunarder fitted from her debut with proper tables and armchairs rather than the communal long tables and infamous swivel chairs

TOP: Aquitania's *funnels 3 and 4 surrounded by bell-mouthed ventilators and a network of guy wires. A row of deck chairs awaits passengers.* (Photograph by Everett E. Viez)

CENTER: *Obligatory mid-ocean photograph. It is April 1922, and the passenger is Penelope Noyes.* (Norman Morse collection)

BOTTOM: *Two Cunarders share Southampton's Ocean Dock, the Edwardian giant dwarfed by the inbound Queen.* (Everett E. Viez collection)

installed wholesale on board *Lusitania* and *Mauretania* in 1907. On this newest Cunarder—the largest built to date—the dining room was elegant and spacious; the inescapable influence of both Carlton Grill and Ritz Hotel dining room pervades all.

Unlike dining saloons on board earlier Cunard superliners, the *Aquitania's* restaurant was not paneled but painted. By 1914, a new interior look was in vogue: painted rather than plain wood-work. Indeed, some of the *Lusitania's* paneled interiors had already been overpainted. The *Aquitania's* dining room gleamed with light color, its columns marble rather than walnut and its floor entirely carpeted in rich blue wool instead of Cunard's traditional, prosaic linoleum intersected by drugget paths. The bronze-trimmed buffet beneath the central open well was pure Louis Seize. Further un-derscoring the Frenchness of things, a mural on the forward wall portrayed the Parc du Grand Trianon, viewed through a charming beribboned colonnade.

Davis's restaurant, I discover, is H-shaped, fore and aft, to fit between funnel casings. Forward entrances from the Foyer are wrapped around casing number 2, while the room's afterend is subdivided by casing number 3. Overhead, between these inescap-able intrusions, adding height and airiness, is what seems at first glance to be a second-story balcony, surrounding an open well up on C Deck. But it turns out to be no more than a narrow decorative overhang, devoid of tables or chairs. Not only was there no room for diners, Davis had also provided no ascent for stewards up to that level. The balcony was an illusion, in reality the exposed cabin corridors achieving C Deck's most elegant midship suites.

Another disappointment awaits overhead as, with neck craned, I survey the restaurant's lyrically painted ceiling. *The Triumph of Flora* serves as an oval window—yet another balcony—into a florid sky where upholstered clouds support bare-breasted goddesses and attendant putti. Alas, Cunard had obviously cut short Davis's soar-ing grandeur: A real painted dome should have protruded on up into B Deck, just as Mewès had done across the North Sea on board the *Imperator, Vaterland,* and *Bismark.* As it is, that disappoint-ingly flat—in both senses of the word—ceiling, rimmed by its *faux balcon,* puts a two-story cap atop what should have been a three-story marvel. Davis's architectural ambition had obviously been reined in by Cunard's practicality. Into the space above that should have accepted the dome, a dozen inside servants' cabins were located instead. Had he been in charge, I am convinced that Mewès would have prevailed; Davis's failure to do so sold short his otherwise splendid restaurant.

Curiously, it was sold short logistically as well. The original table configuration for Restaurant Louis XVI seated no more than 508. More than an additional 100 seats were required to accommodate the vessel's entire first-class passenger load of 618. Denied space on his balcony, Davis fell back on an odd solution, which even the most adventurous of us newly embarking passengers had difficulty in finding: a small mock-Tudor Grill Room farther aft, separated from the restaurant by an anonymous paneled corridor along the port side of the ship. It could also be achieved by descent of a midship staircase, far removed from the main one.

Therein lies the *Aquitania*'s great dining conundrum. Why that supplemental, extraneous 104-seat Grill Room? What was its original purpose, why its detached location, and why, as marked on the vessel's original deck plan, no less than two "Grill Room pantries" just inside the galley to starboard? I am convinced that the Grill Room's *original* designed use, when the vessel's general arrangements were laid out, was as an extra-tariff restaurant.

Architecturally and logistically, it had the right perquisites: just over a hundred covers, an isolated entrance by staircase or elevator, discreet removal from the main restaurant, and support facilities hard by in the galley. Moreover, an extra-tariff Grill Room on board the *Aquitania* would have confronted *Olympic*'s A La Carte Restaurant head-on. In curious point of fact, the handsome "Tudor" plasterwork lining the *Aquitania*'s Grill Room ceiling matched perfectly that surmounting dining saloons on board all three *Olympic*-class vessels.

Yet, obviously, somewhere between conception and completion, Cunard had reneged, aborting their extra-tariff option and turning it instead into an adjunct restaurant for regular first-class dining. I did stumble across one curious clue, a Cunard dining aberration in an *Aquitania* advertisement from the *New York Times*. Appearing just before the vessel sailed eastbound on the return leg of her maiden voyage, a final, mystifying line of copy promises:

GRILL ROOM A LA CARTE WITHOUT EXTRA CHARGE

Its import is unclear. First, to advertise "à la carte" in first class seems redundant: All first-class dishes in Restaurant Louis XVI—

indeed, *all* first-class dishes on every transatlantic ship—were offered à la carte. Second, since the Grill Room was patently required for a regular sitting, how could diners avail themselves of an optional table without discommoding their fellow passengers already assigned there? There might possibly have been an additional, optional second sitting, extending beyond regular dining hours, but if so, it was never articulated, let alone promoted, in any *Aquitania* brochure. Finally, the copy states clearly "without extra charge"; whatever sophisticated Grill service Cunard offered was clearly on the house.

Again, a working extra-tariff Grill Room on board the *Aquitania* was precisely the kind of White Star/Hamburg American frippery that *should* have been part of this great "White Star" Cunarder. But apparently, feeding over 600 first-class passengers in Restaurant Louis XVI was impossible, or at least could not be achieved without either a working balcony or the kind of table crowding that would have been anathema to Cunard's—and Davis's—lavish *Aquitania* style.

The main staircase, completely enclosed on D Deck level, occupies the center of the Foyer, almost obscuring the Bureau forward of it. I can proceed upward either on foot or by elevator, two of which lie across from the stairs. But whichever I choose, the period detailing of staircase and elevator alike is sumptuous: Banisters are as elaborately wrought as elevator grilles, and gleaming white Ionic columns support richly paneled and painted modillons. Underfoot is Cunard's traditional white gutta-percha tiling, accented by small blue inset squares.

Although my destination is only one deck higher, I am still laden with sufficient parcels to summon the elevator, depressing an ivory disk within its handsome bronze rosette. Grille doors swing open, and interior steel gate slides aside. A pink-faced, white-jacketed lift attendant, heavily brilliantined, ushers me in, closes gate and grille, rotates the half-round rheostat control, and with a gentle motored hum, I am lofted briefly heavenward. The *Aquitania*'s lift men are wounded veterans from the Boer War or Northwest frontier; their crackling, starched jackets often bear ribbon flashes or, occasionally, a pinned-up, empty sleeve.

I leave the elevator at C Deck and walk to the port side. My destination is Cabin C-80, conveniently just aft of the main staircase. Though an inside cabin, it is not quite inside, as intriguingly noted in the brochure when I selected it. A small, cheerful chamber, it is fitted traditionally. The bed's headboard and footboard are made of walnut inlay; unlike the pretentious brass beds in the *Aquitania*'s suites, mine has old-fashioned characteristics of a bunk: Incorporated along either side are polished siderails reaching from pillow to thigh, guaranteeing restraint in the event of rough weather. Can this giant steamer, I wonder, be subject to much sea motion?

My parcels are gratefully strewn onto the companion sofa, and I note with relief that my steamer trunk has already been delivered, standing upright on one end. Once unpacked, it will slide neatly beneath the sofa, whose legs, just for that purpose, are precisely fifteen inches above the deck.

Since it is a warm spring afternoon, the steward has left the stirabout fan buzzing in one corner; in another hangs a convenient mahogany cupboard. Cabin wall panels are covered with a slightly too busy floral cloth; fortunately, the brand-new fabric has not yet absorbed the reek of tobacco, which will soon sully it forever. I detect only the faintly antiseptic but not unpleasant smell of fresh paint, mingled pleasantly with the scent of some spring jonquils, already vased on the oval writing table. Completing the cabin furnishings are cane-backed armchair and glistening mahogany wardrobe.

There is no sink, for Cabin C-80 comes with an attached bathroom. Indeed, a glance along the *Aquitania*'s first-class Cabin Deck plan betrays, for Cunard, extraordinary largesse in the matter of cabin baths. There is not one for everybody, but in marked contrast to preceding Cunarders, more are available. On the *Mauretania*'s Upper and Main decks, for instance, almost no first-class cabin boasted its own bath. By 1914, however, self-indulgent Edwardians, no less than their vociferous, hotel-conditioned American cousins—a transatlantic force to be reckoned with!—demanded facilities denied them during the preceding decade. A cursory peek into my bathroom reveals glistening porcelain fixtures and a massive tub lodged beneath a quartet of taps, two salt and two fresh water. The bathroom is shared, alas, with the occupants of Cabin C-74, just forward.

Although ostensibly inside, my cabin has a unique shipboard fixture, as do many of its neighboring equivalents along the midship portion of C Deck. Recessed high atop the outboard wall, well inside a ceiling aperture, is a brass-rimmed window, a rectangular porthole with ventilating louver. Its existence—almost as much as the private bathroom—had not only compelled me to select this particular cabin but had also emboldened Cunard to charge more for it.

Neither quite inside nor outside, Cabin C-80 remains a curious hybrid somewhere in between. The only view I have (when I stand on a chair) is a close-up of some deck-chair legs, for my cabin's port is set within the baseboard, so to speak, of B Deck's Promenade, one deck higher. Muted daylight and semifresh air filter in, as well as the constant tramp of leather-soled shoes, clarion calls of lost or boisterous passengers, and in mid-ocean, more than one indiscreet confidence passed from one deck-chair occupant to another. Housed in a single cabin, I have few confidences to offer in return.

I think this cabin's unconventional window owes its existence, in a roundabout way, to the loss of the *Titanic* two years earlier. Hear me out: On the most ambitious Edwardian steamers, owners felt obliged to provide the first class with two major promenades. On board the *Mauretania*, these open spaces were found along the two highest decks, Boat and Promenade. On both the *Mauretania* and the *Lusitania*, one entered principal public rooms from the Boat Deck. Indeed, the names are misleading, for Boat Deck con-stituted *the* great encircling, open-air promenade; the Promenade Deck one flight below was really a shelter deck that did not circum-navigate the ship.

But because of the mandatory glut of transatlantic lifeboats fol-lowing *Titanic*'s loss, *Aquitania*'s Boat Deck offered no real view over the side. As we have seen, lifeboats lined both flanks; others were stacked inboard as well. Though only two skylights added their top-deck clutter, funnels, ventilators, and blowers badly re-stricted walking space.

So the *Aquitania*'s two alternate promenades lay along A and B decks directly below. Even so, long-distance walkers were further frustrated because so much of A Deck, as we shall see, is obstructed by Garden Lounges to port and starboard. So Davis has devised an additional promenade, unique on the North Atlantic.

It is ingeniously terraced, with a conventional front row—or orchestra—of chairs on the lower level; inboard and higher, a mezzanine accommodates a second row of chairs elevated above the first. Stretching along the face of the terrace riser separating the two levels are square windows, one of which admits light, and air (and noise) into otherwise inside Cabin C-80. Further ingenuity lies inboard: At the bottom of the deckhouse wall behind the mezzanine chairs, Davis has mandated yet another window row to illuminate yet more formerly inside cabins.

Following the Armistice of 1918, when the *Aquitania* went to the Tyne for conversion to oil firing, B Deck's terrace remained intact. Near the end of the 1920s, though, B Deck's deckhouse wall would push out seven feet, engulfing the former mezzanine while at the same time enlarging and enhancing the cabins just inside. B Deck's promenade lost its distinction as both baseboard and riser windows were sealed up.

But stay, a peremptory blast of *Aquitania*'s whistle rouses me from my cabin reverie, and I hasten two flights up the adjacent main staircase. (Cabin C-80 is handily located, I think to myself. But after years of sailing on a wide variety of vessels, I have concluded that every ship's cabin, crossing or cruising, forward or aft, boasts some geographic advantage: high up, near the open deck; low down, near the dining saloon; forward, near the bridge; aft, near the stern, and so on, ad infinitum.)

The main staircase ends on A Deck beneath a glass dome. Since we are pointing downstream, I exit the deckhouse proper into the forward end of the *Aquitania*'s upper promenade, starboard side, resisting a tempting detour into the Garden Lounge just aft; that treat I will save for teatime during the long passage down-Mersey to the Bar Lightship.

I stay outdoors, hanging over the Promenade Deck starboard railing, as the towered gangways are retracted and cables slipped. Despite the much-advertised impact of this huge new Cunarder, our sailing seems surprisingly low-key, suggesting that workaday Liverpool routine outweighs ceremonial debut. The *Aquitania* departs the Prince's Landing Stage unadorned with serpentine or confetti; no band struts alongside, although somewhere aft, I can hear our string orchestra bowing a thin chorus or two of "Auld Lang Syne." My fellow passengers and I wave decorously, gestures halfheartedly returned from below. I suppose much of today's sentimental histrionics when cruise ships sail derives from cruise-staff hype as well as the unjaded enthusiasm of so many neophyte passengers. Far less is made of even maiden-voyage sailings from the Mersey in 1914; and, in truth, that very absence of stage-managed frenzy makes them, in retrospect, somehow more compelling. That towering new *Aquitania* was departing promptly for New York seemed occasion enough.

Once we are away from the pier, I leave the rail and, rather than reentering the main stairway lobby, proceed aft through two sets of brass-studded leather swinging doors into the starboard Garden Lounge. Moving industriously along rows of tableclothed wicker tables, stewards are already setting out teacups, plates, and teaspoons (halcyon shipboard tintinnabulum!); but there is sufficient time to prowl the room before tea is actually poured.

I am taken with this novel space. Boldly, Davis has transformed a sizable length of the ship's Promenade Deck, creating a bower of greenery, treillage, and wicker, its faux stone walls rampant with ivy. Baskets of fern are suspended from the deckhead, and out of brass-rimmed mahogany tubs sprout clusters of palms. Duplicated on both sides of the vessel, these Garden Lounges offer an admirable daytime meeting place and tearoom between open deck and closed public room.

I have always felt that the perfect shipboard chair carries the proviso that one can, while seated, easily enjoy a view of the sea, a refinement met admirably in the Garden Lounges. Their solo prototype on board the *Mauretania* had been an experimental Veranda Café, a sometimes breezy grotto of wicker and palm, sheltered at the Boat Deck's afterend. But here, on this grander Cunarder, Davis has cleverly expanded that popular *Mauretania* feature by placing a pair of full-blown Garden Lounges amidships, protected by windproof vestibules fore and aft. Each is 126 by 21 feet, providing an informal anteroom between indoors and out. In effect, Davis has almost closed the Promenade Deck circle, gentrifying and reintegrating two lengths of it into public room— like my cabin, neither quite inside nor outside.

Although the term "Garden Lounge" would survive in brochure captions and deck plans, Davis had originally used the term "Winter Garden Lounge," oblique acknowledgment of the North Atlantic's forbidding climate. Interestingly, Mewès's Winter Gardens on board the *Imperator*-class trio, though similarly palm-bedecked and located amidships, were insulated from the sea by flanking promenades. Davis had gone his older colleague one better, placing *Aquitania*'s Winter Gardens directly overlooking the ocean.

After two pots of tea, some cucumber sandwiches, a slice of excellent Dundee cake, and a Lehár medley from the *Aquitania*'s indefatigable string orchestra, I brush the crumbs from my lap and wander indoors. Passing from Garden into Georgian Lounge, I enter Arthur Davis's undeniable chef d'oeuvre. An evocative public

room, the Georgian Lounge will be identified by successive generations of *Aquitania* passengers and historians as the Palladian
Lounge. Although solid British resonances of Robert Adam pre-
dominate, the fireplace and piano recesses at either end reveal
the familiar Palladian motif: a central coffered arch bracketed by
companion, subsidiary niches to either side. Richer embellish-
ments—perhaps too rich for Andrea Palladio—include lavish gilt
swags garlanding the wall as well as extravagant plaster molding
framing an elaborately painted ceiling.

That solid ceiling was at inaccurate odds with *Engineering*'s advance discussion of the vessel. Published deck plans in the *Aquitania* souvenir issue show two rectangular blanks up on Boat Deck,
indicating skylights over both Lounge and Smoking Room where,
in fact, neither exists. Only two skylights pierce the *Aquitania*'s
heavily obstructed Boat Deck: a glass dome atop the main staircase
and another illuminating the drawing/writing room.

By 1914, grand skylights on grander and grander North Atlantic
steamers had become almost shipboard clichés. *Umbria* and
Etruria had had Cunard's first skylit dining saloons, while the next
decade's taller *Campania* and *Lucania* were skewered with shafts
admitting daylight three decks down for breakfast and luncheon.
Though the *Mauretania*'s dining saloon was *not* topped with glass,
as though in compensation, all her Boat Deck public rooms were,
even the open-ended Veranda Café. So perhaps we must forgive
Engineering's editors for anticipating that Davis would necessarily
adhere to Cunard tradition. Across the North Sea, Mewès was
decorating his *Imperator*-class vessels with skylights, not merely
over the rooms' central sections but the full width of the deckhouse.

Though a skylight had enhanced the Carlton's Palm Court, Davis
did not include one in the *Aquitania*'s lounge, thereby not only
maintaining Georgian purity but also liberating valuable Boat
Deck teak above. Instead, he topped the Palladian Lounge's central
eighteen-foot section with an allegorical canvas by the Dutchman
Van Cuygen.

What endows the space with especial exuberance is another kind
of skylight, four great lunettes looking out onto the Boat Deck,
alternating with lavishly ornamented oeil-de-boeuf. Perhaps not
surprisingly, Davis's ceiling treatment resembled that on board
the *France* of 1912, although that *"Grand Salon de Conversation"*
boasted a central skylight as well. But regardless of either the

TOP: *One end of Davis's splendid Palladian Lounge. Midway through the ten-second exposure, a steward inadvertently moved the wing chair on the left, hence the blur.* (Photograph by Everett E. Viez)

BOTTOM: *A perfect New York study of the* Aquitania, *taken on June 28, 1939. Two gravel barges are en route upriver and familiar port landmarks bracket the hull. Aft is Colgate's record-breaking clock, and just above the bow lies Jersey Central's terminus.* (Photograph by David J. Kreines)

French or the Germans, Davis's imaginative clerestory was undeniably a British transatlantic first, forerunner of similar treatment to come on board the *Queen Mary*.

Before returning to my cabin for a nap (embarkation tours of new vessels are exhausting!), I venture farther aft on Promenade Deck to find another showstopper, a heroic Carolean Smoking Room. Just when I had thought that there was no paneling on board, I plunge within a brooding sobriety of oak and mahogany. Davis's Smoking Room is derived, my brochure points out, from a Christopher Wren interior at Greenwich's Royal Naval Hospital, in fact, a smoking room from the era of James II. However pervasive Davis's Francophilia in foyer or restaurant, on Promenade Deck he had tactfully drawn the long English bow.

Despite its grandeur—another eighteen-foot central ceiling—an unmistakable naval aura prevails. Marine canvases, cornered with carved scallop shells, face each other across the richly patterned Axminster; standing lamps, dripping with Venetian garnish and topped with dolphins, masquerade as lanterns; in contrast to the lounge, clerestory fenestration here is reserved, reduced to small-paned windows along both upper walls, momentary reminiscence of a fighting galleon's stern.

But the Smoking Room is far more luxuriantly decorated than any warship. Lush cascades of Gibbonesque carving garland the fireplace, and stately chandeliers are suspended beneath the vaulted ceiling. Davis profits from one naval architectural necessity: The divided engine-room uptakes, already referred to, have the beneficial effect of breaking up the room's rectangularity, creating several isolated corner nooks. These lend themselves splendidly to my idea of the perfect transatlantic smoking room, separate snuggeries united nicely within one imposing chamber. Before leaving, I select in my mind a baize-topped table for a game of two-pack patience after dinner.

En route forward to the main staircase, I retrace my steps through the Long Gallery, an asymmetrical space uniting Lounge and Smoking Room. "Asymmetrical" because it adheres firmly to the port side only of Promenade Deck, balanced on the starboard side by a block of nicely situated cabins. It seemed at first an odd choice to place the gallery off the keel line, but I realize that by choosing to site it just *to port of* rather than *in between* the third and fourth funnel casings, Davis has evaded the uptake stumbling blocks and been able to add impressive length. I pace it out at more than 130 feet, in fact, legitimately "Long" and, with a fifteen-foot width, legitimately "Gallery" as well. Indeed, it is wider than many earlier Cunard promenade decks.

I am at once reminded of the Paris Ritz's corridor connecting its Place Vendôme and Rue Cambon entrances. But during the crossing to come, I find that *Aquitania*'s Long Gallery serves as far more than thoroughfare or shopping arcade. Thanks to Arthur Davis's seductive decoration, it shares the Carlton Palm Court's inviting appeal. Deeply upholstered chairs alternate with card tables along its length, attracting passengers day and night. The steward's pantry, servicing the outer promenades, meets the needs of indoor passengers as well. As a result, the Long Gallery remains a favorite gathering place for drinks before and after meals.

Its inboard wall includes a barbershop—the ship's only shop, filled with souvenirs and useful necessities—while next door is a typist's office. The intervening inboard wall serves as an informal picture gallery. Outboard, long windows open onto the port promenade and the sea. In fact, Davis's imaginative Long Gallery would cast a long design shadow forward, leading to shopping arcades on future ships. The great interior esplanade of shops on board *L'Atlantique*, *Queen Mary*'s Bond Street, and *Norway*'s conversion of Promenade Deck into shopping mall all originated with Davis's Long Gallery.

By the time I return to Cabin C-80 and, as a favorite aunt used to prescribe, "put my face in repose," the ship has dropped the pilot. *Aquitania* stands out into the Irish Sea, creaking agreeably and, as only a ship under way at sea can be, fully alive at last. The early-evening breeze is fresh, the sea moderate, and the motion negligible; I will not, that night at least, have any need for my bed's restraining boards. I look forward to my crossing no less than my first *Aquitania* dinner down in Restaurant Louis XVI; but all that will follow the amiable racket of the dressing gong at seven-thirty.

The *Aquitania*'s first season encompassed only three voyages to New York. Thereafter, she was dragooned as an armed merchant cruiser (not a success, due to her excessive consumption of coal), then a troopship to take men to the Dardanelles, a hospital ship to bring home the wounded, and during the war's final year, as troopship again, a fast, dazzle-painted transport bringing Canadian and American troops across the Atlantic to the trenches. After the Armistice, she returned the survivors westbound and embarked passengers for a series of makeshift postwar crossings before undergoing an elaborate conversion to oil firing on the Tyne, as well as restoring her interiors from wartime abuse to peacetime gloss. As a result, RMS *Aquitania* did not return to normal transatlantic service until 1920, six long years after her maiden voyage.

Having devoted so many pages to describing the vessel at the start of her life, I cannot be as indulgent about her long career. The *Aquitania* steamed without interruption from 1920 until her final voyage in 1949, when she was withdrawn from service and scrapped. How does one encapsulate the combined minutiae and drama of three decades and 3 million miles of steaming throughout peace and two world wars?

Readers familiar with my previous works will appreciate that, to my mind, neither the line nor the historian illuminates the careers of these immortal vessels; rather, it is the passengers themselves. Theirs are seldom complete documents, only fragments of memory, scraps of paper, and curling sepia photographs; from these essentially trivial vignettes, I hope to fashion a random composite of an imperishable steamship.

As a child, Jane Winslow traveled to Europe with her family on board the *Aquitania* in the early 1930s. Her remembrance of the crossing is not only typical of a young American's first taste of abroad but also bears witness to the Cunarder's susceptibility to motion during winter crossings:

> We left in January. I was four years old, the middle one of three children. I vaguely remember miraculous miles of corridors lined with brass cuspidors, brass railings, and other brass fittings agleam like the Christmas tree we left behind. When at last we reached our cabins, there were two adjoining, one for our parents and the other for us kids. It was great looking out through the portholes, just the right size for our heads.
>
> We had ginger ale in champagne glasses. And cookies. Lots of family and friends had come to see us off. My mother looked sensational. She'd changed into a slinky silver satin gown cut to expose her magnificently stylish bare back. . . .
>
> As we settled in for the night, a steward came with a wrench to close all the portholes. Storms were predicted, he explained, and open portholes might admit high waves. We accepted this with delight.
>
> Next day, the ship was bouncing about like a toy. . . . Lunch was an adventure. The restaurant had a sideboard in

the middle and columns with funny Greek scrolls at their tops. [*So much for the impact, on small passengers, of Arthur Davis's glorious decoration!*]. . . . There was much talk and laughter as the stewards tried to keep their balance, sometimes unsuccessfully. Plates tended to slip off their trays, which reached wonderful tilts. We'd clap with glee to see a platter shoot across the white starched tablecloth and out into the void, to fall with a most satisfying bang and disorder.

The stately paterfamilias at the table next to ours permitted his children to mix their peas into their sticky mashed potatoes and eat the lot with spoons—surely a reasonable procedure for small children in stormy weather. . . . But Mother saw no excuse for neglecting table manners. We had to carry on with knives in pudgy right hand and fork in proper left little fist, chasing the little green marbles around and around our tilting plates.

Incidentally, one persistent anecdote about that restaurant must be laid to rest. Specifically, I am less concerned with what *was* served there than what was patently *not*. Lucius Beebe started it all in 1966 when he published a panegyric to the superrich called *The Big Spenders*. The author makes much of portly Commodore Sir James Charles, known fondly among regular passengers as "Captain Charley." This legendary master, Beebe suggests, presided at a captain's table (table number 37 on the forward starboard side) whose passengers were obliged at one meal to devour "carcasses of whole roasted oxen"; largesse on an ensuing night included "small herds of grilled antelope."

Picturesque as this may seem, the story lacks any basis in fact whatsoever; who, one wonders, was Beebe's source? These extravagant lies have proved durable: Mythic oxen and antelope resurface within more than one maritime anthology. Dinner on board the *Aquitania*, especially during the fabled 1920s, was splendid enough without recourse to this gratuitous hyperbole.

A young Anglo-American who had emigrated to the United States in 1908, Edward Pulling, served as a Royal Naval Reserve officer during World War I. After graduating from Princeton, he taught school and, in the summer of 1927, embarked on board the *Aquitania*, escorting a young protégé, J. Graham Parsons, who would later become ambassador to Canada.

A glance at the third epigraph heading this chapter will explain why that crossing became so special. The "tall beautiful girl" who volunteered as his deck tennis partner was Lucy Leffingwell, a twenty-one-year-old young lady traveling with her family. A year later, she would become Mrs. Edward Pulling. Their courtship during that summer crossing on board the *Aquitania* was idyllic, the ocean smooth and weather bright. Pulling and his new girl spent all of their days playing deck tennis or shuffleboard and their evenings, he recalls, "strolling the promenade decks," marvelously deserted after dark and just right for ardent new friends.

Whereas Pulling sailed on the *Aquitania* for that single crossing, one of her most loyal passengers was a fanatical transatlantic: Herman Murray, a silk importer from Long Island. Born in 1888, he made his first crossing as a four-year-old and, as an adult, began crossing with a vengeance. He so enjoyed every ship that he had their names engraved on both sides of a slim gold cigarette case that his daughter Peggy treasures to this day. His crossing roster was enviable, beginning with White Star's *Britannic* in 1892 and ending with the Cunard White Star's second *Mauretania* in 1955, ten years before he died.

Of all the ship's names engraved on his cigarette case, none recurs more frequently than *Aquitania*'s: He crossed on her eleven times, starting in the mid-1920s. He was besotted with the ship. "She was always sea kindly," he wrote, "never vicious, and in foul weather as in fair, her behavior was exemplary." As an incurable *Aquitania* recidivist, Murray not only made good friends with the officers but recorded many of their stories as well. He knew the legendary Captain Charley well and also his staff captain, H. A. L. Bond, whom he would often meet in the Long Gallery for a Scotch woodcock and glass of ale before retiring.

The chief steward was Robert Bartram Powell. Though a stickler for perfection and a celebrated martinet among the crew, he had one endearing habit when prowling the vessel: Approaching a corner, he would always whistle the same distinctive air, loudly, to alert potential miscreants around the corner of his approach. All of the officers were devoted to their ship. Commodore Chief Engineer Lewellyn Roberts told Murray one night in the Smoking Room that he had six children—twins at home in Hampshire as well as the *Aquitania*'s four engines below.

Murray's ideal *Aquitania* cabin was up on the top deck. Just aft of number 3 funnel, there was a small deckhouse with a curiously checkered past. In the vessel's original 1914 configuration, it had housed the Marconi office and a cabin for two Marconi operators.

LEFT: *Herman Murray's cele-brated gold cigarette case. Note how eleven* Aquitania *entries have been crowded into the right-hand margin by a dogged engraver.* (Peggy Lovering)

BELOW: *The* Aquitania *first crossed the equator in 1938 on a winter cruise to Rio. Passengers enjoy the spectacle of their bare-headed captain under interroga-tion at the hands of Neptune's court.* (Author's collection)

In addition, there were fourteen small cabins—oddly placed in a rarefied corner of the vessel—that accommodated male servants traveling with and attending to passengers. They ate together in a windowless Menservants' Dining Room at the center of the deckhouse, connected to the galley far below by a special pantry lift that pierced the *Aquitania* all the way down to Upper Deck. En route, the same elevator delivered food to the Long Gallery's pantry (hence, Murray's nocturnal Scotch woodcock) and, one deck lower, the larger Maids' Dining Room directly below on Bridge Deck.

Postwar, during the oil conversion, by which time the number of menservants had dwindled, the deckhouse briefly accommodated engineering officers. (On board all ships, cabins with optimum fresh air and sea views are traditionally assigned to engineers because so much of their workday is spent confined below.) The Menservants' Dining Room now fed the maids; presumably, those menservants still traveling ate in the second-class dining room down on D Deck.

But within very few years, the engineers were moved elsewhere, and the little Boat Deck deckhouse was reconverted into several small but comfortable passenger cabins, christened by the purser's staff "the bachelor quarters." The best of them had been the chief's original cabin. It was situated in the deckhouse's after starboard corner, and deck plans identified it as Cabin O.

The only one up there with a private bathroom, Cabin O was Herman Murray's perennial favorite. Throughout his crossings, he would summon the Long Gallery's crack steward, Tizzard, to mix cocktails in Cabin O for gatherings of shipboard chums. On the last night of a westbound crossing—at seven-fifteen on June 16, 1927— he distributed a copy of the following poem to all the guests who had joined him for a drink:

> *Such is the* Aquitania
> *Beautiful, wondrous, real;*
> *Every old ocean loves her,*
> *Knows the caress of her keel.*
>
> *Away up on top on the Boat Deck,*
> *In a nice little suite lettered O,*
> *The Manhattans, Martinis and Bronxes*
> *And good fellowship, Ah cheerio!*

How clubby our cocktail parties
How gorgeous our sunset shows;
And tonight's our last one together
Where again shall we meet, who knows?

So here's to your Health and Happiness,
Whither in the world you may go;
Remember our own Aquitania
And my cabin, lettered O!

In September 1939, *Aquitania* went to war for the second time
in her career. Turning instantly to trooping, she was seen on oceans
of the world where her builders had never conceived she would
sail. Part of one memorable convoy from Sydney to the Middle
East, she sailed in a vast wartime assemblage that included both
Queens, the *Nieuw Amsterdam*, and the *Mauretania II*. Service
personnel all over the South Pacific who might be confused about
which gray-painted *Queen* was which had no problem identifying
the only four-stacker still afloat.

Early on during hostilities, conditions belowdecks retained peacetime perquisites. J. Lennox-King, part of a naval detachment sailing
from New Zealand to the Clyde, recalled the cabin he shared with
only one other officer in May 1940:

> The two-berth cabin was unchanged from its first class condi-
> tion—thick carpet, its walls covered with silk brocade, com-
> fortable arm chairs, mahogany furniture. The public rooms—
> smoking rooms, lounges, and so on were still in their peace-
> time opulence. The officer's dining saloon still had its full
> complement of stewards (as did the cabins) and of peace-
> time fare. Menus were printed in the ship's printery fresh
> each day. . . . With the starched tablecloths and napkins of
> snowy linen and array of table silver, meals were pleasurable
> occasions.

Once past Capetown, Lennox-King remembers the *Aquitania*
passing a stricken tanker on fire, abrupt reminder of their entry
into the war zone. The film entertainment on board was marginally
topical: Four-year-old newsreels were screened, doubtless vacuous
reassurances from politicians that the war was not likely to take
place.

But by November 1943, when the *Aquitania* returned to the North Atlantic, her peacetime patina had worn thin. Robert McCormick, part of the Forty-fourth Evacuation Hospital, was scheduled to board for passage to the United Kingdom. His unit assembled by train at Camp Kilmer and Fort Dix in New Jersey. There, long before boarding, they were briefed at length about the possibility of torpedo attack and coached in a facsimile boat drill. Some units were even bused to the YMCA pool in New Brunswick for a jump into the deep end of the pool, wearing bathing suit and life jacket.

They crossed the Hudson from Hoboken on November 16 and, laden with duffel and musette bags, clambered aboard the vessel after dark, part of a draft of 8,000 men. (The *Aquitania*'s trooping capacity was about half of the *Queens'*.) As the last unit to board, the enlisted men of the Forty-fourth were accommodated, incredibly, up on Boat Deck, on standee bunks packed within wartime plywood shelters open at both ends to the weather. Despite gales that occasionally swept through their quarters, they avoided the overpowering reek of fuel oil that many of their fellow passengers complained about down below.

So much for the "cabin"; what about conditions in the dining room? Records Joe Brandt, another member of the Forty-fourth: "Let me describe the meals aboard ship—terrible." For much of the crossing, he and his friends made do with Coke, candy bars, and cookies instead.

The vessel was still fast enough to travel alone, unhindered by slower fleetmates in a conventional convoy. All the crowded tedium of a wartime crossing was there, including the amateur talent shows that traveled from compartment to compartment—a yodeler and a Hindu fakir who poked needles into his flesh without wincing. There were alarms and daily boat drills; progress was monitored by an amateur navigator called Captain McNutt.

But despite fear, discomfort, and bad catering, Robert McCormick's reaction to the *Aquitania* sounds like any proud passenger's:

> She was strong and steady and soon she had awakened a positive affection in the hearts of all. . . . The weather was excellent most of the time. The view of the wake of the ship from the stern was beautiful to watch. It remained an exquisite aquamarine where the rest of the sea was usually a dull lead. The white caps were lovely. A wave would come rolling along

and as it reached its crest, a brisk wind would whip off the top in a whirl of light spray which looked like the eruption of a miniature volcano. Towards the end of the crossing, the weather grew a little stormy and the ship pitched and tossed a bit. One felt in a topsy-turvy land looking at others standing on a deck slanting at a 20-degree angle.

Captain McNutt had been acting as our unofficial navigator throughout the voyage, with his compasses and strings, and on the afternoon of 24 November, he announced if his figures were right, that a certain lighthouse would be sighted at ten o'clock that evening. Within four minutes of that hour, he started rushing around with the tidings that the light had actually been seen.

Their crossing ended off the Tail of the Bank that night. The following morning, *Aquitania*'s passengers saw that the ship shared the anchorage with both *Queens*. In fact, the *Mary* had been in New York when they sailed but had beaten them across.

Westbound crossings during this period were quite different, carrying small assortments of service personnel or German prisoners of war to America. One such passenger was an Englishman, Geoffrey Barraclough, now a doctor who lives in Kyoto, Japan. In February 1944, he sailed out to America for pilot training:

She was almost empty. I can't even remember where in the ship we slept, except that it was in one of the public rooms which had been filled with bunks in tiers and divided up by light partitions. You could see quite well how the public rooms must have looked; the parts which were out of reach were more or less unchanged, but the lower parts—which I think were unprotected—were much defaced and vandalized. Most of the ship was out of bounds but we managed to have a good look around. . . . Two things about the food: one, it was wartime British rather than American; and two, if we wanted a snack between meals, there was an unlimited supply of Nestlé's condensed milk, but just about nothing else.

We sailed up toward Manhattan at sunset of a perfect evening, everything looking exactly as I had imagined it would. However, the doorway from which we were gazing was blocked by one John Bell from Glasgow, who was sitting with his back to the view, reading the Bible. We asked him to move to the side, and he said "What are you staring at? It's all in here." He did move, but he didn't turn around.

After V-E day, the *Aquitania* never regained her prewar status. By the late forties, she had become an Edwardian anachronism eclipsed by the *Queens*. "The Ship Beautiful" during the 1920s and 1930s, "Old Granny" during the war, she now became "Old Reliable," a kindly if geriatric sobriquet.

The inevitable scarring and deterioration of her paneling, as well as its defacement at the hands of thousands of bored soldier-passengers, would remain an embarrassment until the end of the *Aquitania*'s life. Perhaps that decay was merely symptomatic of the times. Throughout the United Kingdom during the latter part of the war, British manufacturers churned out products in "utility" mode—makeshift, no-nonsense goods that were, if practical, only marginally attractive. The same pejorative could have been applied to the *Aquitania* during that dreary postwar period, the former distinguished Cunarder now a utility transport kept in harness to bring the troops home and then Canadian emigrants to Canada. Her first-class dining-room floor was still covered with wartime linoleum; Davis's rich blue carpeting was never reinstalled. She remained exclusively on the Canadian run for the four peacetime years left her; that unique four-funneled profile was never again seen in New York harbor.

Not surprisingly, for a generation of dispirited postwar British teenagers, the *Aquitania* represented the means to a new life in the New World. So rather than either of the two more prestigious (and probably more secure!) *Queens*, she became the target of choice for stowaway emigrants. One such illicit passenger was Charles Radley, whom I met on board the *Crown Princess* in 1990. Back in 1948, at the age of seventeen, he had been employed in London making coffin moldings. Anxious for a better life at sea, he and two friends had tried joining the merchant navy but, without a job offer, could not get a union card. One weekend in September 1948, after they had been paid their week's wages, the three of them made their way, partly on foot, to Southampton. After dark, they scaled a wall onto the docks and reached the side of a large ship that they found out later was indeed the *Aquitania*. The three stowaways crept on board via an unmanned gangway and bedded down temporarily in a crowded storage room filled with brooms and buckets.

After a few hours' sleep, they emerged to search for a better hiding place. They passed some generators enclosed within wire cages (doubtless refrigerating plants) and, opening several other doors, stumbled into some crew quarters. The alarm was sounded, and Charles and his friends scattered, leading their pursuers a merry chase all over the *Aquitania*'s lower decks. One by one, they were caught and brought before the master-at-arms.

He gave them a proper dressing-down before handing them over to the Southampton Police, who, because they had committed no crime other than trespassing, put them in charge of the Salvation Army. Planning to stow away again, the determined trio set out for Liverpool *on foot*. After several nights of "sleeping rough" and with their money running low, they split up and thumbed rides back to London. Wrote Charles Radley years later:

> Looking back on this adventure, it was doomed from the start. I often wonder what would have happened to me if I had been successful in getting across the Atlantic. I never in my wildest dreams in those far-distant days thought that, in later life, I would be able to enjoy cruising on the luxury ships of today.

During the postwar forties, the *Aquitania* merely marked time. Service standards that had delighted Murray, the man with the ship's name lovingly engraved so many times on his cigarette case, had sadly declined. Geoffrey Coughtrey, now a senior bedroom steward reigning supreme up in *QE2*'s penthouses, began his Cunard career as a *commis* waiter in the *Aquitania*'s tourist-class dining saloon after the war. He recalls that decorum was so lax that he and his dining-room colleagues indulged in all kinds of impertinent horseplay with their inexperienced emigrant clients; nobody seemed to care anymore.

Arthur Joseph Davis outlived his favorite vessel by a year, dying at the age of seventy-three in July 1951. He had designed three more ships for Cunard—the *Laconia*, the *Franconia*, and elements of the *Queen Mary*. In fact, that first *Queen*'s decorative scheme was vitiated by a conflict of tastes between young moderns and a timid board of directors: A sort of art deco ship resulted, with none of the Davis touch so evident on both the *Laconia* and the *Franconia*. There was one extraordinary omission: Davis's obituary in *The Times* of London made no mention of *Aquitania* whatsoever, even though an outpouring of nostalgic grief had occurred when she sailed for the scrap yard. Perhaps there was little regret for a tattered Edwardian sensation in Britain's bleak postwar years.

The inevitable came in early 1950. Having completed thirteen round voyages to Halifax the year previously, the *Aquitania* was laid up at Berth 108 in Southampton's New Docks to "await a survey," chilling words that could only presage the end. Berth 108 had always been death row for superannuated tonnage: The *Mauretania*, the *Olympic*, and the *Homeric* had all tied up there successively before sailing for the scrap yard in the thirties.

"Out with the old . . ." This last four-stacker's departure from Southampton occurred as the port's proud new Ocean Terminal prepared to open alongside the ocean dock. This great art deco structure, now, sadly, gone, was a land-based extension of the *Queens*, planned in the thirties but not completed until 1950. A quarter of a mile long, it seemed part vessel itself: The four-story, semicircular tower greeting incoming vessels at its southern end had the unmistakable shape of a bridge screen.

Cunard charged Hampton & Sons, the London firm, to auction off nearly three-thousand lots of the *Aquitania* furniture and fittings during a sale on the pier. It started on February 13 and continued until Tuesday the twenty-first. A glance through the catalog indicates not only a vast assortment but also a multiplicity of objects spread out for inspection in the piershed. Lot number 529, for instance—"Two polished oak chests of four long drawers, each with compo-lined tops, 29"—was followed by two and a half pages bearing the repetitive legend "A similar lot."

Other lots hinted at the variety of life on board. Lot number 1146, for example: "Six cream enamelled small bunk ladders." Lot number 1185: "Three dog kennels with canvas covers." Lot number 1538:—"Six interior sprung mattresses of striped tick, 6 ft × 2 ft"—was followed, again, by pages of "a similar lot" as the lowest decks' meager bedding was brought out into the light. Lot number 1944 consisted of "40 metal cuspidors." What happened, I wonder, to Lot number 405: "A head-waiter's Louis design mahogany high desk, 25 in. And a stool"? And what about Lot number 980, the next day: "A mahogany crucifix, 36 in."? Lot number 2565, included within the catering equipment sold on the sixth day, sounded like a tongue twister from a purser's competition for young passengers: "Three butter cutters, and three pickle kidds with lids."

During the weekend between the fifth and sixth days' sale, "Old Reliable" was scheduled to sail from Southampton forever on the fog-shrouded morning of Sunday, February 19. Her final destina-

TOP: *Near the end, the* Aquitania *tied up at Southampton's Berth 108, her interiors already stripped. In the foreground is the dry-docked* Queen Elizabeth. (Fox Photos)

BOTTOM: *The auction begins, the auctioneer perched on one of hundreds of ship's armchairs. The newsreel camera just over his podium indicates that it is the newsworthy first day.* (Southern Newspapers)

tion was the Clyde, at the breakup yard of Metal Industries, very near Clydebank, where she had been built. In effect, the great ship was going home to die.

On the bridge stood her last master, Captain R. B. G. Woollatt, and the company's senior choice pilot, Captain George W. Somerwill, a Trinity House veteran of thirty-six years. On board also were James Elder, an *Aquitania* crewman since 1920, and sixty-year-old James Drysdale, a beloved dining-room steward; he had joined the vessel when she first sailed for New York from Southampton in 1919.

Chief Engineer John Moffatt presided down in the engine room. On that last voyage, only three of *Aquitania*'s four funnels would actually smoke (final *Olympic* parallel); for the past year, six boilers had been out of service. Moffatt planned steaming to the Clyde at a respectable fourteen knots.

Six tugs, the *Hornsby, William Poulson, Romsey, Palladin, Canute,* and *Wellington*—port stalwarts that had nudged the *Aquitania* in and out of the ocean dock for decades—assembled off Berth 108 at the scheduled departure time of 0900. But the fog was so thick that Woollatt did not slip her cables until just before one. Impatient with the delay, many of the early-morning crowd drifted away; no more than a hundred chilled spectators, mostly crew wives, finally waved her off.

The vessel was not strictly empty: Two dozen reporters were on board, in high spirits as they embarked for the last run north. But they had signed ship's articles as supernumerary ordinary seamen, and so their contracted wages were a shilling a month. They had to bunk in deserted junior officers' cabins, since all passenger accommodations and public rooms had been stripped for the auction.

Aquitania swung majestically around in the turning basin and began her last passage to sea. Along the Union Castle docks, the *Edinburgh Castle* and the *Durban Castle* dipped their ensigns in salute. A chorus of whistles rent the air not only from the *Empire Windrush* and a dredger offshore but also from locomotive engineers in the New Docks.

But it was the farewell signals that tugged at the heart. R. P. Biddle, docks and marine manager, flashed as the ship passed:

> We at Southampton docks bid farewell to the *Aquitania,* grand old lady of the Atlantic. She will be sadly missed but always remembered.

Messages continued throughout the mournful passage to Scotland. GOODBYE WITH REGRET signaled a shore station en route down-channel, and a passing tanker spelled out GOODBYE OLD FAITHFUL. Later, up near the Clyde, two Royal Navy ships chimed in: WE'RE PROUD TO HAVE MET YOU made a frigate, and a submarine was even briefer, blinking simply "RIP."

On board, the reporters made notes of the incoming signals but had little else to do. They found the uncarpeted public rooms depressing, voices and footsteps echoing over stained parquet. Curiously, many paintings and all of the Smoking Room paneling remained in place. There had been vague talk of a "later sale"; but to my knowledge the paneling went to the breaker's. One ex-passenger wrote to the London *Times*, lamenting that the Smoking Room in particular should have been saved intact: "There is no room afloat," he lamented, "to touch it for beauty and dignity."

The supernumeraries were fed indifferently in one corner of Arthur Davis's now derelict Restaurant Louis XVI, which for the past five years had been clumsily divided in half to encourage tourist-class bookings. Jimmy Drysdale solemnly delivered two dozen table d'hôte plates to their makeshift communal table. After dinner, they stretched out self-consciously in adjacent deck chairs that the company had pulled from auction at the last minute. Deck chairs in the dining room—what would Arthur Davis have said?

Tuesday morning early, they saw to port the snow-covered hills of Arran. Then *Aquitania* steamed past John Brown's measured mile along Skelmorlie's cliffs at only slightly better than half the speed she had made on sea trials there thirty-six years earlier. At 10:00 A.M. sharp, she anchored off the Tail of the Bank and waited for four hours for the flood tide that would permit her to continue under tow up into the Gare Loch.

She arrived off Faslane that evening; the last voyage was over. Carrying their own luggage, the reporters/crewmen assembled in the ship's foyer for the last time. The purser presented them with discharge certificates and conduct reports. There was much guffawing as each signed off, accepting a buff manila envelope containing his pay packet—three days' wages of three ha'pence.

From ashore, they watched the *Aquitania* vanish into the winter dusk. Local children had been let out of school early to watch her go. At the same time, down in Southampton, the last auction item, Lot Number 2875—"a Glazed Ware Shanks lavatory basin"—was knocked down; ship and sale ended at precisely the same moment.

Within a year, 600 Metal Industries workers would burn, cut, and wrench "Old Reliable" into 30,000 tons of unrecognizable steel scrap. Bits of the *Aquitania* that were never auctioned turn up everywhere. Some paneling—but not the Smoking Room's—graces the dining room of an Isle of Wight hotel. Her wheel is in Halifax's Museum of the Atlantic, and her largest bell can be found to this day in *Queen Elizabeth 2*'s wardroom, where it is tolled only once annually, at midnight on New Year's Eve.

I like Herman Murray's suggestion of *Aquitania*'s Southampton finale:

> Her wonderful profile stood out in bold relief against the morning sky, and her majestic presence made itself felt by all. Men raised their hats to her in a final salute, and from her forward funnel, a white plume of steam followed by the deep-throated roar of her siren acknowledged the tribute.
>
> There were few dry eyes among those who bade her farewell. And so *Aquitania* passed on her way to the great beyond, where Captain Charley, Roberts and Powell awaited her.

Chapter 4

Status distinctions would be inimical to the charter yacht tourists who share a sense of "being apart together in an exceptional situation." The distinctions that matter and that are addressed are not the distinctions among the charter yacht tourists themselves but between the charter yacht tourists and the rest of the world of "non-players."
—James W. Lett, Jr., Ludic and Liminoid Aspects of
    Charter Yacht Tourists in the Caribbean

The arrival of the Stella Polaris *caused excitement. She came in late in the evening, having encountered some very heavy weather on her way from Barcelona. I saw her lights across the harbor and heard her band faintly playing dance music, but it was not until next morning that I went to look more closely at her. She was certainly a very pretty ship, standing rather high in the water, with the tall pointed prow of a sailing yacht, white all over except for her single yellow funnel.*
—Evelyn Waugh, A Pleasure Cruise in 1929

Miniships: Extravagance of Scale

In today's buoyant cruise market, why has the luxurious small ship proliferated? Perhaps the best way to answer that question is to consider the other end of the spectrum: Why are there so many big ships?

Megaships are in vogue because the demand for cabin space has mandated a principle called economy of scale. In words of one syllable, it costs cruise lines less to book a horde in one huge hull than to split the same horde in half on two small hulls. At stake is the expensive duplication of salaried posts as well as the cost of fuel. Every vessel requires a captain, a staff captain, a first officer, navigating officers, a chief engineer, assistant engineers, a cruise director, a chief steward, a projectionist, a master-at-arms, and so on—an essential crew list regardless how many passengers are carried. So, accommodating 2,000 passengers in one enormous vessel means that one salaried crew can look after that much larger a number; dividing them in half on two smaller ships would require two captains, two first officers, two chief engineers, two cruise directors, and so on. Additionally, it takes less fuel to power one large vessel than to bunker two smaller ones. Therein lies economy of scale, the inescapable financial logic that propels the *Sovereign of the Seas*, the *Fantasy*, the *Star Princess*, the *Norway*, and increasing numbers of megaships around the Caribbean every week.

(But what, one might inquire impatiently, does this have to do with small ships? A little more patience will achieve the connection.)

Thousands of megaship cabins must be filled, day in and day out, fifty weeks a year. (Like most of their clients, cruise ships get a fortnight's rest each year, spent in dry dock.) As a result, a wide marketing net must be cast to fill the hulls with a populist clientele. Many of these Newpassengers have no prior shipboard experience, limited funds, and easily fulfilled expectations, what one might describe as Carnival cannon-fodder. Since megaships can afford larger entertainment budgets, there are either bigger names at the lounge microphone or, inevitably, longer chorus lines grinning throughout more elaborate, Las Vegan show rooms.

Indeed, the seven-day megaship offers its passenger overload an unrelenting shipboard surfeit: traditional nonstop food that is free, drink that is not, and, in addition, gambling, fashion shows, beauty tips, grandmother gatherings, service-club meetings, television games and interviews, pool games, sun-drenched, primary-colored deckscapes, masquerade parties, horse racing, and bingo; and throughout the clamor of their dizzying week, passengers will enjoy just adequate digs ingeniously stacked within the honey-combed bowels of their hull.

Periodically, on-board glitter is abandoned for island excursion: Half the megaships' cruise itinerary is spent ashore, feeding a persistent Newpassenger craving for yet another port; neophyte passengers like to go home at the end of their cruise laden not only with comic hats and souvenir leis but also port memories hanging like scalps from their cruising belt.

That hyperactive seven-day regime does not necessarily enchant every passenger. In general—and how dangerous it is, ever, to generalize about *Peregrinator americanus*—the more experienced the passenger, the less he or she enjoys being part of a shipboard herd. The problem persists on the metaship, what used to be the standard cruise ship—20,000 tons and 600 passengers. In fact, these are an endangered species nowadays since the few remaining often have their interiors and schedules upgraded to resemble small-scale megaships.

So the only alternative is the miniship, everything the megaship is not: It is small, quiet, select, and luxurious, has a high servant ratio, and is, perforce, expensive. Involved here is the very reverse of economy of scale, a contrary marketing principle that I have christened, for the purposes of this chapter, extravagance of scale. As a means of megaship-miniship comparison, it is worth remarking that the entire *fleet* capacity of Sea Goddess and Wind Star combined could be accommodated—doubtless unhappily—with room to spare on *Sovereign of the Seas'* A Deck.

There are, of course, less splendid miniships, conveyances for what is called adventure cruising, destined for rugged or remote ports, from which passengers disembark on Galápagos or Antarctica. Although well run and eminently seaworthy, they cater largely to academics and amateur scientists; extravagance of scale does not apply. Also, since I have never sailed on one, I must regretfully exclude them from consideration here.

Miniships are not necessarily snob ships, although their hefty passenger per diem narrows their appeal, spawning an aura of exclusivity. Whereas passengers sailing on megaships in the early 1990s could manage a week in an inside cabin for about $1,000 apiece, that same $1,000 would last less than two days for a suite on board the *Seabourn Pride*, which, like every miniship, has no inside cabins. In terms of on-board ambience, miniships pride themselves on being understated. Evening diversion is confined to a minimalist casino or lone combo.

In the mid-eighties, a Norwegian, Helge Naarstad, conceived, designed, and built the first pair of miniships, which his advertising agency subsequently called the *Sea Goddess I* and the *Sea Goddess II*. It is a lamentable fact of miniship newbuilding that ships' names incorporate the company name: Royal Viking started the trend two decades ago, but at least they added a short distinguishing suffix name—the *Royal Viking Star* or the *Royal Viking Sun*. Sea Goddess Cruises used numbers only, as does an octet of Renaissance Cruise Line vessels numbered simply *Renaissance I* through *Renaissance VIII*.

Sea Goddess ships were designed as elegant yachts, carrying at most 116 passengers in identical suites deluxe. Food and service were—and still are—exquisite, with unlimited caviar and all drinks, save the most recherché vintages, on the house. More-over—and this was the class clincher—there was to be almost no regimented passenger life or entertainment whatsoever—no "shows," bingo, or horse racing, none of the megaship's Brue-ghelian hugger-mugger. Sea Goddess passengers would make do with book, deck chair, swimming pool, sun, food, and refreshingly, conversation.

That low-keyed shipboard regime, together with its steep tariff, discouraged mass-market cruise clients. They would not have any shipboard fun (as they are perceived to perceive it), nor could they afford to pay so much more for, apparently, so much less; and less, balanced on the socioeconomic fulcrum of extravagance of scale, is definitely more.

Perhaps it was no accident that the Norwegians pioneered the current small-ship market, for more than six decades ago, Norway's Bergen Line launched their legendary *Stella Polaris* from the Go-taverken Shipyard of Gothenburg. Although she sailed on her last cruise in 1969, she should be remembered as cruising's prototypical small ship, conjuring up old-fashioned cruising resonances long vanished.

The *Stella Polaris* was an ingenious anachronism: a modern 170-passenger cruise ship that seemed, from over the water, a throw-back to Edwardian luxe. By 1927, the year of her debut, contempo-rary passenger ships' funnels had already been shortened by the squat modernity of the motor ship. In one breathtaking vision, *Stella Polaris* turned back the maritime clock, her single tall buff 'midships stack, bowsprit, and masts giving her passengers the impression that they had booked on board a turn-of-the-century steam/sail yacht. In fact, she could not sail at all—masts and bow-sprit were merely decorative. This was merely nostalgic legerde-main, a faux sailing yacht with rococo, gilt-encrusted prow and pristine, white-awninged decks. Lacking only a figurehead, the *Stella Polaris* remains perhaps the most visually striking cruise ship of all time.

Her looks were derived from the *Empress of India*, built in 1891 for Canadian Pacific Railway's express mail service between Vancouver and the Far East. Though that graceful white vessel had an additional funnel and mast, she might otherwise have seemed the *Stella Polaris*'s double. Curiously, those earliest *Empress*-class vessels came equipped with working sails, as though dependence on canvas might prove a necessity. But since they enjoyed the fail-safe of twin screws (several years, incidentally, in advance of Cunard's *Lucania*), they never hoisted sail at all.

At just under 6,000 tons, the *Empress of India* was almost exactly the same displacement as the *Stella Polaris*, longer—485 feet as opposed to 416 feet—but with an identical beam of 51 feet. Below-decks, she was not luxurious throughout, since she carried a whopping 900 passengers in three classes: 160 in an admittedly lavish first class, 40 in a less lavish second class, and a teeming 700 in steerage. Yet, despite that conventional late-nineteenth-century density, cruising seemed intrinsic to the graceful new ship. The *Empress of India*'s first voyage—delivery from her Scottish yard to Canada's west coast—sold out as a round-the-world cruise, as though nothing were more natural for that sheer white hull and soaring bowsprit, beneath which Queen Victoria's figurehead smiled benignly over the sea.

Another yachtlike *Stella Polaris* forebear was Hamburg American Line's *Prinzessen Victoria Luise*, a two-funneled, bowspritted cruise ship equally at home in turn-of-the-century northern fjord or Caribbean island; less at home, alas, off Jamaica, where she came to grief on underwater coral in 1906.

Both *Empress of India* and *Prinzessen Victoria Luise* served as obvious role models for the Bergen Line when the *Stella Polaris* was laid down in 1925. She would fulfill every embarking passenger's dream wish as *the* cruise ship of all time; her 1935 brochures heralded the *Stella Polaris* as "a pleasure cruiser par excellence" and the power she exudes in passenger memory is formidable.

In July 1935, Bill Morris, a young Princeton undergraduate, booked the *Stella Polaris*'s inside Cabin 220, down on C Deck, the lowest passenger deck at the bottom of the afterstaircase, "crowded but adequate," he recalls. It was also inexpensive, even allowing for retrospective inflation: Cabin 220 on the *Stella Polaris* during the summer of 1935 cost only $135 for an extremely comfortable fortnight.

Passengers for that summer's four North Cape cruises boarded at either Calais or Harwich. Bewitched by the vessel's haunting profile, Bill had booked to see the fjords. A devoted, lifelong passenger on dozens of vessels as well as an avid collector of memorabilia, Bill kept every scrap of paper issued on board. One of his dinner menus is, like all *Stella Polaris* early ephemera, as simple as it is revealing and invaluable for the historian.

The choices are not lavish. Bill Morris's dinner began with caviar

TOP: *Festooned with signal flags right down to the water, the* Empress of India *lies at anchor off Victoria at the end of what seems to have been a testing maiden voyage.* (Royal British Columbia Museum, Historical Collections)

From William Morris's Stella Polaris *album:* CENTER: *A pretty cruise ship awaits offshore.* BOTTOM: *Where the girls are: a party of attractive fellow passengers ensconced in one of the company's open tourers.* (William H. Morris collection)

molossol, two soups, a fish course, followed by either sweetbread or roast chicken, salad, dessert, and cheese; "Coffee served in deck saloons" ends the column. On the opposite page, the menu is reproduced in French. (Although overwhelmingly booked by Americans, there were a dozen Frenchmen on board.) On the back cover are listed the orchestral selections played that evening under the direction of bandmaster Heinrich Pecht.

Most striking is the menu's simplicity—the margins broad, the typeface conservative, the choices adequate but not overwhelming—almost table d'hôte and far more modest than almost any cruise-ship offering today. But beyond its typographic and gastronomic significance, it conveys to me conditions in the dining saloon that sunlit July evening so many years ago. I can hear the gentle table chatter, the discreet clatter of cutlery, and the strains of Strauss's "Artist's Life" as the stolid, white-gloved stewards set *Coup Glacé Vanille* before each diner. And through white-painted casements to either side, the incomparable coast slipped by, awash with gold.

Norway's coast in high summer remains without question my favorite cruising ground. I have enjoyed it from half a dozen vessels, from coastal steamer to *QE2*, and never tire of those extraordinary fjords, the increasingly spectacular, if forbidding, shore farther north, and everywhere, that haunting, unending summer light. I only wish that I had been able to enjoy it from the decks of the *Stella Polaris*. Just forward of the bridge was a large, square observation deck, running the full width of the vessel, unobstructed forward save by the mast, an ideal space from which to view that magical progression through the fjords. Later in the ship's career, a small swimming pool would be added down on Promenade Deck just forward of that observation deck, undoubtedly the pool with the best view in the world.

Shore excursions from the *Stella* were elegant as well. One went ashore in the earliest days on board handsome, half-decked launches, with parasoled passengers in an after cockpit and white-clad crewmen brandishing boat hooks atop a mahogany foredeck. Ashore, passengers transferred for land tours into the open tonneaus of four-doored touring cars, which, since they only saw use two months a year, retained their pristine, if dated, good looks well into the fifties.

Eighteen-year-old Peter Spang encountered them during his *Stella Polaris* cruise in the summer of 1953. By then, interestingly enough, the vessel's decor had lost some of its earlier charm. "The whole ship seemed cramped and dark for one used to travel on the *Queens*," he recalls. He loved it nevertheless, especially the incomparable sight of the *Stella* across the limpid expanse of a fjord with snow-covered peaks in the distance.

That was two years after the Swedes had taken over the vessel, and they had not yet redecorated the ship. Inevitably, fellow-passenger holdovers from the old days insisted that "things had been better" under the Norwegian regime.

Irreplaceable fragments from those long-gone *Stella Polaris* days survive, thanks to the recall of correspondents. Peter remembers the hardness of the (Norwegian) water on board, so hard that shampoos were avoided because rinsing out the soap was almost impossible. Perhaps the laundry soap was removed more easily from his Brookscloth shirts, novel wash-and-wear travel clothing new that very summer. He also remembers fishing over the stern and hooking an enormous cod.

Mary Jane Luke and her sister Betty had been on board five years earlier, in 1948. Both recall rumors, at the time, of World War II mines still lurking in Norwegian coastal waters. Though their parents were up on A Deck—boasting the luxury of a private bathroom—the two girls berthed down on C Deck and used to invite visitors to come down and "watch the mines float by" through their almost waterline porthole. It was into that same (open) porthole that the girls used to stuff an extra pillow to thwart the pervasive glare of the midnight sun when and if they ever decided finally to get some sleep. And that same cabin played unhappy host to some souvenir Lapp reindeerskin moccasins from Hammerfest, which soon gave noisome indication that they were uncured; Mrs. Luke consigned them, regretfully, overboard.

Pointing up the perennial shortage of private bathrooms, Cloty McMasters Hughes's father, a keen deck-plan aficionado, had carefully selected his family's cabin accommodations adjacent to a large public bathroom. Sadly, the bathroom in question turned out to be male only; though McMaster père was happily situated, Cloty and her mother had a long trek for bathing. Several South American diplomats were on board, and Cloty remembers with amusement inevitable corridor encounters: Though bathrobed and laden with sponge bag and towel, they always managed an impeccably elaborate bow.

Hard by the *Stella Polaris* when Bill Morris visited the North

Cape was Hamburg American's *Monta Rosa*. The German vessel's entire passenger load—"several hundred Nazis"—climbed to the top of the cape (everyone went up on foot in those days) and established a kind of *Feldlager*, goose-stepping in formation all over the top. It was an eerie preview of unpleasantness to come.

Mary Jane Luke pens perhaps the most heartfelt tribute to her favorite cruise ship: "There was a sort of spirit about the *Stella Polaris* and she has remained in my memory as might a lovely friend long gone, whose face and voice have dimmed with time."

The *Stella* had been designed for long-distance cruising as well. Each year, she circumnavigated the globe, carrying no more than 120 passengers out of New York. Her silhouette was familiar in dozens of ports all over the world, a sparkling Scandinavian dream ship for all seasons. Evelyn Waugh wrote that "she exhibited a Nordic and almost glacial cleanness. I have never seen anything outside a hospital so much scrubbed and polished."

In truth, architecturally, the *Stella Polaris* only just achieved her yacht image. However extravagant the tycoon, privately owned pleasure craft seldom run to 6,000 tons, with dozens of passengers rather than scores. The *Stella Polaris*'s 170 passengers were tended by nearly that number in crew, an enviable servant ratio that required accommodations for 300 souls, in varying degrees of luxe within one graceful hull.

This is a perennial catch-22 of the high-density cruising yacht: Pampered passengers demand many hands. For example, one of the *Sea Goddess*'s design shortcomings is distressingly crowded crew accommodations, because, inadvertently, hull dimensions had been established before crew noses were sufficiently well counted. Her original passenger capacity was projected at 120, but so crowded was *Sea Goddess I*'s backstage that two original passengers' cabins had to be reassigned to officers. Lower down in the maritime hierarchy, Sea Goddess crews are inevitably crowded in dayroom, deck space, and cabin.

It was a curious coincidence that having been originally built in a Swedish yard, the *Stella Polaris*'s ownership would pass to Swedish interests in 1951. Changes in Norway's maritime laws made it uneconomical to fly the Norwegian flag, so the *Stella Polaris* was transferred to Clipper Line, registered in Malmö. Subsequently, the vessel was completely air-conditioned by her new owners—a boon in the Caribbean and the South Seas—and, late in life, was radically refitted belowdecks to remedy the inadequacies of 1920s passenger plumbing. Thereafter, every cabin on board had a private bathroom, and more suites were created.

But the changes came too late to attract enough passengers, and after forty-two years of memorable service, the *Stella Polaris* was withdrawn. She survives as a floating hotel in Japan, moored permanently in Kisyo Bay, an hour south of Yokohama. She is still painted white and, given her Nordic/Swedish antecedents, has an appropriate new name, *Scandinavia.*

I visited her in 1988 during a Yokohama stopover, having crossed the Pacific on board the *Royal Viking Star.* En route, I discovered that our master, Captain Helge Brudvig, was as keen as I to visit the venerable *Stella Polaris* because his father had served briefly on board her as a steward in 1928.

So early one humid morning at Yokohama's railway station, we boarded a bullet train, having been instructed solemnly by the ship's agent to disembark smartly after three stops. (Bullet trains waste no time calling at stations.) We did so and next endured an interminable taxi ride through that combination of lush greenery and industrial sprawl that is present-day Japan to a winding, almost fjordlike stretch of seacoast. By the time the taxi's meter had racked up a terrifying total of yen, we suddenly encountered *Scandinavia-ex-Stella Polaris*, moored to shore by stout chains and looking essentially unchanged save for an inoffensive blue logo on her buff funnel.

Captain Tsujio Date and Hotel Manager Hiroshi Anraku welcomed us on board, and we joined them for lunch in the ship's dining saloon, scrupulously preserved and offering an excellent smorgasbord. Tables soon filled with touring bus parties of Japanese who consumed their smorgasbord, I was interested to note, exclusively with knife and fork rather than chopsticks. We sat at the captain's table in the vessel's original chairs, Helge Brudvig occupying the lighter-colored captain's chair. All the dining-room chairs boasted seats of relentlessly Spartan surface; *Stella Polaris* passengers must have been either hardy or well upholstered themselves to linger long at table.

After lunch, we were given a complete tour of the vessel by genial Mr. Anraku, encompassing Veranda Café, Smoking Room (the names alone are redolent of another era), several cabins, including the long-since-closed captain's quarters, the bridge (apart from the wheel, devoid of navigational equipment), and the engine room, still providing service electricity and, during the winter, heat, in a hissing, steaming simulacrum of its former self.

The open decks and lifeboats were still covered by taut white awnings. Although everything showed the passage of time—the varnished teak bridge screen had been overpainted brown (since scraped and revarnished), and tourist souvenir stalls crowded the midship lobby—a sense of what the *Stella Polaris* had once been remains hauntingly intact. Ships in retirement, whether hotels or museums, suffer a lack of vitality; there is no sea presence, neither movement nor light, and the overcast Japanese skies betrayed the vessel's interior ambience. Again, though, that day's on-board gloom could have been identical to that half a century earlier during a Norwegian coastal stop as *Stella Polaris* passed a rainy day tied up at Tromsø.

Hiroshi Anraku has remained on board the *Scandinavia* ever since sailing from Lisbon to Japan twenty years earlier. October 28, 1969, marked the start of the final voyage of "the white queen of the seven seas." On board were forty Japanese hands, a Japanese master, Captain Michitsugu Tanaka, and in an advisory capacity, her Swedish master for the previous ten years, Captain Lennart Nilsson, as well as six fellow officers. She sailed from Lisbon into a gray storm-tossed Atlantic, finally profiting from warm, calm waters in both the Caribbean and South Pacific, where, en route to Hawaii, Anraku remembers being especially grateful for the vessel's pool.

Beyond Hawaii, back in the Northern Hemisphere's winter, the *Stella Polaris* changed course several times to avoid threatening low pressure—"dark gray skies, gray rough sea and strong wind." Ten days before Christmas, the sight of Mount Fuji on the horizon, traditional benison for homecoming Japanese, did not please the hotel manager: "I would not mind keep sailing another forty-five days at all," he remembers wistfully.

Hiroshi Anraku is not alone in regretting the layup of his favorite cruise ship. Legions of passengers all over the world recall the *Stella Polaris* with special fondness. That she is still preserved and giving pleasure to new generations while still marginally afloat is satisfying, for it is extremely doubtful that anything like the *Stella Polaris* will ever be built again. Contemporary passenger expectations have surpassed her.

As a case in point, I well remember the summer of 1982 when,

TOP: *The vessel as she is today, a permanently moored hotel in Japan renamed the Scandinavia.* (Hiroshi Anraku collection)

BOTTOM: Sea Goddess I *from aft, showing "roll-bar" and tall single funnel.* (Author's collection)

in a garden on the Oslo Fjord, I saw the *Sea Goddess I*'s projected hull taking shape. The garden and its adjacent house belonged to Helge Naarstad's designer, Petter Yran, a stocky, bearded, and brilliant Norwegian who has since created a wide range of stunning shipboard interiors for an apparently endless list of clients.

Helge had brought me to Petter's house because beneath the summer trees, set out on a table, lay a five-foot Styrofoam *Sea Goddess*. It was one of those sculpturally adaptable models with which a designer can experiment, similar to the clay mock-ups that Detroit automakers favor when working the design kinks out of next year's cars. Two of Petter's assistants were transferring his design corrections from drawing to model, literally reshaping the miniature profile with their own hands, shaving off a millimeter of hull here, fashioning a more rakish railing slope there, or giving the bows a more generous flare.

Quite honestly, first sight of that Styrofoam maquette disappointed me. I had cherished the vain hope that Naarstad might resurrect the *Stella Polaris*'s haunting grace. But the *Sea Goddess* emerged instead as a miniature of a contemporary cruise ship. Bow and bridge screen were joined in a conventional 1980s wedge; there was a very tall pyramidal funnel aft towering above a cramped but jazzy afterdeck with what seemed a roll bar soaring over the stern. Three and a half decks of identical cabins occupied amidships and forward, with public rooms and galley aft; hence, there would be no indoor view over the bow because, in the world of contemporary cruise-ship design, cabins and public rooms never mesh, so that late-night music does not disturb early retirees.

Overall, Naarstad's and Yran's *Sea Goddess* profile looked high tech—squat, businesslike, and densely superstructured. The elevation above the strength deck was crowded to the rails, so that the ship's sides rose from water to top hamper as a wall, balconied, to be sure, but revealing that interior space rather than open deck had been given priority.

So, farewell to the *Stella Polaris*'s classic central deckhouse, surrounded by open teak culminating in that forward observation deck. This look, alas, can no longer be achieved; we are all— owners and passengers alike—victims of creeping material and technological acquisitiveness. Today's accommodation expectations have so surpassed the Bergen Line's ordinary of 1927 that cabin dimensions and facilities must be larger. For, in truth, however glamorous *Stella Polaris* was from across the water, the harsh realities below deck told a different tale. Originally, only fifteen of the eighty-five staterooms had private bathrooms; all of them, private and public alike, dispensed salt water only. The *Stella*'s cabins in those days were endearing yet modest sleeping chambers; none of their perfectly contented occupants felt any need for the television, VCR, sofa, icebox, bar, safe, coffee table, double bed, and mirrored dressing table that every passenger takes for granted on board Sea Goddess vessels.

Perhaps there's a capsule cruise history lesson here. The contrast between what the Norwegians had incorporated into their exquisitely comfortable ship of the twenties and what Helge would incorporate into his exquisitely comfortable ship of the eighties speaks volumes not only about contemporary luxury cabins but also about the tenor of life on board the two ships. The *Stella Polaris* passengers would be more inclined to take their ease in the vessel's public rooms rather than languish in their cabins. As a result, I suspect they mingled more readily with their fellow passengers, promoting a greater homogeneity on board.

In sum, those tweeded and booted originals of the twenties and thirties embarked for shared experience rather than isolated luxe. Admittedly, once the Swedes took over, their drastic upgrading—air conditioning, more private baths, and the questionable advantage of brass beds rather than bunks throughout—meant that the vessel, according to a Malmö brochure, boasted "the atmosphere of a private yacht and the comforts of an ocean liner." But had it not lost something in transition, a kind of Spartan bonhomie that would never be recaptured? The *Stella Polaris*'s passengers made do with an honest bunk, porthole, and deck chair; their miniship successors luxuriate in floating resorts, withdrawing from poolside chaise longue to queen-size bed in a televisioned suite illuminated by plate-glass window. Perhaps the key to *Stella Polaris*'s appeal was her no-nonsense practicality; sybaritic yet seaworthy, her gilt-edged comfort never negated the basic shipboard niceties. Whereas today's miniships are either hyperluxurious or adventurous, the *Stella Polaris* seemed somehow both.

Built in the Finnish shipyard of Wärtsilä in 1982, the *Sea Goddess I* sailed on her maiden voyage two years later. I was a passenger on her first westbound positioning crossing in the fall of 1984. At the time, as detailed in *Liners to the Sun*, only thirty-five passengers were on board, so we were cradled in pampered luxury across a smooth Atlantic from Las Palmas to St. Croix. Since then, I have sailed twice more with Sea Goddess cruises, but, on both occasions, under a new owner.

In the summer of 1986, battered by a crucial loss of Mediterranean business, Sea Goddess Cruises was taken over by Cunard. The British company just beat out Kloster Cruises by a scant margin. I had first heard talk of Cunard's takeover during an eastbound *Queen Elizabeth 2* crossing that summer but had discounted it as inevitable shipboard gossip. Two days later, however, seated in the bar of London's Ritz, I suddenly saw Helge Naarstad walking past the Palm Court. In an instant, without having to inquire, I knew that rumor was fact—why else would Helge be a guest in one of Trafalgar's (the giant that owns Cunard) hotels in midsummer?

Since then, I have been pleased to find that Naarstad's original concept and high standards remain scrupulously in place. It amused me recently to read a *Town & Country* article that described Sea Goddess life as "crisply British"; in fact, though Cunard's rampant-lion house flag flies from the masthead, there are scarcely any Brits on board: The officers are still Norwegian; the hotel staff, by and large German, Swiss, and Austrian.

Every miniship, whether Sea Goddess, Wind Star, Seabourn, or Renaissance, is ideally suited for Mediterranean sailing, a cruising arena that has made a remarkable comeback from the disastrous episode on board the *Achille Lauro* in the summer of 1985. One aftershock of that notorious hijacking was a passenger embargo throughout the region: You could not give Mediterranean cabins away the following summer, and loss of that crucial market guaranteed Sea Goddess's Cunard takeover. They were not alone in their distress: Every line normally operating in those waters—Sun Line, Royal Viking, Royal Cruise Line, Cunard, and Sea Goddess among them—suffered losses at the hands of those bumbling but murderous terrorists. The only winner was the Alaskan market: So rich was the diverted glut of vessels swarming to America's West Coast that Colonel Mu'ammar al-Qaddafi was pronounced, only half in jest, Alaska's patron saint.

Ever since the *Achille Lauro*, the cruise industry has waited for the other shoe to drop; so far, thank God, it has not, although the Gulf War of 1990–91 provoked an identical Mediterranean embargo. Terrorism is a unique hazard, separate and apart from historic disasters plaguing mankind. A hurricane, an oil spill, a red tide, or a drought all have finite ends: The glass rises, the oil is cleaned up, an organism imbalance is corrected, or the heavens open. Terrorism, the grimmest concomitant of travel by air, land, and now sea, hovers perpetually, an interminable air-raid warning with no "all clear."

Most far-reaching of all, the *Achille Lauro*'s hijacking and murder jolted shipboard's traditional serenity. Cruises will never again be quite the seagoing sanctuaries they once seemed. Though airplanes have always been vulnerable, cruise ships were perceived as inviolate; alas, no longer. In that sense, one can equate Leon Klinghoffer's murder with the loss of the *Titanic* for its chilling impact on an entire way of maritime life.

When I first saw the *Sea Goddess I* tied up at her Las Palmas berth, a truck was delivering some Heineken beer to be loaded on board for our crossing. There was no forklift or crane, only a truck driver, who, standing atop the pier, slung cases one by one across the water to a deft barman on the *Sea Goddess*'s stern platform. This vignette symbolizes the vessel's innate smallness, a characteristic pervading every aspect of the Sea Goddess experience. Everything on board is within as easy reach as the Heineken beer. If one is on deck or in the dining room and needs something from the cabin, it can be retrieved instantaneously. Similarly, when the ship's pianist plays at the bottom of the open well piercing the three decks above, his music suffuses the entire vessel, like a sonata drifting throughout a country house in summer. One can reach Lounge, Dining Salon, Library, purser's desk, afterdeck, or bridge in a matter of moments. That small-ship aspect recurs again and again.

It recurs most painfully at sunset, when the day's beach, snorkeling, and windsurfing activities wind down and passengers gather on the open stern for a drink and one of those devilishly good sandwiches dispensed from the outdoor bar. The last time I sailed, the *Sea Goddess I* carried a near-capacity passenger load of 110. In the late afternoon, with water-logged diehards still immersed in the pool, readers immersed in a final chapter, and others immersed in the hot tub—that dense gathering, however jovial, overfilled the available space uncomfortably.

The same crush recurs in the cabin, or as the company prefers to call it, the suite. Splendid as it is, there are two woefully inadequate and, if you will, unsuitelike limitations: closet and bathroom. Astonishingly, there is less hanging space in a *Sea Goddess I* suite than in any cabin on board Carnival's megaship the *Fantasy*; and *Fantasy* is designed for three- and four-day cruises only!

Sadly, short of a major interior-cabin refit, there is no easy rem-

LEFT: *The diminutive shelter deck connecting pool aft and purser's lobby amidships. Everything on board Sea Goddess vessels is conveniently nearby.* (Author's collection)

BELOW: Sea Goddess's *afterdeck, outdoor social focus of the vessel. Only at sunset, with the day's beach activities over, does it tend to overfill.* (Author's collection)

edy. In his original design, Petter Yran obviously felt that larger closets would diminish the living portion of his suite. It's part of every stateroom's trade-off: Apportioning those 200 square feet, Petter opted for smaller closet and bathroom in favor of larger cabin. In the bathrooms—every one of which contains a tub, incidentally—standing space is restricted to one person.

Two other Sea Goddess cabin notes are worth recording. The television set, positioned almost at floor level in the cabinet wall, is awkward to watch from in bed, well-nigh impossible for the outboard partner. But nearby, my wife, Mary, discovered a happy design accident: The cabin safe is housed directly above the icebox's motorized compressor. Hence, pearls or necklaces kept therein are inadvertently prewarmed to skin temperature.

As already advised in *Liners to the Sun*, Sea Goddess passengers should "think yacht"; only then do those cabin limitations make sense. Moreover, they are solitary aberrations in an otherwise superbly designed vessel and do not detract from an overwhelmingly rewarding cruise. Food is first-rate, caviar unlimited, drink is on the house, service is courteous and impeccable, and—perhaps the luxurious miniship's most profound but unspoken advantage—passengers are treated like grown-ups rather than children at camp.

Of course, they don't always *behave* like grown-ups. A stewardess told me the following shipboard morality tale. During one particularly late, exuberant party—common to every passenger vessel—too many passengers drank too much champagne too late in the hot tub. When she came on duty the next morning, the stewardess found a supine, snoring gentleman stretched out in the corridor outside his cabin door. His infuriated wife, tired of waiting for him to come to bed, had refused him entry; so he had slept peacefully on the cabin threshold instead.

It was specifically Sea Goddess's smallness that Warren Titus was determined to avoid on board his two (larger) miniships that sail under the banner of Seabourn Cruises, the *Seabourn Pride* and *Seabourn Spirit*. The company was originally to have been called Signet Cruises, but it turned out that the name Signet had been copyrighted earlier by another company.

When I heard the news, it occurred to me that Warren could have, effortlessly and advantageously, merely changed the spelling of "signet" to "cygnet," a rather pleasing and evocative word for a young swan. I suggested this to him, but he said that he had considered but rejected the thought unequivocally. "I wanted to avoid any inference of baby swan or, indeed, baby anything," he explained. "When you sail with us, you'll see what I mean—these ships are not miniature at all; they're substantial vessels, and I don't want to convey any other impression."

Warren Titus had cut his cruising teeth with American President and P & O lines before founding Royal Viking Line. His first vessel, the *Royal Viking Star*, sailed on her maiden voyage in July 1972. The three Norwegian owners were the Bergen Line (which had originally launched the *Stella Polaris*); A. F. Klaveness; and Nordenfjeldske. Every aspect of life on board the company's first three vessels, the *Royal Viking Star, Sea,* and *Sky,* reflected Warren Titus's patrician taste, and the handsome, up-market sisters were dispatched on choice worldwide itineraries.

Titus is a ruddy, distinguished-looking man with a thatch of silver hair, living incarnation of the breed of relaxed, successful Americans his vessels instantaneously attracted. Indeed, his hands-on involvement in the day-to-day operation of the line often made him a sitting target for disgruntled clients; many telephoned him at the company's San Francisco headquarters if they felt that things on board were not up to snuff. That kind of appeal to the top, a hot line to God, is symptomatic of Old Guard passenger directness: They are ruthlessly specific about what they like and do not like and are seldom shy about making their wishes known. Few, if any, New passengers would telephone their line's president after Miami disembarkation; they would probably not know his name and, in any event, he would probably not be available.

Throughout the 1970s, Royal Viking's formula worked; standards were high, on-board life was traditional, entertainment was low-key and oriented toward a largely middle-aged (and up) clientele. But at the start of the eighties, changes crept in, part of an effort by Royal Viking's Norwegian owners to attract more and, they hoped, younger passengers. The most immediate and visible change was expansion of each hull. Starting in 1980, all three were "stretched," one after the other, at A. G. Weser, a Bremerhaven shipyard. A ninety-three-foot section was added amidships (see illustrations, pp. 416–17, in *Liners to the Sun*), raising the fleet's capacity by 40 percent and each vessel's passenger load from 550 to 750.

Hard-core Royal Viking reactionaries felt it to be a mistake: 200 additional passengers, crowding their lounges and decks, destroyed the line's carefully cultivated ambience. Years later, Warren Titus said pointedly about that lengthening decision: "When you think in terms of that market segment, you were taking perhaps a little step backward." The on-board feeling of family—an attribute dear to Royal Viking's heart—had been diluted.

In another sense, the naysayers were right: A less discriminating marketing effort was necessary to fill those extra berths, and inevitably, the new Royal Viking passengers wanted something more exciting than Royal Viking's traditional shipboard regime. Keeping Old Guard cabins filled with Old Guard passengers is demanding. Owners always wonder if there are enough of them, searching in addition for a younger yet equally affluent clientele; I wonder if there are enough of *them*.

Not enough additional passengers were attracted, and by the mid-eighties, Royal Viking's cash flow had diminished so alarmingly that the line was up for grabs. Knut Kloster and his Norwegian Caribbean Line grabbed, absorbing Royal Viking into an otherwise exclusively Caribbean fleet, under the banner of Kloster Cruises. (Norwegian Caribbean Line became Norwegian Cruise Line in 1987; conveniently, the initials "NCL" remain intact as a shorthand moniker.) News of the alliance between the two companies—one Newpassenger, the other Old Guard—sent further temblors through Titus's alarmed constituency. A querulous outcry arose from every Royal Viking vessel: Would their elegant San Francisco line meld with tourist buses sailing out of Miami? It would not; apart from an abortive attempt at mingling passenger pools, the companies are allied only in purchasing and office space. Royal Viking abandoned San Francisco for Coral Gables at the end of 1988, precipitating another Old Guard bombshell. Today's most visible RVL/NCL interaction is transferring both fleets' Norwegian officers back and forth; their marketing strategies remain sensibly separate.

Shortly after the merger, Warren Titus became Royal Viking's chairman rather than president. But after only a year as chairman, in February 1987, he "retired from Royal Viking Line," the company with which his name had formerly been synonymous; his growing disaffection had been fueled by the expansion of his ships, their absorption within NCL, and the loss of a separate, San Francisco identity.

A month later, Titus was in Athens doing some consulting work when he received a telephone call from Norway. It was Erling

Rostad—a former president of Kloster Cruises—asking if he would mind going home to California the long way, via Oslo. Titus did so and was introduced to a phenomenally successful Oslovian by the name of Atle Brynestad. Brynestad wanted to establish a new, special marketing-niche cruise line and wondered if Warren Titus would serve as consultant.

Within a month, Titus had agreed to handle the hotel operations and American marketing effort as president, and Seabourn-ex-Signet Cruise Lines was born. Petter Yran, the man responsible for Sea Goddess, would design Brynestad's high-luxury miniships. (It will not be lost on readers how small the cruise world is. Owners, operators, and designers all know one another; the Nordic-American linkage is pervasive.)

Unlike Helge Naarstad, who had needed a cadre of shareholders to push Sea Goddess off the ways, Atle Brynestad would be the line's sole investor. One of Norway's most prosperous young entrepreneurs, he had started his career in the early 1980s with a single knitting machine; within ten years, he had amassed a fortune and a business empire that included textile mills, glass factories, travel agencies, and shopping malls. Now he was intent on founding a cruise line, in Petter Yran's words, consisting of "extremely comfortable cruise ships for a small number of guests going worldwide." By enlisting Warren Titus, Brynestad had chosen a man with exactly the right cruising credentials. Warren and Seabourn were made for each other: The new company president not only had his finger on the pulse of America's upscale passengers but also a name that would attract bookings from disenchanted Royal Vikings.

The two ships were built at Schichau Seebeckwerft AG in Bremerhaven. Although reminiscent, at first glance, of Sea Goddess's Wärtsilä hulls, they are, at 10,000 tons, twice the size. Their passenger capacity is almost double as well—a total of 212 can be accommodated in identical cabins. And whereas Sea Goddess suites, as we have seen, must be faulted for a lack of spacious largesse, the same cannot be said of Seabourn ordinaries; in fact, ordinary, as I was to find out, they are not.

Mary and I sailed eastbound from Fort Lauderdale on the *Seabourn Pride* in April 1989, the vessel's first repositioning from Caribbean winter to Mediterranean and Baltic summer. The crew hoped fervently that their vessel's second Atlantic crossing would be better than her first. Brand-new *Seabourn Pride* had departed

Bremerhaven the previous November, her only passengers some shipyard workers embarked to complete the vessel's interiors before landfall in Fort Lauderdale.

Two days out, the *Seabourn Pride* ran into a storm, a low-pressure system that would savage her for nine days. Traditional Thanksgiving was aborted once the turkey flew out of the oven; cold cuts were served instead. Even they slid off the table, and the refrain heard most often during *Seabourn Pride*'s first Thanksgiving was "Forget the food, grab the wine!" David Green, one of four entertainers on board, suggested that more than once he felt he was on board the miniature boat that comes to grief in a Ty-D-Bol commercial. One hapless engineer spent a night inadvertently locked inside a refrigeration space; no one could hear his frantic knocking.

Walter Berg, the ship's Norwegian first officer, showed me the stubborn radar track of the storm that had paralleled the vessel's southwest course toward Bermuda. The *Seabourn Pride* made an unscheduled stop there to refuel and lick her wounds. The storm had blasted off most of the hull's new white paint, and five bridge windows had shattered, not from an onslaught of green water but because repeated impacts of hull against sea had wracked their frames. The same shocks had flexed the sloping forward windows of the owner's cabins below. Four months later in the Canaries, caulking crews, roped with lifelines, were still trying to seal up glazing margins forward, legacy of *Seabourn Pride*'s North Atlantic baptism.

The most far-reaching damage of that delivery crossing was less structural than logistic: The storm was so prolonged and the sea motion so abrupt that the Seebeckwerft personnel on board had not been able to work at all; more than a precious week was lost, and in predictable consequence, Florida's inaugural cruise had to be postponed.

Two things struck me as we boarded the *Seabourn Pride* the following April. First, so many faces were old friends from Royal Viking; crewmen no less than passengers had been wooed by Warren Titus from his former domain. Second, Titus was right: The ship did not seem small at all. As I stood in the entrance lobby and looked forward down a cabin corridor, it receded to a vanishing point rather than ending abruptly in the middle distance. The *Seabourn Pride* was, as Titus had been anxious to convey a year earlier, a proper ship. Petter Yran has summed up his brief from the owner:

> The ship should have all the amenities that the much larger ship has and itself be large and seaworthy, enough to carry her guests around the world in comfort. In other words, we had to design a real ship with no resemblance to a yacht-like vessel.

The Warren Titus/Petter Yran Seabourn cabins are, in a word, incomparable, large (277 square feet), comfortable, and exquisitely finished. Oak paneling is interspersed with vertical mirrored accents. The space is divided by beautifully wrought cabinetry and curtains into sleeping and sitting areas: inboard, a large double bed and dressing table; outboard, beneath a huge window, a sofa, coffee table, and comfortable chairs. Farther inboard is a white-marble-and-oak bathroom, with tub and twin sinks; for once, there are almost too many shelves and cupboards. Next to the bathroom is a capacious walk-in closet, about the size of a Sea Goddess bathroom.

Rather like opening a collection of Russian dolls nested one inside the other, additional cabin perks kept coming to light. The window boasted two intriguing features: At night, it can be rendered (alas, not quite) opaque by a motorized shade; every morning, exterior freshwater jets sluice off any salt accumulation.

Furthermore, Petter Yran has installed workable and efficient reading lights. Modest twin-bullet fixtures, centered midway on the headboard, provide pinpoint lighting for insomniac readers while leaving a sleeping mate in the dark; the only one I have ever seen like it was in the Hotel Majestic in Cannes.

Throughout, he has lit the cabin with a network of recessed ceiling fixtures that spill radiance on every marble surface. A tall ottoman footstool conceals an interior compartment; I was never sure what Petter had in mind—it seemed like a bottle stash from Prohibition. We found it an admirable laundry hamper.

The cabins are wonderfully quiet. Because of the large windows, *Seabourn Pride*'s three passenger decks are high above the sea, so that the lowest of them is still insulated from the engines by two intervening decks. Complaints are limited to two. Petter chose to give his Seabourn desk/dressing table more surface area than its equivalent on Sea Goddess by bulging its margin; when anyone sits

ABOVE: Seabourn *transatlantic: Passenger Jean-Claude Murat takes a postprandial siesta, and passenger Anne Lincoln reads in the sheltered well-deck amidships.* (Author's collection)

LEFT: *Roomy and lavish, the vessel's marble-clad bathrooms are a sybarite's delight.* (Author's collection)

at it, passage past the foot of the bed is awkwardly obstructed. Another minor flaw involves the cabin door, approached through a short alleyway from the corridor; a doorbell, situated on the corridor wall, is often rung by a stewardess who cannot see if a DO NOT DISTURB sign hangs on the doorknob. Apart from this nit-picking, those Seabourn cabins excel, the best I have ever seen— well thought out, supremely comfortable, pleasing to the eye, and sumptuously elegant. One disembarks with a wrench.

The same perfection permeates the public rooms. As on Sea Goddess vessels, dining-room seating is permanently open—one dines where one will at tables of varying size throughout the restaurant. The only slight disadvantage is that no continuing steward learns your routine over the course of the voyage; but, interestingly, I note that most passengers always gravitated to the same table—and, hence, the same steward—regardless of the open seating policy.

The great advantage is that one can dine with new friends on impulse. Single travelers find the system awkward, but only, I must assume, for a day or two, after which time they will either have attached themselves to congenial couples or, better yet, organized their own dinner parties. Two women friends who sailed on the *Seabourn Pride* came down to dine their first night at sea and were seated at a table for six near the restaurant entrance. When the maître d'hôtel proffered succeeding couples seats at the same table, the newcomers refused, indicating firmly that they wished their own table. Once again, before the cruise was over, the two women had a choice of dinner companions, but it points up a problem of permanently open seating: Clearly, passengers who have been promised optional dining choices prefer to keep it that way. As it was, we used the system to organize a different dinner party each night with fellow passengers as well as officers and staff.

While Seabourn does not lavish as much caviar as Sea Goddess ships and charges only a (refreshingly) modest tariff for drink, its food is, without exception, glorious, whether in restaurant, cabin, or the Veranda Café. That informal gathering place, high atop the ship, offers a splendid buffet each day. Curiously, seating is limited to less than fifty chairs, and I wonder what it must be like with a full passenger load. There are additional tables outdoors overlooking the stern, but they tend to be overbright and windy in mid-ocean and, I would guess, humid in port. Of course, the dining room is open for lunch as well.

Tea was served daily up in the Constellation Lounge, reminiscent of the forward-facing, top-deck lookout bars of Royal Viking's fleet. This lounge has a dividend, a crescent of exterior deck reachable from the interior. Would that the cups of tea matched the view! I have discovered, after half a century at sea, that only British lines know how to make tea; Continentals do not have the knack.

From the pier, *Seabourn Pride*'s bullet-shaped profile seems almost menacing, in Petter Yran's words, "a sleek, elegant, stretched design." The two upper decks of cabin windows are clad with a supplementary plastic skin, rather like storm windows, that imparts an almost indescribable, futuristic sheen: The vessel seems almost more rocket than ship. On either side of the hull aft, twin funnels rise sinuously above a soft, rounded transom from which, at anchor, a sharkproof swimming enclosure emerges, as well as Petter's distinctive "Venetian taxi" tenders.

I was frankly mystified by two fixtures on board, one atop the deck, the other atop the keel, one for peering up, the other for peering down. Sited on tripod legs high above two midship Jacuzzis rears a large, clamshell pod. Inside it are three reclining armchairs (one is reminded of astronauts preparing to be shot into space), each with its own telescope for scanning the heavens through glass panels in the top of the pod. It was apparently lost on Seabourn's dreamer/planners that the most modest telescopes cannot survive the slightest vibration: Even moored at a pier, using Seabourn's observatory is impossible; at sea, unthinkable.

Far below, in a sepulchral "lower lobby," lurks another fantasy gone wrong. Once again, passengers gather on curved sofas, searching for sea life through a large circular viewing port in the ship's bottom plating. It has all the animation of an extinguished television set: One sees nothing save one's own reflection. Presumably, passage over the right reef in the right light might make sense, but the idea seems, together with the unobservatory above, an elaborate—and expensive—waste.

Wind Star sail cruise ships were the brainchildren of two men, Karl Andren, a Finnish-American shipping man and owner of Manhattan's famous Circle Line, and Jean-Claude Potier, a Franco-American who was the last French Line North American passenger manager and, more recently, an executive with Sun Line.

The two men formed Wind Star Sail Cruises, and in December 1984, an artist's rendering of the prototype was first revealed, appropriately, at the New York Yacht Club; even so, very few of

TOP: *Second-of-the-class* Seabourn Spirit *is ready for sea trials.* (Schichau Seebeck-werft AG)

BOTTOM: *Seen from over the water, Petter Yran's supplementary plastic sheathing gives the superstructure a futuristic sheen.* (Author's collection)

the dozens of journalists present realized, until the actual unveiling, that sails would drive Wind Star's vessels.

Not since the turn of the century have passengers embarked on a scheduled sailing steamer. Andren's and Potier's contemporary sail ships boast a sophistication undreamed of in 1900. Four masts tower eighteen stories above a capacious hull that, at 440 feet, is almost exactly the same length as Seabourn's vessels. No sailors scamper aloft; instead, Wind Star sails are operated remotely from the bridge by push button, allying the sea's oldest technology with its newest, canvas effortlessly controlled by computer. With the touch of a finger, the master or officer of the watch can spread, jibe, trim, reef, or furl any or all of six soaring triangular sails. The sight of those sails "hoisted" on cue from the bridge and materializing overhead like time-lapse photographs of a blossoming rose is a sublime vision.

Only 148 passengers can be accommodated along two passenger decks, and clearly Messrs. Andren and Potier were intent on selling their sailing cruise ships to vigorous and nimble passengers exclusively. The one telltale clue? There is no elevator anywhere on board. With one wave of their wand, Wind Star Sail Cruises banished the handicapped, the infirm, and the frail elderly from their decks forever.

We sailed on the *Wind Spirit* in the fall of 1988. Suiting the no-elevator regime, the vessel's on-board mood is rigorously *sportif*. Most passenger life revolves about a lowered stern platform, around which jet skis, Sunfish, Zodiacs, and the like flock all day while the vessel is at anchor. In fact, though all three miniship companies— Sea Goddess, Seabourn, and Wind Star—boast this convenience, on board Wind Star especially the hyperactive watersport passenger is most relentlessly preoccupied. Indeed, the activity around the *Wind Spirit*'s stern brought to mind Ratty's endearing observation from *The Wind in the Willows*: "There is nothing—absolutely nothing—half so much worth doing as simply messing about in boats. . . ."

The same indulgently modish life-style extends into the evening as well. Mine was the only dinner jacket on board that week and, presumably, forever. In the matter of shipboard dress, the ship's program encouraged passengers to dress in a style they described as "casually elegant," a baffling sartorial recommendation. What do "casually elegant" passengers look like? Holland America refers to their preferred passenger archetypes as "active relaxers," just as oxymoronic as the sign I once saw in a Bal Harbor milliner's window: "Active sportswear for leisure-minded people."

"Casually elegant" apart, I was saddened, as were many of my fellow passengers, that the *Wind Spirit* spent relatively little time under sail: Too much of our week passed at anchor. Nearby, admittedly, were tranquil island beaches well off the beaten cruise ship path; in fact, Sea Goddess and Wind Star vessels shadow each other around the enchanting Grenadines in season. But since those consecutive island stops are adjacent, the Caribbean itinerary seems confined, laid out more with beach time rather than sailing time in mind.

Elsewhere, I am told, things are better. On the run from Rome to Venice, Wind Star's Mediterranean itinerary includes at least one sea day between Taormina and Corfu; but in the South Pacific and Caribbean, during standard seven-day circuits, there are none whatsoever. Of course, those short hops, together with occasional bursts of sail power, are extremely economical: at worst, Swiss chief engineer Henri Staaeli advised me, one week's fuel consumption seldom exceeds forty tons.

Lack of sea days on board a rare sailing cruise ship seems curious. Surely most Wind Star clients have booked with sailing in mind, not only on a windsurfer off the stern but on board a large vessel under a full press of canvas. I recall with special delight one glorious afternoon of perfect sailing weather. A strong southerly breeze sundered the Caribbean's gleaming indigo with tossed whitecaps. The thrill of feeling *Wind Spirit* heel and surge to the wind, no less than the spectacle of white sails bellying forward overhead, was exhilarating. Although Wind Star computers are programmed to restrict extended heeling to no more than six degrees, that sailing experience and sail-driven progression should play the star part during one's Wind Star week. For those who feel similarly deprived, a positioning crossing or Panama transit might make more sense.

There is certainly room enough to enjoy it all. The *Wind Spirit*'s spread of open decks is magnificent; no other 148 passengers afloat anywhere have such generous deck space at their disposal. Directly forward of the bridge—which remains, incidentally, accessible to passengers at all times—lies the same broad observation deck that was such a successful feature of the *Stella Polaris*. Aft, a small pool is available; directly aft of that, incorporating a nice resonance from traditional sailing ships, is a domed mahogany-and-glass skylight that illuminates the main salon below; directly aft of that, passengers enjoy a broad spread of unencumbered teak. One deck higher an auxiliary afterhelm has been installed where passengers can take a short trick at the wheel under Captain Tormod Hansen's genial supervision.

Out on deck, Wind Star Cruises' color scheme embodies a pleasing mélange of brilliant emerald-turquoise, white, and teak—a palette carried out nicely from logo to scupper. Below, different colors but the same pleasing touch obtain: a cool, blue-gray scheme with mahogany-and-teak accents. All interiors are the work of Frenchman Marc Held. I asked him at the New York Yacht Club unveiling about his design idiom, whether it would be sailing ship, yacht, or early steamer. At that juncture, Held was frank enough to admit that he had no idea.

What has emerged is a splendidly serene, yachtish 'tween decks with a specific high-tech patina. The feeling is not the traditional cliché of brass-and-mahogany Edwardian but a contemporary synthesis of naked steel and aluminum, airplane cable railings, bone-white walls, and teak grating. Reflecting the vessel's birthplace— Le Havre—no less than the designer's nationality is a spacious, *chantier naval* interior. Here and there are undersea relics, amphorae and the like, displayed to advantage. The whole effect is at once civilized, trim, and inviting.

All seventy-four staterooms are identical, and though not luxurious suites, they are perfectly roomy, well planned, and stylish. For reasons unknown—perhaps so that daytime bed may masquerade as sofa?—stewardesses store pillows in deckhead lockers high above the bed, overhead bins reminiscent of those used for hand luggage aboard jets; passengers who want to use the bed by day either for reading, a siesta, or a look at television must stand awkwardly atop it to retrieve their pillows, a cumulative annoyance by the end of the week.

Adjoining cabin bathrooms are, in my experience, unique, wrought in the shape of a cloverleaf: toilet to the right, shower to the left, sink straight ahead. The decorative materials are pleasingly high tech, brushed aluminum and teak set against curvilinear walls of glitter-flecked blue composition, as chic as it seems practical.

The cabins are situated along two passenger decks; in fact, the paneled, swelling curve of every bathroom cloverleaf intrudes frankly into the corridor, forming pleasing architectural breaks along its length. But it must be acknowledged that passengers

Three deck scenes, forward, amidships, and aft: TOP: Surrounding the bridge is an expanse of open deck. CENTER: A rare crusing treat: Wind Spirit *under full sail in the Caribbean.* BOTTOM: *Leaning against the handsome mahogany skylight, a lady passenger enjoys the sun. Wind Star Cruise's open decks are the most amply generous afloat.* (Author's collection)

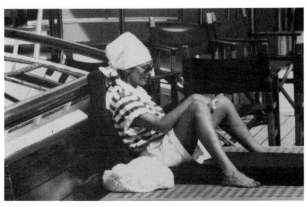

booked on the upper deck enjoy a more peaceful cruise than their shipmates one deck down. Those lower cabins, especially aft, one of which was mine, lie directly above the engine room, so that the only sour note of that *Wind Spirit* cruise (a very loud note at that) was an engine symphony—*allegro sostenuto*—while under way. To be charitable, it was appalling.

The *Wind Spirit's* propulsion is diesel-electric, and I am told that the whining string section was scored for hydrophore pumps that circulate engine coolant; according to my old friend Willem Koopman, vice-president for operations out in Seattle, they have been silenced since my cruise. But short of hoisting sail exclusively, I doubt that the diesel's obtrusive brass pedal point can ever be rendered *piano*.

Of course, no contemporary sailing ship ever offers unalloyed quiet, even with main engines stilled. Service electricity must be generated around the clock for light, air-conditioning, and refrigeration. Wind Star's evocative promise points up a fine sociotechnological dilemma: Can one combine the winsome charm of yesterday's canvas power with today's competitive cruising comforts? This question brings us back to our miniship, full circle, linking up again with the vanished simplicity of the dear old *Stella Polaris*.

Wind Star comes close, I think; the key, again, is the unique feel of movement powered by the ocean's wind. Before I joined the ship, I talked with two discriminating friends, both experienced passengers, who had just come back from separate Wind Star cruises. They might have booked on two different vessels. The first dismissed the sails as "a joke," mere window dressing. The other raved nonstop about the sails as well as the ship and everything on it. In sum, I agree with the second and hope that in future, when I sail with the company again, the itinerary will have more sea time and my cabin will be located, so to speak, on the mezzanine rather than the orchestra floor.

Wind Star has two successor sailing cruise lines, one slavishly derivative, another refreshingly different. Potier's contract with his Havrois yard, the Societé Nouvelles des Ateliers et Chantiers du Havre (a jawbreaker happily reduced to ACH), forbade it from building any additional sailing-cruise-ship replicas until after they had delivered the third Wind Star hull. The yard abided by that condition until they had completed the *Wind Song*, the third of the class. Then they signed a contract with Club Med to duplicate both Wind Star's look as well as its technology in creating a larger but almost identical class of vessel. The result was the *Club Med I*, which boasts five instead of four masts, a larger passenger capacity, and hence, another deck. I encountered the vessel recently coming into St. Thomas under sail at sunset. ACH's necessary hull amplification damages the vessel's looks. Her extra deck creates a dense, overburdened hull with cumbersome freeboard, disrupting any possible balance with mast and sail above. Whereas *Windstar* just manages to be graceful, *Club Med I* misses the boat. Life on board, I am advised, is similar to Wind Star's.

But the second new entry into the sailing-cruise-ship market offers impressive aesthetic promise. The *Star Flyer*, first vessel of the Star Clipper Line, arrived in the Caribbean during the summer of 1991, the first of a two-ship fleet owned and founded by Mikael Krafft, a Swedish-born businessman-yachtsman now residing in Belgium. Krafft hired a Scotsman as his naval architect, Robert McFarlane, who has since signed on as vice-president in charge of operations at the company's Miami headquarters. McFarlane and Krafft pored over the designs of legendary clipper-builder Donald McKay before laying down a trim sailing hull on the ways of Ghent's Langerbrugge shipyard.

At 360 feet, the *Star Flyer* is 80 feet shorter than the Wind Star prototype but compensates visually with a 60-foot bowsprit. One hundred and eighty passengers can be accommodated inside an extremely graceful hull. She carries a crew of sixty on board, no more than eight of whom are required to handle the sails, which are hoisted and set by hand but furled remotely by sophisticated hydraulic mechanism.

Examination of the *Star Flyer*'s deck plan reveals that aftercabins change shape toward the stern, conforming to the hull's taper. On board both the *Windstar* and the *Club Med I*, ACH's building philosophy seems to have encouraged the reverse. Their hulls adapted to the rectangularity of cabin modules; hence, the French ships' boxiness, designed from the inside out, as opposed to the Belgians' pleasing contiguity contained within traditional clipper form.

However, in commending the *Star Flyer* adherence to tradition, perhaps I am hoist with my own petard: Should a vessel be designed primarily for distant observers or its occupants on board? Are naval

All sails set in the lightest Caribbean breeze, the Star Flyer *makes for a splendidly evocative sight. The proportion of hull to sail is near-perfect.* (Star Clipper Cruises)

architects obliged to create a beautiful at the expense of a comfortable ship? Ideally, he or she should do both. But it is a vexing dilemma and one that will arise later in these pages.

My week on board the *Star Flyer* was exhilarating. I am a passenger rather than sailor but enjoyed the company of three dozen keen yachtsmen and their wives from the Royal Swedish Yacht Club who were completely entranced. Cabins are compact and shipshape, service cheerful, and food excellent, served in a dining saloon that might well have been transplanted intact from an Edwardian sailing steamer. I particularly enjoyed two additional public spaces: an open, permanently awninged deck in the waist of the ship that served as continual meeting place and its adjacent Library/Cardroom, complete with working Belgian fireplace. This latter has been rendered electrical for U.S. waters but is ready for live coals should the weather warrant it elsewhere.

But what pleased me more than anything was being on a real sailing vessel that really sailed, with cambered decks, soaring masts, and a fine spread of canvas; lines and halyards are secured on belaying pins and, astonishingly, there is no creaking whatsoever. She will appeal to a broad range of passengers, including those who like to lend a hand at a rope or serve a trick at the wheel; however, no maritime qualifications are required at all. One first-rate aspect of the *Star Flyer*'s itineraries—departure on alternating, complementary cruises every Sunday from St. Maarten: One returns always to St. Maarten, leaving the master sufficient option to choose the most favorable winds. There is one full day (and two nights) of sailing during each incredible week.

Now we leave miniship cruising and its extravagance of scale for what must be described as extravagance of style, characteristic of a historic transatlantic megaship from the thirties. I refer, of course, to the *Normandie*. Apart from the *Titanic*, she summons up more nostalgic lament than any other liner, hallowed favorite of millions. *Normandie* cruised twice during her brief life, to Rio and back, documented *in extenso* in *Liners to the Sun*. But my concerns now are her design as well as her North Atlantic service during those part-halcyon, part-ominous days before hostilities engulfed the world, the Atlantic, and, alas, that extraordinary one of a kind.

Chapter 5

The need for luxury on board our ocean liners is legendary. Let us consider Normandie, *which was the world's most beautiful ship. The structure of* Normandie *was certainly luxurious: the purity of her design, the elegance of her line, the power of her machinery, her technical perfection, were themselves elements of quality and breeding. The price of "standard" decorations, which would have contrasted regrettably with the beauty of her construction, would have represented at least 6 percent of the vessel's cost. By devoting 10 percent, the* Compagnie Générale Transatlantique *achieved a result that was entirely sensational.*
   —André Leleu, French designer

Mais où est le bâteau? Je veux voir le bâteau!
   —A baffled young passenger after embarking on board
      Normandie

The French Line, while doing its utmost to give every satisfaction to its Guests, is aware that perfection is a very difficult achievement and would welcome any suggestions for making the ship as agreeable as possible to her patrons.
   —Extract from Normandie's passenger list

Once & Future *Normandie*

Of the hundreds of ocean liners that have sailed into the port of New York, none has made a more profound impact than the *Normandie*.

Her June arrival in 1935 was an enviable debut: Everything came up trumps for the French Line's new flagship. Before she left France, President Albert LeBrun had journeyed to Le Havre in full pomp for a gala dinner on board; the LeBruns were already inextricably involved with the vessel, for Madame LeBrun had christened her two and a half years earlier at St.-Nazaire.

The *Normandie* took the Blue Riband comfortably from the *Rex* on the first, westbound leg of her maiden voyage, the only French liner ever to do so. She was also history's first 1,000-foot liner, hence, maiden occupant at the southernmost of three 1,100-foot North River facilities called the superpiers. Moreover, she was a year ahead of her cross-Channel rival the *Queen Mary*, and priority in this regard was perceived somehow as crucial. Had it not been for the calamitous work stoppage on the Clyde earlier in the decade, the Cunard White Star vessel would, in turn, have arrived a year earlier than the *Normandie*.

Yet despite that aura of unassailable success, several glitches might well have delayed the *Normandie*'s departure on her record-breaking performance. Just after the vessel had arrived in her home port of Le Havre, Transat crews went on strike, doubtless hoping to hold the completed vessel hostage; the same labor unrest was troubling completion of the vessel's transatlantic destination, newly extended North River Pier 88. But the French strike was settled after only four days by the arbitration of William Bertrand, France's minister of the merchant marine; that he himself was scheduled as a passenger on the maiden voyage may well have added impetus to his negotiations.

The day after the strike was resolved, there were reports of attempted arson: Two painters ignited a pail of gasoline in an officer's cabin, whether by accident or design was never established. An alert *veilleur* not only apprehended them but put out the fire as well. Finally, an ominous mechanical failure occurred at sea, twenty-four hours after passing Bishop Rock lighthouse in pursuit of the record. Down in the boiler room, a condenser tube fractured, disabling the starboard central generator for twenty-four hours, temporarily reducing speed. As history has recorded, the vessel's peerless maiden voyage continued unchecked, but the incident illustrates the slender margin separating *Normandie*'s successful quest from failure.

Most memorable of all, the *Normandie* remains, long after her untimely demise, a paradigm of elegance, style, and taste, the culmination of naval architecture as well as shipwright's art. Half a century after her loss, mention of the *Normandie*'s name still conjures up extravagance of design, of food, of service, and inevitably, of imperishable glamour. Quite simply, for the cumulative total of her 132,508 passengers, for thousands of pierside spectators who gazed enviously in Le Havre, Southampton, New York, and Rio, and for generations of marine historians and ship buffs since, *Normandie* remains, simply, *the* ocean liner.

Though I share this almost mystical reverence, I am at something of a loss to explain why. What engenders our consuming *Normandie* preoccupation, this unswerving loyalty toward a vessel that entered the port of New York only seventy-two times? Is it the brevity of her life span, longer than the *Titanic*'s but shorter than most? Is it the unforgettable hauteur of her profile? Or is it the lure of her unique interiors, combining, as they did, stunning monumentalism with brilliant detail, like a cascade of rich ormolu adorning the corners of a Louis Quatorze chest?

One is tempted to answer: "All of the above." But I am never quite sure and, in all probability, will be no closer to a definitive response when this chapter is complete. I only hope that something to follow may add fresh insight or substance to the *Normandie*'s legend, if leaving unresolved the eternal riddle of her appeal.

Final *Normandie* caveat: Readers should be alerted that this chapter is divided into two parts, one scrupulously factual, the other blatantly fantastical. The first part will reexamine the *Normandie*'s design as well as her North Atlantic service. Rather than dwelling on the *Normandie*'s first and last crossings—both have been well documented by Harvey Ardman in his *Normandie* volume—I will concentrate instead on minutiae from unsung intervening years, when normal Transat crossing routine obtained, long after the triumphal maiden entry into New York and well before that final refugeelike berthing at Pier 88 on the eve of World War II.

This chapter's second part will consist of a fictional coda. I am going to play with the facts, or, rather, one specific fact governing events on board the *Normandie* that hectic wartime afternoon of February 9, 1942. In so doing, I claim a precedent of sorts. My dear friend Walter Lord, the *Titanic*'s renowned historian, once commissioned a painting from *Titanic* artist Kenneth Marschall. By direction, his canvas depicts the White Star liner steaming serenely past the Statue of Liberty on the morning of April 18, 1912, *as though nothing had happened*. There is RMS *Titanic*, her quartet of black-topped buff funnels intact, arriving unscathed at her North River destination on schedule. Walter's commission was, after all, nothing more than wish fulfillment. And it often seems to me that much of the marine historian's task in recapitulating maritime events involves some degree of wish fulfillment as well. We are dealing, after all, with ghosts manning ghost ships, and since she is one of the great ghost ships of all time, I propose bending the *Normandie*'s truth just a little for this chapter's coda.

But for now, let us dwell on the team that designed the *Normandie*. They achieved a miracle in creating a vessel whose exterior look reflected the chic of her interiors. Consider, by way of contrast, the *Normandie*'s great predecessor, the *Ile de France*. For *Ile de France*, company president Jean dal Piaz had decreed a refreshing new look, the debut of *le style paquebot*. In so doing, the French Line's—indeed, *all* ocean liners'!—traditional museum mentality was abandoned. Rather than recycling land-based originals, the *Ile de France*'s designers created interiors of a kind never before seen. Furniture, trims, moldings, brackets, grilles, capitals, fabrics— every scrap of decor was new; nothing had been derived from the past.

But regardless of that 'tween-deck commitment, the *Ile de France*'s exterior profile adhered firmly to tradition. She seemed an admittedly larger carbon copy of her predecessor of 1921, the *Paris*. Although her three red-and-black funnels were spread out more pleasingly than the *Paris*'s atop the superstructure, the *Ile de France* remained yet another Transat clone, firmly entrenched within the company's traditional steamer form.

(In fact, ever since 1912, each French Line flagship had been unique, and it is not surprising that no word exists in the French language for "sister ship"; was it, perhaps, because the Compagnie Générale Transatlantique stopped building them just after the turn of the century? The *France*, the *Paris*, the *Ile de France* and the *Normandie*, the *Liberté*, and the final *France* were all one of a kind.)

Then, in 1935, came the *Normandie*. St.-Nazaire's naval architects had fashioned in steel a profile that matched in daring what other innovative hands belowdecks had fashioned in glass, leather, bronze, lacquer, and marble. For the first time in transatlantic history, an ocean liner generated from afar the same excitement engendered inside her hull and superstructure.

It is the specifics of that art deco profile that concern me. Quite naturally, the naval architects started at *Normandie*'s summit, or- daining three extraordinary funnels, each one receding in height to convey an impression of speed. It is interesting that the French Line stayed with three funnels. By the mid-thirties, trios were already dated. With the exception of Cunard White Star's *Queen Mary*, rival shipping lines had reduced funnel numbers to two: The *Bremen*, the *Europa*, the *Rex*, the *Conte di Savoia*, the *Manhattan*, and the *Washington* were all adorned with twin stacks; so, too, would be the projected *Queen Elizabeth*. But at St.-Nazaire, the *Normandie*'s designers sensibly mandated a third funnel, even though it was a dummy, erected for purely aesthetic reasons. The

Normandie's ample length demanded a row of three to satisfy the Sun Deck's horizontal *longueur*.

But working or fake, those funnels were wrought in an imposing, freestanding shape. The *Ile de France's* conventional Transat cylinders were displaced by substantial ovoids that might more accurately be described as semi-elliptical. In plan, the *Normandie's* funnels taper to a fine point aft while at the same time presenting a purely circular aspect forward. In elevation, they were cleanly sculpted as though of one piece with neither guy wires nor intervening horizontal bands betraying plate margins. The rims surmounting them were plain, as simply finished as the funnels' sides.

Though plain at the top, the funnel bases had a unique refinement at the bottom: Rather than disappearing into the deck, they were flared with a sloping steel skirt. That flange was practical, to accommodate the rejoining trunks of the vessel's divided uptakes where they emerged from the deck. That foundation suggested masonry, as though those three red towers with their black battlements required a plinth for support. As a result, the *Normandie's* funnels seemed rooted, growing from the teak plain surrounding them. Never had any funnels appeared so inextricably wedded to superstructure; they gave the effect of malleable clay mock-ups that, dropped from a great height, had splayed out on contact with the deck. Their massive diameter communicated overwhelming puissance.

This *Normandie* funnel fixation is, chronic Maxtone-Graham readers will appreciate, an ongoing preoccupation. Writing in *Liners to the Sun* nearly a decade ago, I hazarded that the *Normandie's* funnels were inspired by land-based architectural sources, perfect maritime re-creations of the awesome fortress towers at Angers. If true, was this not antithetical to dal Piaz's stern design credo for the *Ile de France* about creating new steamship forms? Surely, Angers towers perched atop a 1930s Sun Deck at sea represent retroheresy at its worst, a return to the company's supposedly discarded museum mentality. But in fact, we are not discussing the slavish re-creation of a period room but, rather, inference of a subtle naval architectural resonance.

I feel confirmed in this medieval hypothesis because the same thought obviously occurred to the artists executing the *Normandie's* brochure graphics. The cover of every *Normandie* deck plan features a knight in chain mail, in the school of Howard Pyle. Adorned with a patterned tabard, he stands atop crenellated battlements

TOP: *The cores of funnels 1 and 2 reveal the emergent divided uptakes. Note the extremely graceful curve of the original bridge wings, later to prove inefficient.* (Chantiers de l'Atlantique)

BOTTOM: *With trials only a week away, the* Normandie's *familiar profile during final days at the yard.* (Chantiers de l'Atlantique)

ABOVE: *The company's new flagship as seen from the bridge of the* Champlain. *The new vessel's funnel trio seems rooted to the deck.* (French Line)

LEFT: *On the cover of every* Normandie *first-class deck plan, a* chevalier normand *greets the inbound vessel. Two supplementary stone towers seem obvious funnel facsimiles.* (Author's collection)

overlooking the sea. He raises one gauntlet in greeting to the approaching *Normandie* (steaming full tilt toward shore); the other rests atop a shield bearing the twin rampant lions of France's *département* of Normandie. Knighthood was in flower belowdecks as well: In front of the ship's chapel, forward on B Deck, was a retractable cloisonné screen by François-Louis Schmidt, depicting a *chevalier normand*. (Presently, it decorates the lobby of a Manhattan apartment building.)

But for the vessel's most persistent design clue, leave *Normandie*'s open decks for a moment and come with me down to Main Deck. The first-class purser's desk was surmounted by a freestanding, bilingual chrome legend, RENSEIGNEMENTS INFORMATION. The typeface is serif-free, modified Theatre Bold. What strikes my eye is the sign's first letter, specifically the upper portion of the R of RENSEIGNEMENT: a simple, clean semicircle that typified the vessel's entire design scheme. In fact, the purser's desk itself, mirrored by an identically shaped novelty shop facing it, was pure semicircle as well. Indeed, a semicircular motif recurred all over the *Normandie*, throughout her naval architecture, deckscape, signage, interior decoration, and funnel. That simple, uncluttered art deco arc evokes the *Normandie*'s consistent design idiom.

Up on deck, the complex junction of *Normandie*'s whaleback that concealed mooring machinery, with the hull strakes incorporated semicircles of sorts but in reality twin curving apophyges; the line of deck plating seemed to reverse itself. (This was a curious visual phenomenon, unseen from pier level, apparent only if one's point of view were as high as the central bower anchor.) One found the boldest semicircle form forward in the bulge of Winter Garden windows. The bridge wings matched it until they were revamped during the *Normandie*'s winter refit of 1935–36. Although those original wings suited the vessel's slipstream profile to perfection, they had proved impractical for in-port navigation, and the company reshaped them to jut out more angularly from the wheelhouse; though the master and pilot had better sight lines, the restructuring violated a marvelous sweeping flow.

Aft, a veritable feast of semicircles came to light, but en route, perfect half-rounds plate each funnel's forward slope and the rounded terraces surrounding them. A stunning cascade of afterdecks fell to the stern from Sun Deck down to Main Deck, terminating in a glorious half moon. In fact, tourist class's Smoking Room at the afterend of Promenade Deck repeated in reverse the handsome crescent of windows illuminating the first-class Winter Garden forward.

We shall resume our semicircle hunt belowdecks momentarily, but while we are back in tourist-class country, it is worth examining the general arrangement of their public rooms. Though the *Normandie* could unquestionably be described as an outstanding first-class vessel, it is harder to rhapsodize about conditions in tourist class. Tourist-class brochures hinted: "Here on this beautiful flagship of the French Line, a large section has been planned '*pour touriste*,' at astonishingly low rates." Not large enough, I fear. All the space, all the luxe, and, especially, all the light seemed to have been expended on first class. Leftovers for the *Normandie*'s humbler passengers were less rewarding.

In fact, tourist-class life on board the *Normandie* was confined to the stern. Rather than a smoking room with flanking promenades, their Smoking Room—together with the *salle à manger*, their only handsome public rooms—faced aft on Promenade Deck. Stretches of Promenade Deck forward that would, on other vessels, have been assigned to tourist class were occupied instead by a row of splendid first-class cabins boasting private promenades. So tourist class was, in effect, sited athwartship, with views over the stern rather than the sides. One insulating belt of enclosed deck surrounded the Smoking Room (as always, semicircular) and another glass-enclosed promenade was available one deck below. Though tourist-class passengers could stroll on an open-air crescent one deck higher on Boat Deck, none of them ever ascended (legally, that is) up onto Sun Deck. Tourist-class passengers' view of the *Normandie*'s famous funnel trio was restricted to an unsatisfactory vantage point from far behind. Small wonder that the *Normandie* recorded probably more persistent tourist-class incursions into first class than any other vessel: Most of their ship's much-vaunted luxury clearly lay forward and off-limits.

Admittedly, those deprived passengers did have exclusive use of an outdoor pool down on the stern, but the number of crossings during which it could be comfortably used was limited. Although their dining saloon down on C Deck was exposed to the sea on both sides, their Grand Salon was not. Once again, intruding first-class cabins were at fault: Running aft along Main Deck, uninterrupted rows of first-class cabins denied outside window access to tourist class's Grand Salon as well as Salon de Thé and Library.

Despite this shabby treatment of the *Normandie*'s tourist-class

Normandie's semicircular syndrome: TOP: *The purser's desk.* BOTTOM: *The bar down at the indoor swimming pool.* (Author's collection)

ABOVE: *One of the vessel's original glories, the Café-Grill's esplanade, complete with lamp stanchions and double-backed benches. Proposed supplementary glass panels atop the bench backs were never added.* (French Line)

LEFT: *The view from tourist class, always behind and rather out of things.* (Hardy Graham)

clients, a year after the maiden voyage, they would extract a devastating revenge from their first-class shipmates. The same renovations that "improved" the vessel's slipstream bridge wings saw the construction of a new deckhouse on the afterend of Boat Deck, an elevated and much-improved tourist-class lounge with a semicircular sweep of windows. Here were tourist-class ocean views with a vengeance, cloaked in sufficient foliage to duplicate the Winter Garden forward.

But at what fearful cost to first-class occupants of the Café-Grill! The new deckhouse obliterated their handsome esplanade, the great outdoor extension that had served, previously, as culmination of the *Normandie*'s unique Promenade/Boat Deck sweep, about which more later. Moreover, the ship's look from over the water had been flawed forever, the extravagant perfection of her after-descent violated. Although earlier I descried the present-day convention of designing ships so that they look well from over the water, this particular *Normandie* renovation irreparably damaged two first-class perks, a view as well as passenger flow.

At the Café-Grill's afterend, centered in its semicircular wall, steps led up to double doors, through which one could exit onto the esplanade, as though leaving a country house's *salon* for an afternoon stroll in the garden. Now those doors, their arc of windows to either side, and, most important, the Grill's light and prospect existed no longer. First class's afterview had been given over to tourist class.

Presumably, that intrusive addition was the line's only solution, short of expanding the original Grand Salon to either side and losing more than a dozen revenue-producing first-class cabins. There was an addional and urgent impetus to overbuild the Grill Room's esplanade. A new structure there might stiffen *Normandie*'s afterdecks sufficiently to quell tourist class's final *sottise*, the bone-rattling, water-slopping, bunk-shaking vibration that inundated the vessel's stern anywhere near full speed. It was no better, confessed Commandant Thoreux, at twenty-eight knots than at thirty.

The *Normandie*'s appalling vibration and its cure had remained an unceasing preoccupation for the company ever since the first sea trials off Brittany in May 1935. After the maiden voyage, American engineers were enlisted during subsequent crossings in the desperate quest to banish it: Sophisticated sensors were mounted all over the afterdecks in an effort to localize and identify the most offending areas. (Almost any insomniac tourist-class passenger or crewman could have told them.) In fact, the problem was finally solved in the spring of 1936 by substitution of four- as opposed to the original three-bladed propellers; all those stiffening elements, including the offending new lounge, had made precious little difference.

Now, back to our semicircles. Follow me belowdecks through the vessel as we check off motifs that repeatedly crop up. Our entry level, incidentally, depends on our port of embarkation. In Southampton, where the *Normandie* saved invaluable crossing time by never docking, the tender would bring us alongside the anchored vessel off Cowes, and we would clamber through gaping ports down on C Deck. There, just through the Foyer, we would emerge into the lowest complete level of the great hall; two huge, semicircular niches faced inboard. Down one level there were semicircles galore—not only the pool's forward wall but also the lighting fixtures looping overhead. Circular poolwide steps lead from the shallows into the deep end. Centered on the afterwall, a great semicircle of mosaic enfolds the half-round bar, another duplicate of the purser's desk above.

In New York or Le Havre, one entered the *Normandie* on A Deck and, once past an (almost) semicircular information desk in the Foyer, would be directed up one level to Main Deck *pont principal*. Let us climb one more flight to Promenade Deck, highest level of the great hall. There the inset carpeted seating area is rounded, semicircularly, at either end. Inside the cinema, a miniature Radio City Music Hall, overlapping plaster arcs layer the ceiling. Lining both sides of the gallery as we proceed aft are semicircular sofas. Then, through the Grand Salon and into the adjoining *fumoir*, or Smoking Room, we find that the outboard ends of the four principal banquettes are rounded off. Then we ascend an unforgettable staircase up toward the Café-Grill, its entry from the smoking room leading between two rounded corners; columns line the walls to either side, set within semicircular niches.

Pause for a moment—that staircase is such a noble thing! Via a gentle, almost languid slope, passengers mounted thirty steps, making a unique progression *within the room*, from Promenade Deck to Boat Deck. This enviable architectural treat is equally ceremonial in either direction, up to the Café-Grill or down into the Smoking Room. The formidable climb up was tempered: Every five steps, landings were flanked with convenient benches. In the tradition of the Carlton House's Palm Court, one was encouraged to *linger* en route.

Before and after: TOP: *The epic staircase connecting* fumoir *and Café-Grill under construction. Note brackets awaiting Dunand's lacquered panels.* BOTTOM: *Completed, the finished ascent is flanked with lights and greenery; at the top is Baudry's* La Normandie, *now in the bar at Miami Beach's Fontainebleau Hilton Hotel.* (Chantiers de l'Atlantique and author's collection)

Shipboard stairs of this ambition have always been rare, almost impossible concessions from naval architects. They prefer that their hull be divided into strictly horizontal compartments. Grand staircases raise havoc with fire prevention; moreover, they create wasted space above and below, awkward triangles unusable for passengers. But in the *Normandie*'s Smoking Room, little space was wasted. In the redundant triangle belowstairs, the naval architects managed to shoehorn the service pantry. The upper triangle was, perhaps, a useless but glorious component of an inspired interior.

Wrote an impressed Harold Nicholson to his wife, Vita Sackville-West, after a summer crossing in 1935:

> What they have been so clever about is the arrangement on the different levels. That makes the boat look even more enormous than it is. You know how the big rooms on the *Bremen* were all on one floor. Here they are on different floors communicated by vast decorative staircases.

With the possible exception of descent down to *L'Atlantique*'s first-class dining room, the *Normandie*'s Smoking Room/Café-Grill connector remains without question the most elegant staircase treatment ever devised on board ship.

Up in the Café-Grill, there were a circular dance floor and two matching semicircular bars to either side, slightly elongated along one axis but essentially clones of the information booth down on Main Deck. The stewards' stations were round ended, and overhead, *"une vaste arabesque"* concealed indirect lighting. And every floor-level stretcher of the leather-and-chrome armchairs arced into semicircular form.

The list, as you may gather from this lightning tour, is endless. On board the *Normandie*, the ancient, the traditional, and the conventional decorative disciplines were banished. Oval frames, egg-and-dart encrustation, quirked ogee, fluted column—all had been swept away and replaced with the vessel's design signature, the clean, uncluttered half-round.

Before we embark on *Normandie*, another of her great spaces deserves comment: It is, of course, the dining room down on C Deck, separated from the great hall by another grand staircase as well as immensely tall bronze doors, each bearing five bas-relief medallions. Those medallions have been preserved to this day on exterior doors at Brooklyn's Our Lady of Lebanon Church on Remsen Street. Although one must laud Chor-Bishop Mansur's zeal in preserving these splendid relics, one can only deplore the spurious vine-and-grape appliqués he devised for the discs' interstices. Raymond Subes, the original designer, must have been appalled by this gratuitous embellishment, for they do his work a terrible disservice.

The *Normandie*'s dining room had been designed by Patout and Pacon. Its glory was its height, rising grandly through three decks. But that breathtaking height was no less striking than the room's length. The uptakes on the *Normandie* were divided; in other words, the chimneys piercing intervening decks between boiler room and funnel adhered to the sides rather than the center of the ship. That was the structural device permitting the room's impressive uninterrupted length as well as dictating its lateral configuration. Sited along either wall, those inescapable trunks arbitrarily misshaped the dining room's lateral dimensions at both the entrance and far end. Uptakes for number 2 funnel narrow what should have been a grandiose entrance. Passengers came down the staircase and passed through a kind of vestibule before reaching the great room itself. (Never mind—tables in that entryway, heavily trafficked and farthest from galley access, were the most eagerly sought-after on board.)

The room was narrowed farther aft by number 3 funnel's ventilation trunks. That second narrowing was christened by the dining-room stewards *le couloir polonais*, or the Polish corridor, a term borrowed from uneasy prewar headlines. Along the sides of the room between numbers 2 and 3 uptakes were eight private dining rooms as well as port and starboard escapes to the galley one deck below. In first- and tourist-class dining rooms alike, both on C Deck, stewards rode escalators up and down with their heavily loaded trays to and from the pantry.

Perhaps the dining room's most extraordinary conceit was that it had, unashamedly, no access to fresh air or daylight: Both sides were devoid of window or porthole. *Normandie*'s first-class diners, if you will, suffered the same shortcoming as tourist-class passengers in their original Grand Salon. This parallel begs the question: Did lounge occupants have a greater need for daylight than dining-room occupants? They probably did, since a lounge is used throughout the day and a dining room only periodically. Then again, since the *Normandie*'s first-class dining room was the vessel's only air-conditioned space, a novelty in 1935, perhaps the French felt justified in eschewing fresh air.

But Patout had provided mock windows in the form of vertical, hanging lamp fixtures lining both sides of the room; the effect was one of a bank of glass admitting daylight. To give even more light, a dozen huge Lalique cascades were scattered among the tables. Two more hung inverted as chandeliers, enriching both narrowed sections of the room. And a final decorative extravagance, a thirteen-foot gilded bronze figure entitled *La Paix*, by Dejean, loomed above the master's table.

Two decorative thrusts made the *Normandie*'s dining room work: extravagant scale and extravagant color. Just as the *Normandie*'s frankly overscale funnels dominated the profile, so those twin ranks of imposing crystal cascades filled the dining room to perfection. Gold predominated everywhere. The deeply coffered ceiling, the banding around each waiter's station, the caps and bases of the columnar wall lights, as well as the frosting, so to speak, on Lalique's glass wedding cakes. The gilded statue gave the impression of dining room as pagan temple, a vast, ordered space of paradoxical simplicity and richness: One dined importantly. Perhaps its most striking contemporary equivalent in New York would be a dinner reception within the glass-walled chamber housing the Metropolitan Museum's Temple of Dendur.

Down in the galley below, Chef Gaston Magrin ruled with an iron hand, a demanding perfectionist; no photograph ever showed him smiling. He once asked a subordinate how a new galley trainee was working out. "He's doing well," reported the subordinate. "Doing well is not enough!" was Magrin's curt rejoinder. He was so abusive a martinet that just before the maiden voyage, the *Normandie*'s cooks and stewards threatened a sit-down strike in Le Havre if he did not mend his ways. He tried but never could. Nevertheless, the results of his ruthless dominion were what made the *Normandie*'s cuisine—offerings in that dining temple—so memorable.

One of my favorite but doubtless apocryphal shipboard stories took place in that dining room. Boarding in New York, an American and his wife asked to be seated with a French couple so that they could improve their French during the crossing. They descended to dinner the first night out and met, awkwardly monosyllabic, a pleasant young French couple as requested. Throughout the crossing, the four of them conversed in bursts of execrable French. Only at the final breakfast off Le Havre did the New Yorkers discover that their tablemates were Americans who, like themselves, had requested of the same tricky maître d'hôtel that they be seated with French-speaking companions.

The *Normandie's* conventional sailing day was Wednesday, on her maiden voyage and thereafter, departing on a midweek afternoon from both Le Havre and New York, exactly a week apart. Westbound sailings originated in the Gare St.-Lazare, at track 24 by the side of the station wall. Each carriage of the boat train to Le Havre was identified by removable enameled plaques suspended from the right, or platform, side of the train. Passengers bound from Paris to the *Normandie* made the same anticipatory pilgrimage across Paris, transferred luggage from taxi to blue-clad porter's care, then followed him through the station's jostle to that out-of-the-way track that seemed such an inauspicious starting place for such a sumptuous journey. Once porter had been tipped and luggage and owner ensconced on board the boat train, one felt enfolded within the caring hands of the French Line. The *Normandie* crossing had begun.

The train ride from Paris to Le Havre is longer than the one from London to Southampton, so there was always time for a leisurely lunch. Indeed, scarcely was the train out of the city and gathering speed through Parisian suburbs than the cheerful tinkle of the restaurant-car manager's bell—"*tocsin of the soul*" Byron once called it—invited one to book a table. Is there any more gratifying meal than that taken aboard a well-manned French train swaying through the Norman countryside? Whether, as at maiden-voyage time, cloaked in May green or, before crossings to follow, shrouded in autumnal murk, that comfortable overland journey seemed an essentially fitting prelude. There is a way that French train waiters, encumbered with enormous table d'hôte platters, deliver portions unerringly from platter to plate, balanced against the sway of the train, that I have always admired.

Hanging forgotten on the wall of Le Havre's railway station is a bronze bas-relief showing railway tracks converging into the distance; at their widest, in the foreground, an anchor is supported by two diaphanously clad Edwardian nymphs; they are struggling to sustain a garland of fruits and vegetables atop the anchor. The whole thing seems a pleasing allegorical union of land and ocean no less than rail and ship. When I first saw it, I presumed it was a relic of 1912 and the second *France*. But I was amused to note that it dated from the construction of Le Havre's new railway station,

TOP: *The vessel's incredible dining room, devoid of passengers and stewards.* (Author's collection)

BOTTOM: *Brass on the bridge: Commandant René Pugnet* (right), *the vessel's first master, with Commandant-Adjoint Pierre Thoreux, who would be her second. Note how rings of rank on the sleeve are duplicated around the cap.* (French Line)

the cornerstone of which was laid in 1931; what stubbornly old-fashioned art for the *Normandie*'s decade!

It bore no relationship or resemblance to the port's new mid-thirties Gare Maritime, a towering pale yellow concrete structure hard by the pier that could absorb four trains simultaneously. Three trains had brought the *Normandie*'s 1,261 maiden-voyage passengers down from Paris.

As in every well-designed Gare Maritime, they descended from the carriages protected from the weather, mounted a broad escalator, and proceeded by bridge directly through an embarkation hall and onto the vessel. On Wednesday afternoon, May 29, 1935, the day of maiden-voyage departure, a steady stream of matériel was still coming across the *Normandie*'s working gangway: Lamps, furniture, and carpeting were loaded on board up to the last moment. Plumbers and painters were still at work throughout the vessel; in fact, fifty of their colleagues remained on board during two ensuing voyages in order to finish up every cabin.

Among the crew, stewards were delighted that the demanding week of preliminary pierside festivities was over at last. Although the maiden voyage would be challenging, it would at least establish the *Normandie*'s normal seagoing routine, away from the grime and company kibitzing in Le Havre. Along every corridor, stewards on their knees were scrubbing scuff marks off the linoleum with cloths dipped in turpentine; for some reason, true to the present day, visitor feet exert far worse shipboard wear than passenger feet.

The indoor pool was empty; at its deep end, plumbers, balanced atop ladders, were still fussing with last-minute adjustments to the pipes. Intermittently, over the ship's speakers, fire- and lifeboat-drill alarms added their intrusive clamor.

Those same speakers delivered their ultimate warning for two hours: *"Les visiteurs sont priés de quitter le navire dès maintenant!"* The vessel sailed an hour late, at 5:30 P.M. As tugs pulled her from the pier with her first passenger load, in-port vessels saluted, the *Paris, Ile de France*, and *Manhattan* among them.

That late departure from Le Havre delayed Southampton's festivities until midnight. The *Normandie* did not drop anchor in the Cowes Roads until eleven-thirty. She made no rendezvous with the pilot station, for two Southampton *pilotes de choix* were already on board, having crossed the Channel and embarked at Le Havre. One of them, Captain Somerwill, was the Trinity House veteran who would take the *Aquitania* out of Southampton for the last time, in February 1950. It was he who ushered the new French Line flagship into British waters for the first time; his colleague, Captain Holt, would take her out.

The *Normandie* had been due to anchor for only an hour at Southampton, but the apparition of four tenders out of the midnight gloom ruled out any thought of a prompt departure. Two contained British passengers and their luggage, one the press, and another Southampton's official greeting party. Complete with carefully written speech and gold chain of office, the mayor, his elaborately coiffed and hatted wife, and an extensive municipal entourage clambered through the shell plating down on C Deck. With cautious, hushed expectancy, they ascended by elevator to Promenade Deck for a midnight champagne reception. Although Commandant René Pugnet and his senior officers greeted them wearily in the Grand Salon, Madame LeBrun had already retired.

Despite the hour, the carefully prescribed ritual of the maiden call was endured: Speeches were read and translated, presents were exchanged, and toasts were drunk. Then, with discreet urgency, the port functionaries and their wives were ushered out into the great hall, down the elevators, across the gangplank, and into their tenders. As they churned back up toward Southampton, they could hear the rhythmic "clunk, clunk, clunk" as *Normandie*'s anchor cable was winched up into the hawsepipe. And before they had disembarked at the pier, the great French liner was steaming past Spithead en route to the Channel.

Although a satisfying glimpse for the official party, *Normandie*'s brief nocturnal visit was scant comfort to thousands lining the shore. At Southsea, searchlights were thrown onto the vessel as she passed, but for the most part, she appeared only as a distant enchantment, a twinkling, elusive vision capped by floodlit funnels.

Once the sensation of her record-breaking crossing to New York was history, the *Normandie*'s schedule would settle down. She took her place with fleetmates *Ile de France, Paris, Lafayette*, and *Champlain* in regular Transat service between Le Havre and New York. For some of her first eastbound crossings, the *Normandie* disembarked London-bound passengers and mails at Plymouth, farther down the Channel coast and a fast four-hour train ride to London. But thereafter the Plymouth call was intermittent both ways, and she customarily discharged her passengers at Southampton on the Monday morning of her afternoon arrival back at Le Havre. Passengers booked through to Le Havre rather than South-

TOP LEFT: *Fifteen-year-old Albert Rose in the uniform of his first post,* mousse de sonnerie *on board* Lafayette *in 1933.* (Albert Rose)

TOP RIGHT: *One of his contemporaries on board* Normandie *in the new uniform.* (Paul Hollister)

LEFT: *Elsa Lanchester perches atop a Winter Garden table for the photographer.* (French Line)

ampton were charged an extra ten dollars, for the cost of a final luncheon on board.

One of the treats of lecturing before Les Amis des Paquebots in Paris is a delightful septuagenarian called Albert Rose, who officiates at the projector. During a *Normandie* talk there two years ago, he excitedly identified several *mousses*, or bellboys, in my pictures. It turned out that he had been a *mousse* himself half a century ago and he readily agreed to share some of his memories with me.

Albert grew up in Le Havre, born a month after the Armistice, in December 1918. He was the only child of a soldier killed in the trenches before Albert was born. His widowed mother, denied a pension, took a job collecting tickets on the Le Havre tram system.

After school, young Albert was often left to his own devices. He haunted the docks and piers, a true *enfant du port*. When the boy was thirteen years old, his uncle enrolled him in the Stage à l'Armement, a Transat training school with classes held in what was called the Tente de New York; years earlier, transatlantic passengers had assembled beneath a tent, and the name, if not the canvas shelter, had stuck. There he was taught the basics of French maritime service. He also learned rudimentary shipboard English: "How do you do?," "Let me assist with your luggage," and "Here is your cabin."

Upon matriculation, as a *groom*, young Albert started climbing the Compagnie Générale Transatlantique's ladder of promotion, assigned to the *Lafayette* as one of a dozen *mousses de sonnerie*, or bellboys. His working uniform was a source of immense pride to both mother and son: a fitted dark blue jacket and trousers with half a dozen brass buttons, topped by a *polo*, the little round pillbox hat made famous to generations of Americans by an earlier Johnnie, the bellboy of Philip Morris fame.

Later, he was assigned to both the *Paris* and the *Ile de France*. But when, in the spring of 1935, he was transferred to the *Normandie*, he joined a corps of seventy fellow mousses. And there was a new uniform for the new ship: A vivid scarlet jacket was decorated with no less than forty-nine brass buttons: Three vertical bands of fifteen each covered the chest, and two highlighted each epaulet. All had to be kept polished by Albert; he had also to iron the shirts he wore beneath the jacket. A matching scarlet polo above and blue trousers below completed the dashing uniform. A pin emblazoned with his crew number—313—adorned the left breast of his splendid scarlet tunic.

In those days on board vessels of the French Line, whereas deck and engine-room personnel were paid year-round, hotel staff was not. Albert's pay of 245 francs a month was further reduced because only days at sea or in a foreign port were salaried. The moment *Normandie* tied up in Le Havre, his wages ceased until the following Wednesday, when the vessel sailed again for New York.

As *mousse de sonnerie*, Albert Rose shared a dormitory cabin with only a dozen of his peers, a vast improvement over his quarters on board the *Paris*, where all mousses bunked in one huge berthing compartment. Reveille or, as the French say, *branle-bas*, came just before six every morning: The cabin lights turned on abruptly, and a cooking pot filled with spoons rattled deafeningly until everyone was on his feet. In a frenzied rush, the boys dressed and were fed an indifferent breakfast in the crew mess. Half an hour of exercises followed out on deck. After a shower, the mousses had to be on duty no later than seven-fifteen. Face and shoes glistening, nails trimmed, and uniform spotless, Albert Rose and his fellows clattered up crew stairs to Main Deck and reported to one of the resplendent *sous-chefs de réception* on duty at the purser's desk. A long day had begun; the contrast between Albert's day and that of most of the *Normandie* clients was marked: At the same time that he undertook his first assignment of the morning, most passengers were either sound asleep or thinking groggily about breakfast.

He was on call, literally, all day, apart from hasty interruptions for meals snatched on the run. The ship's daily newspaper, *L'Atlantique*, had to be slipped under every cabin door; flowers had to be delivered, doors ceremonially opened and closed, cigarettes brought, and written messages dispatched. For every voyage, each mousse was assigned, in addition, a specific *corvée*, or extra duty. For some, it might be maintaining the polish of a brass stair rail or keeping a pair of plate-glass doors jewel clean. Or one could be assigned gong duty, marching up and down the ship's corridors sounding a Chinese gong, warning visitors ashore on sailing day or summoning passengers to lunch and dinner. Midafternoon free time was not spent off duty but in required attendance at hotel-school classes; promotion depended on it.

On one voyage, Albert Rose reported each morning to the Winter Garden, forward on Promenade Deck. This was *Normandie*'s handsome lookout lounge just under the bridge. Albert's daily task during that crossing was feeding the tropical birds as well as "mucking out" the bottom of their cages. The ship's tropical aviary was confined within a pair of elaborate, man-high facsimiles of the Lalique lamp standards lining the dining room. (Students of design, take note: Rose-covered pergolas, soaring above each cage, were, as was the Winter Garden itself, flawlessly semicircular.) Sometimes birds would escape and roost in the surrounding greenery; Albert Rose would race to close both outer doors before embarking on a mad scramble over wicker, fountain, and hydrangea in hot pursuit. Although the birds could be extremely noisy, the cages were never covered at night; instead, the Winter Garden was *Normandie's* only public room in which lights did not burn overnight. They were rigorously turned off at dusk, partly to improve visibility for the bridge above but also to put the raucous flock to sleep.

Within a year, Albert Rose had been promoted to *mousse de deck*, assisting deck stewards in keeping deck-chair occupants happy. Each morning, once the sailors had finished washing down the black rubber tiling, Albert and his colleagues would set out and arrange in perfect order more than six hundred deck chairs, logoed mattresses, and the company's distinctive tartan blankets. Since a number of French passengers took breakfast in their deck chairs, Albert delivered hundreds of *cafés complets* each crossing. Americans, whose breakfasts tended to be more substantial, either broke their fast in their cabins or descended to the dining room.

But they invariably showed up for consommé at eleven or tea at four; just as predictably, many were seasick. "*Hopla, Rose, encore un renard!*" the sharp-eyed *chef de deck* would mutter out of the corner of his mouth. (*Renard*, or, in English, fox, was sufficiently obscure slang for French crewmen to use for vomiting passengers.) And it was Albert's job to clean up the mess.

One renard did not require his services. Coming out on deck one afternoon in August 1939 (the ship's last eastbound crossing), Albert saw the great French actor Michel Simon leaning over the rail, apparently very sick. Albert leaped to his assistance, only to hear an exasperated director cry, "Cut!" Overly solicitous Albert had interrupted the shooting of a location scene for *Paris/New York* being filmed on board.

Some passengers lunched, and a few even dined in their deck chairs, which meant that deck stewards and their attendant mousses remained on call long after dark. Then all mattresses and blankets had to be stowed away in lockers, the chairs folded and lashed into ranks against the deckhouse wall. But the day was not over yet. In the Grand Salon, red-jacketed bellboys were required to move the wooden animals around an oval baize track during horse-racing sessions every other evening.

Another venue to which Albert Rose was occasionally assigned was one of the cabin pantries, keeping an eye on the annunciator board for passenger calls. A *garçon de cabin* was summoned by a yellow light, and in the man's absence, Albert was instructed to respond, but he was forbidden to answer a green light requesting the presence of a *femme du chambre*; he had to hunt down and inform the appropriate stewardess instead. Once, before a gala dinner, when the stewardess was occupied elsewhere, Albert finally answered a green summons of such persistence that he felt justified in disobeying standing orders. As a result, he solemnly helped do up what seemed as many buttons on the back of an impatient lady passenger's dress as adorned the front of his tunic.

Older mousses served as elevator operators. All *Normandie* elevators in first class were extravagantly manned by a team of two: One ran the controls; the other was a kind of *chasseur* who transmitted deck requests to the driver. At journey's end, the chasseur would open the gate with a flourish, leap out, and bow the dazzled passengers on their way.

Albert Rose, at the age of eighteen, was assigned to the first-class dining room, again on the lowest rung, as *commis débarrasseur*—in English, a busboy. Throughout every meal, he retrieved dirty plates and platters from the gold-rimmed service stations and carried them down to the galley. Subsequently, he was promoted one grade higher to *commis de rang*, charged with delivering full dishes from galley to dining room.

On one occasion, he was leaving the pantry with a full platter covered with a steel cloche to keep it warm. Autocratic chef Magrin always stood by one of the pantry doors, his baleful eye alert for the slightest infraction. On this occasion, Albert's tray had tipped slightly, and a telltale crescent of sauce had flooded out onto the platter's rim. Magrin exploded. Kicking Albert savagely in the backside, he barked: "Rose, go back to the counter and change that plate! And next time you lift a tray, carry it the right way!"

Perhaps Albert's most dramatic experience on board the *Normandie* was helping restrain an American who was trying to jump over the railing. With a team of stewards and mousses Albert helped wrestle the beserk man from the Boat Deck down to the hospital. However, while the doctor's back was turned, the determined suicide stood on an examining table and began squeezing himself through an open porthole. He had his torso out before the doctor and crewmen could grasp his legs. With his arms firmly outstretched on the shell plating, he effectively prevented them from dragging him back inside. Finally, using that half of the passenger still, literally, in his clutches, the medico administered an injection into the buttocks through the trousers; only then could the sedated passenger be drawn back inside. He completed the crossing in full restraint.

Albert disembarked from the *Normandie* for the final time in Le Havre on August 22, 1939. He had been called to duty in the navy, but at Cherbourg, his enlistment center, he did not qualify physically. In December, he married Claudine Coquin and spent the war working in France. After V-E day, he went back to sea, but never on a French Line vessel.

Regrettably, Albert Rose has no picture of himself on board the *Normandie*. A very good one that was taken by a journalist used to sit unframed on a shelf at home, but his young daughter Evelyne, missing her steward papa, kissed the photograph so ardently in his absence that she finally obliterated his image for all time.

During Albert's last crossing, the one during which *Paris/New York* was being filmed, one American passenger was Everett B. Moore, a textile executive from Lowell, Massachusetts, abroad for the first time and traveling alone on business. His wife, Charlotte, and only son, Richard, had accompanied him down from Boston to Pier 88 to see him off.

News from Europe was alarming; the prospect of war, only too real. To relieve his worried wife, Moore dropped a daily letter into the writing room's mailbox. The unvarying salutation read "Dear Sweetheart and Son"; the unvarying signature, "Hubby and Dad." That entire one-way correspondence, as well as his daily journal (a bon voyage gift from his wife) have survived intact in the collection of Wayne G. LaPoe, who was kind enough to lend them to me for inclusion within this chapter.

Everett Moore's letters clearly show the impact the *Normandie* made on a first-time passenger. Coincidentally, they throw into sharp relief Moore's unusual isolation from his fellows. Surely there was never a greener or less socially interactive client on board any ship. Everett Moore was all cautious detachment, shy and unsure: He watched passengers playing shuffleboard or horse racing or Ping-Pong but apparently never joined in. Indeed, he remained a perennial loner throughout the crossing.

TOP: *At teatime on board the* Ile de France *in the winter of 1934,* mousse de deck *Rose, on the left, shrouds a passenger's feet in the company's traditional tartan rug.* (Author's collection)

BOTTOM: *A passenger trio, coats draped over chairs, caught in the Café-Grill. An* unnamed *chef de rang* hovers *to the left; on the right is* commis de rang *Charles Anquetil.* (Albert Rose)

He did talk with his cabin steward, Frimeaux Ridet, with the help of a French phrase book that Charlotte had also given him on sailing day. The only indication that he enjoyed any additional conversation on board comes from notations in his passenger list. Next to "M. le Marquis d'Assche" and "Mr. and Mrs. Sidney Benedito," he penciled the words "Next deck chair." In fact, he may never have spoken to them at all, merely ascertained their names from the cards identifying the adjacent chairs' owners.

Additionally, in his copy of the passenger list, there are check marks next to his name as well as those of three celebrities: Helen Hayes, Michel Simon, and Erich von Stroheim. Otherwise, the columns of 174 cabin-class names are pristine, a sure giveaway of a noncommunicative passenger. Moore apparently made no friends, met no cabin neighbors, chatted with no one at a bar, and had none of those engaging chance encounters endemic to shipboard. Certainly, there was a raffish mix on board, from the president of the company, Edmond Lanier, and the maharaja of Tripura to the Earl of Carnarvon and Lord Eustace Percy; the only film star Moore missed was Ramon Novarro.

After his first full day at sea, he confesses to Charlotte in his initial letter: "I am as lonesome as I have ever been in my life." He had awakened early, long before anyone else, even Albert Rose and his fellow mousses:

> I didn't know what time people got up so figured with break-fast posted from seven to eight and I woke up at 6:45 . . . I dressed and went up to the Prom deck and the crew was swabbing deck—no-one in the dining room and apparently not ready so I went back to my stateroom. The stewart [*sic*] asked if I would have breakfast in my room so I said yes in pretty good french. I found out from him—no-one gets up until 10 or eleven. I guess you have to learn.

But I think Everett Moore never did. He spent some time that first morning in his deck chair on a still-deserted Promenade Deck, keeping one eye cocked for celebrities: "Some of the Maharaja's company came later but few others." He read in his deck chair again that afternoon—a biography of Coolidge—and then saw a Bette Davis film in the theater.

He dressed carefully for the second night's dinner, reporting in the dining room that there were "more black tux's than white but

I wore white." Afterward, he only watched but did not bet on horse racing in the Grand Salon. "Two pages move the horses," he told his wife and son; I wondered at first if one of them could have been Albert Rose; but then I remembered that by 1939 he had become a *commis de rang* in the dining room.

From Moore's letter of the following day, August 18:

> We got the war news in the ship's paper but don't worry, as I won't be near where they are planning if at all. The French people aboard that I have talked with don't seem concerned and go right on having fun as unconcerned as can be. . . . I never did so little or do so little for such a long time and for the first two days I couldn't get used to it.
>
> People on the boat certainly wear clothes—different dresses every night—sports things all day. A ballet dancer from Philadelphia and another dancer gave solo dances in the Grill tonight. . . .

It was symptomatic of the *Normandie*'s light passenger load that all of cabin class could be accommodated at once in the Café-Grill. During that performance, Erich von Stroheim was seated at a neighboring table; "Looks like Mussolini," Everett confided to Charlotte. Nevertheless, he sent a waiter over with his program to have it autographed.

The following day, a party of tourist-class passengers was conducted through cabin class. "Pretty nice-looking folks," recorded Everett wistfully:

> I think I would have met more Americans there. Apparently a lot of titles and professionals in the Cabin Group. The last day or rather today one or two warmed up a bit but I don't know where they keep themselves.

Between every line, one is reminded continually that poor Everett Moore not only missed home and family terribly but, in a literal sense, missed the boat as well. I think he was hopelessly out of his depth. Who were those "one or two" who "warmed up a bit"? They are never identified, nor, curiously, are any table companions. Though he admired the *Normandie*'s food enormously, it seems to have been a solitary indulgence. From an early journal entry:

I thought as long as I could still eat and as we approached mid-ocean I might not have as good an appetite I better eat well—so I ordered a nice steak with baked potato, salad and carrots—of course, with soup. And for desert [*sic*] the famous crepe-Suzette which is as much enjoyment to see prepared as to eat and are delicious, I had heard of their fame and so without knowing whether they were soup, fish or nuts knew it was the thing to have.

There follows a detailed description of the maître d'hôtel's labors in producing his special dessert; one only wonders if Moore shared it with unnamed table companions. I suspect he must have eaten alone. Certainly the ship was empty enough—179 passengers must have been very thin on the ground, rattling about in that vast chamber; a table for one would have been easy.

Underscoring his malaise, on the next day a pronounced "groundswell" set *Normandie* rolling. While Everett was dressing for dinner:

You remember how large the portholes were, about 24″ to 28″. I stood over by the bath and we were rolling so the horizon would disappear at the bottom and then go a little above the top and when I was shaving, the water in the bowl would be up an inch from the top and then go down 2 or 3 inches, then reverse. If I had roller skates, I could have rolled down hill in the cabin in 15 seconds each way. And then in the foyer in front of the dining room, also up by the theatre they roped up all the chairs and put balustrades of rope toward the dining room to hold onto. In the dining room they pour water on the cloths.

The next day, it got rougher:

All chairs, tables and every moving thing is lashed down as the heavy roll continues. On the dining tables, they have riggings to hold everything from sliding shaped like this [sketch]. This sets up about 2 inches above the table with holes for oil, vinegar, water bottles, drinking glasses, even a band an inch high for your plate.

Earlier in that same letter, he remarks on his difficulty in meeting people. Here is Everett Moore's *cri de coeur*:

You forget what day of the week it is but believe it when I say they are all long ones. . . . Most all of the regular Americans seem to be families or business men who have known each other before or came together and you probably wonder why I have not met them but you can't break into a twosome or group without some letdown from them too. On a longer trip, the ice would be broken easier for sure.

One result of Everett Moore's chronic aloneness is the care with which he describes the *Normandie*'s interiors, even though one must assume that Charlotte and Richard must have explored them when they saw him off in New York. Never mind, in his Sunday letter, he documents the Promenade Deck, starting with what he calls the conservatory (Winter Garden) forward:

The walls and floor are all white and gray grained marble, all kinds of growing plants and two large bird cages of glass and gold frames with 15 or 20 different kinds of song birds in each. . . . Just back of this room which is almost a continuation of a Promenade Deck is a room on one side for bible study and the other a business reference library.

Unless there was a party of missionaries on board, it seems unlikely that the *Normandie*'s library would have been devoted exclusively to "bible study." Moore continues his travelogue, describing how one side of the Promenade Deck is for deck chairs, the other for Ping-Pong tables; obviously, the low passenger count made the task of the *mousses de deck* that much easier.

The theater catches his attention, and the textile executive, punctuation still awry, comes into his own:

The theatre is very pretty a cerise plush curtain red plush chairs the walls and ceiling all pure gold. The ceiling steps back so all the lighting is indirect and I have sketched the Chinese pattern which looks as though it has been carved in with a stick.

The main foyer is domed. Ivory walls Gold grilled elevator shafts and open both sides with windows to the Prom Deck. The Grand Salon is gold and has walls of black gold and white glass pictures of old shipping . . . there are 4 towers modernistic glass pedestals for lighting and surrounded by seats, all of which are rich rose and needle point in floral colors.

(There is something haunting about mention of those fatal lighting fixtures in the Grand Salon.) Everett Moore commented on the ones in the Dining Room:

> . . . six tremendous floor pillar lights of glass about ten feet high and five feet in diameter.
> The dinner gong which sounds like a musical metal pan is just ringing. A man makes the rounds of corridors and you can hear it a mile. I'll have lunch and then continue the description.

But he never did. The weather deteriorated, and Moore's guided tour ended. In fact, he had already covered the ship adequately. His last letter from the *Normandie* begins: "Here I am in S. Hampton . . ." and from then on, he is preoccupied with matters awaiting him ashore. He would be met at Le Havre by a business colleague from a Swiss firm called Elastic, headquartered in Basel, his ultimate destination.

Moore had been booked to sail home on the *Normandie's* westbound passage of September 6, but as we all know now, it was a crossing that never took place; he returned on the *Nieuw Amsterdam* instead. The *Normandie* would steam westbound for the last time on August 23, staying put forever, as it turned out, at Pier 88.

So it was that both passenger Moore and *commis de rang* Rose disembarked from the fabled vessel for the last time in Le Havre on the same day, August 22, 1939, by different gangplanks and for different reasons. But their respective experiences on board serve, I trust, to illuminate some aspects of the great ship during that tragically brief peacetime career.

Now for the war. Suppose that ghastly fire had never happened; suppose Clement Derrick and his chain gang had contained those molten steel fragments while cutting down the Grand Salon's fourth light stanchion on the afternoon of February 9, 1942: If there were no fire, there would have been no fireboats, no capsize, and no immolation. Instead, *Normandie's* productive life would have continued.

With that enviable postulation a reality, join with me in a leap of faith as, quite shamelessly, I fabricate the ship's subsequent career. That graceful, camouflaged trooper will steam halfway around the globe before resuming, as the *Normandie* once again, peacetime transatlantic service.

The *Lafayette* left New York for Boston under command of Captain Robert Coman, USN, on the afternoon of February 16, two days later than scheduled. Civilian dredges under contract to the navy had worked around the clock to shift accumulated silt from the south side of the slip between Piers 88 and 90. Regardless, Captain George Seeth, the Transat's *pilote de choix* for New York, ordered his tugs to favor the slip's northern half as the *Lafayette* exited, over the portion where so recently the *Queen Mary* had been moored.

The *Lafayette* was under way for the first time in nearly two and a half years. The vessel proceeded downstream and out through the Narrows. In the early winter dusk off Ambrose, she rendezvoused with a destroyer escort. Overhead, a pair of Martin PBYs and a blimp were on station to accompany her up the coast.

The Boston Navy Yard, containing the largest dry dock in the Western Hemisphere, was the vessel's inevitable destination. As recently as 1940, it had been enlarged and improved to handle vessels of the *Normandie*'s dimensions; the *Queen Mary* had been in only a month earlier.

On board was Admiral Adolphus Andrews, commanding officer of the Third Naval District, sailing as a specially invited guest. His fellow passengers included a large contingent of Robin's dry-dock personnel, working in twenty-four-hour shifts to complete welding and painting as well as installing bunks and mess tables. They also gathered up vast piles of accumulated rubbish and stacked them in the A and C Deck entryways for off-loading in Boston.

The work force was fed in a corner of the first-class *salle à manger* by a cadre of Military Sea Transport Service (MSTS) cooks and messmen who had boarded only two days before the vessel sailed. They had begun the Herculean task of converting the *Lafayette*'s D Deck galley into an efficient navy facility that would churn out rations for over ten thousand men twice daily.

In anticipation of those hungry battalions, the dining room had actually been enlarged. Acting on early Navy Department specifications, workers had breached the bulkhead separating first- and tourist-class dining rooms on C Deck. This not only increased the resulting room's capacity but improved traffic flow. The vessel's enlisted passengers (who would increase to nearly sixteen thousand before war's end) could be fed in shifts, 2,600 at a time, entering from the afterend through the old tourist-class entrance and exiting up the staircase into the lowest level of first class's great hall. All eight private dining-room walls were gone, expanding the dining room. Long port and starboard steam tables were installed in their place, flanking chow lines that cooks could replenish conveniently by escalator from the galley below.

The Grand Salon looked like a rectangular warehouse. In place of handsome glass murals, prosaic steel walls remained, painted utilitarian gray. The color only added to the perennial gloom, for in New York, paint crews had painted over all flanking Promenade Deck windows; even had they been left clear, festoons of life rafts, hung outside, blocked the view.

As in the Dining Room, adjacent ancillary chambers had been dispatched. The walls of both forward music rooms had come down, enlarging the Lounge's capacity. Underfoot, red linoleum had displaced parquet and carpet. The only things left to sit on were four circular banquettes, vestigial remnants of the space's quartet of central light stanchions cut down in New York. All 10,000 troops' life preservers had been unpacked, stenciled, and distributed throughout the Promenade Deck dormitories to either side as well as down to every cabin below. It was no longer the Grand Salon; it was the Troop Recreation Compartment and would be so identified on thousands of makeshift mimeographed deck plans handed to embarking commanders.

Troop officers would mess in the Grill Room and yarn and relax in the darkened tourist-class Lounge directly aft; all of its windows had been painted over as well. Workers had refashioned a connecting door between the old first- and tourist-class spaces. The elegant staircase ascending from Smoking Room to Café-Grill was no longer a thoroughfare, since the military discouraged traffic between enlisted men and officers. However, because of the necessity of retaining it as an evacuation route in case of an emergency, doors at the top of the staircase remained unlocked by order of the master-at-arms.

The *Lafayette* arrived off the Boston pilot station at first light on March 18. Apart from the *Queen Mary*, she was the largest vessel to use the facility since White Star's *Majestic* in the early twenties. At that time, a battalion of marines had to control avid sightseers, but with wartime security, no spectators were permitted inside the yard.

Once the vessel was positioned over the keel blocks, the dock was drained. As the water receded, overalled workers, bundled against the bitter New England cold, stood atop floating scows and scrubbed accumulated slime off strakes of exposed plating. Over the next two weeks, the *Lafayette*'s entire underwater hull was sandblasted and primed, then repainted with U.S. Navy–compound antifoul paint. All four anchors—three forward and one àft—were lowered to the dry-dock floor for scaling and painting. Every link of cable was also lowered to the dock floor for chipping and painting.

Workers atop a ladder unbolted the access door to the *Normandie*'s rudder, and a foreman-inspector entered, dragging a cabled work light behind him. Fifteen minutes later, he emerged and pronounced the interior in excellent condition. The rudder's outer surfaces were sprayed with a defoliant agent. One blade of the outer port screw of the *Lafayette*'s quartet of manganese propellers was newly chipped (legacy of an overenthusiastic dredge master in New York); the opposite blade was chipped to balance, and all four props were rotated, balanced, and cleaned. The hull's final wartime addition was the fat belt of a degaussing cable to repel magnetic mines.

The *Lafayette* sailed from Boston on the first of March, topping up her fuel tank from a navy fleet oiler alongside the port's celebrated Commonwealth Pier, now packed with anonymous gray navy tonnage. Once clear of the harbor, the giant troopship steamed north. She stayed at sea throughout the first week of March for exhaustive sea trials off Portsmouth, New Hampshire. A vigilant antisubmarine cordon surrounded the area, overseen by ubiquitous blimps. By week's end, the vessel had achieved thirty knots through a stiff, force 7 gale.

The *Robin*'s dry-dock workers, still toiling on board, downed tools, complaining that they were too seasick to continue working. Scornful navy supervisors gave up as the grumbling civilians retired to their makeshift standee bunks. Others yarned and smoked out on the bitter decks. Early next morning, six-inch ordnance on the stern was test-fired by navy gun crews, alarming the civilian supernumeraries; no one had notified them that test-firing was taking place, and the more fanciful among them were convinced that German torpedoes had bracketed the *Lafayette*. A delegation delivered a letter of grievance to the bridge.

On March 7, fully operational now, the troopship returned to Pier 88's north side. On board from both pier and lighter came more steel mess tables, thousands of blankets, and tons of provisions. A full complement of MSTS messmen boarded, helping to supervise stowage of the ship's newly arrived commissariat.

The last of the Robin's workers disembarked. "Good riddance," muttered the ship's executive officer as the last one walked across the old French Line gangplank onto the pier. They had proved an unruly, slovenly lot of plank owners, racking up more overtime pay in two weeks than the exec earned in six months. Moreover, the combination of their oxyacetylene torches and overpowering paint fumes worried every officer on board.

Now, finally, the *Lafayette* was almost an all-navy ship. Fully manned for carrying 10,000 troops, the *Lafayette's* crew was divided as follows: navy deck officers, engineers, and deckhands, MSTS catering and service staff. Peacetime holdovers included two French engineering officers serving as consultants to the navy who, it turned out, would remain on board for the duration. One of them had wept emotionally during the first day of sea trials off New Hampshire when his beloved diesel-electric motors were finally throttled to full power.

By late March, New York saw the last of the *Lafayette* for a year and a half. Her immediate destination was top secret. But despite tight security, disembarking Captain Seeth reported to his colleagues on the pilot boat that she had veered south before disappearing into the early spring mist. Thirty-six hours later, a coastal vessel spotted the *Lafayette* off Nassau. She refueled at Trinidad's Port of Spain before racing eastward across the Atlantic, bunkering again at Freetown and yet once more in Capetown. Then she disappeared farther east, arriving at Trincomalee, where she boarded her first load of troops. Fifteen hundred wounded Anzacs from the Western Desert, bound home for Sydney, were carried on board in litters by Sinhalese orderlies. A detachment of Royal Australian Army Medical Corps boarded with them.

A week after an additional fueling call at Fremantle, the *Lafayette* made a triumphal entry past picnickers atop the Sydney Heads in mid-May. Several of the more knowledgeable identified the camouflaged three-stacker instantly as the *Queen Mary.*

The wounded Anzacs disembarked into lighters and thence ashore. Then the *Lafayette* was towed across Sydney Harbor to the Cockatoo Docks and Engineering Works, where painters covered her camouflage coat with standard battleship gray; antiaircraft guns appeared on the stern and just aft of each bridge wing. A week later, nearly three thousand British and American dependents, civilian refugees from the Philippines and Malay, came on board. The Yanks would disembark in their homeland at San Francisco, the Brits on the west coast of Canada.

The *Lafayette* sailed from Sydney, not in convoy but traveling alone at high speed, skirting the war zone through deserted reaches of the South Pacific. She refueled at the Marquesas Islands. Many of the 2,800 on board were children who enjoyed running up and down the main staircases, badgering the elevator operators for rides and resenting the adult-sized life preservers that Captain Coman had insisted all passengers wear until the *Lafayette* was safely east of the Marquesas. A committee of parents organized storytelling sessions for the children and bingo games for all. From some forgotten recess in the purser's office, those same mothers unearthed a peacetime treasure trove of gala paper hats for a noisy farewell party in the dining room one day out of San Francisco.

On June 3, 1942, the American civilians were off-loaded at San Francisco. Then, under navy escort, the *Lafayette* sailed north for the Canadian naval base at Esquimalt and another dry docking; on orders from Washington, improved minesweeping paravanes were added to the hull. Yet more armaments—Bofors guns this time—were added aft, and the tourist-class swimming pool was armored over to become a magazine for six-inch naval ordnance. All British dependents were off-loaded onto lighters for passage across the straits to Vancouver and thence onto transcontinental trains for the next interminable stage of their trek to wartime Blighty.

The *Lafayette* returned south and picked up her first full load of troops in San Francisco a week later. Just over ten thousand infantrymen came on board at heavily guarded Pier 35. With no fast-loading system yet devised and with no advance parties to guide troop commanders inside the vessel, embarkation alone consumed nearly twenty-four hours. Bound for down under, many of the GIs clambering across the gangway thought, once again, that they were boarding a Cunarder; the *Queen Elizabeth* had been in the port only months earlier.

Down on D Deck, the galley was put to the test for the first time. Since the theater was too small, Special Services personnel on board showed films each afternoon and evening in the Troop Recreation Compartment; the screen was viewed from both sides, navy fashion, a length of canvas lashed within a steel rectangle suspended in the opening separating *fumoir* from Grand Salon. Hundreds of soldiers camped out on the staircase for each screening. A canteen, fashioned from the combined novelty shop and barbershop on Main Deck's square, dispensed bottles of warm Coca-Cola and candy bars. Gum was verboten, and empties were scrupulously gathered up. The troop commanders were advised to discipline anyone throwing bottles or trash of any kind over the side. Smoking was restricted to specific decks and ruthlessly prohibited after dusk.

The voyage to Sydney lasted more than two weeks. Several yellowing copies of a mimeographed ship's newspaper, written and edited by the chaplains, remain extant. The paper was called *Lafayette Laffs* and contained reams of bad poetry, interservice jokes, crude cartoons, heavily censored war news, and announcements of general interest and safety. "Troops must wear life jackets at all times" was a running head recurring across the top of every page. One article urged troops not to linger over their meals in the air-conditioned dining hall. This would remain a perennial catering problem, especially during Indian Ocean passages to follow.

The *Lafayette* made one more trans-Pacific crossing before joining several convoys carrying Aussie troops from Sydney to Trincomalee. In one evocative gathering of expatriate Atlantic tonnage, she joined the *Aquitania*, the *Queen Mary*, the *Mauretania*, and the *Nieuw Amsterdam*, as though celebrating a New York harbor reunion in the gray Pacific. But after her third westbound run to Trincomalee, the *Lafayette* was ordered to dead-load across the Indian Ocean, around Capetown, and back to New York. She traveled alone, without air cover or escort, and arrived without incident, tying up at Pier 90 on New Year's Day, 1943.

She was urgently needed back on the North Atlantic: The great transatlantic push was on, and the *Lafayette* took stalwart part in that relentless GI buildup anticipating D day. Gangs of shipyard workers swarmed back on board to install yet additional standee bunks. This time, GIs filled every conceivable cranny—the theater, the swimming pool, and the Winter Garden. Larger first-class cabins, arranged to accommodate no more than half a dozen men, doubled their capacity. With the neighboring *Queens* as example, the *Lafayette*'s troop load was nudged above fifteen thousand.

Once again, the *Lafayette-ex-Normandie* returned near her home waters. On the eastern end of the run, she dropped anchor off the Tail of the Bank at Gourock in Scotland, where fleets of Dutch lighters—refugee tonnage from Holland—off-loaded troops ashore.

The *Lafayette* and the two *Queens* sailed in triple tandem. One of them was always at sea, an efficient shuttle of giant gray liners, each carrying an entire infantry division. After the D day landings, the *Lafayette* embarked wounded men for westbound voyages to the States. For these lighter crossings, the upper levels of standee bunks were lashed upright, and hospital mattresses were added to supplement the lowers. On one crossing, she made her first (and last) call at Halifax with several hundred Canadian casualties.

Although Le Havre had been liberated within a month after D day, retreating German sappers had left the port in such ruins that it was not until after V-E Day that the French Line's flagship made an emotional reentry into her home port. It took place, by curious coincidence, on May 29, 1945, exactly ten years from the day that the brand-new *Normandie* had sailed on her maiden voyage. Now the *Lafayette* steamed slowly into the *avant-port*, a battle-scarred veteran, with radar tower rising above the bridge and tubs of Oerlikons and Bofors antiaircraft guns dotting her battered gray superstructure. War-weary Havrois crammed every waterfront vantage point, weeping unashamedly as their *Normandie* came home. Troopship or not, she seemed somehow a harbinger of peace and better times to come, an infusion of hope into their shattered port.

But she was still officially the USS *Lafayette*, still a working navy vessel with a task to complete. Acting on General de Gaulle's heartfelt request, navy planners transferred her eastern terminus from Gourock to Le Havre, despite the difficulty of restoring destroyed rail and embarkation facilities. U.S. engineers as well as Le Havre's Porte Autonome wrought miracles, however, and for thousands of GI veterans returning home, the way lay through Paris and Le Havre.

The *Lafayette* was in port the day that the German *Europa* arrived to be handed over to the French. It was her first postwar reunion with both a Teutonic rival and future consort. Luckily, she was safely out of port and en route to New York when that catastrophic Channel gale sank the *Europa* upright alongside the hulk of the capsized *Paris*.

Not until February 1946 did the *Lafayette* unload her last contingent of returning troops. The bands and confetti had long since stopped; New York troop arrivals had become commonplace. At the same time as the last GIs went ashore, civilian workers boarded to remove all U.S. Navy property, including thousands of standee bunks and mess tables. Towed by a tug, a derrick barge churned up from the Brooklyn Navy Yard, moored under the *Lafayette's* counter for a week. Naval dock workers dismounted all the vessel's armaments, not one of which had ever fired a shot in anger. Corroding ammunition was gingerly off-loaded as well.

Once again moored empty at Pier 88, the navy decommissioned the *Lafayette* on January 16, 1946. They planned handing her over to the former French Line captain, Commandant E. Payen de la Garanderie, who had sailed over from France with a specially recruited French merchant marine crew. The simple handing-over ceremony took place atop the bridge in a snowfall. A twenty-four-hour blizzard had dumped more than a dozen inches of snow up and down the coast: New York and the Northeast Corridor were paralyzed. The snowstorm had closed airports and stalled trains. Neither the French ambassador nor the secretary of the navy, due up from Washington, could attend.

Yet somehow it seemed fitting that principals only should officiate. Old Glory came down, and the tricolor and CGT flag were restored. The French commandant said a few heartfelt words that were echoed by his U.S. Navy predecessor. The two captains shook hands for those few photographers who had made it across town through the drifts. Then the entire party—naval and French merchant marine officers as well as the press—retired gratefully below-decks to the warmth of the master's cabin, where, now that it was no longer a U.S. Navy vessel, cocktails were served legally before lunch. That afternoon, *Normandie* sailed for St.-Nazaire.

Two years would elapse before she became her prewar self. Severe postwar shortages persisted in France, particularly supplies of the appropriate structural steel needed by shipbuilders. Penhoët's hard-pressed management was frantically busy: an *embarras de richesses* of gray liners awaited their turn for civilian restoration. The *Ile de France* had tied up in the fitting-out basin, already under reconversion; major revamping of her engine rooms and uptakes resulted in a two- rather than three-funneled profile. The grimy hulk of the salvaged *Europa* arrived under tow from Le Havre. But *De Grasse, Ile de France*, and *Normandie* had first priority, so the German conversion was delayed; four years would elapse before the newly wrought *Liberté* came on line.

There was neither the time nor the money to restore all of the

Normandie's former glories. The Grand Salon's glass murals, for instance, were replaced by panels of anodized bronze, and the fumoir was clad in bleached pearwood. Lalique did reproduce facsimiles of the dining-room lamps, and resurgent Aubusson studios rewove original upholstery fabric for both salle à manger and Grand Salon.

In the spring of 1948, the *Normandie* left St.-Nazaire for her third session of sea trials, off the Brittany coast. Then she picked up a capacity load of passengers at Le Havre to take to New York. During the crossing, every one of them received a blue-boxed medallion especially created at Paris's Hôtel de la Monnaie; on the obverse, the official three-quarter ship's profile, on the reverse, an inscription about the *Lafayette*'s U.S. Navy career, crossed American and French flags, and the date of the vessel's return to Transat service.

A tremendous reception awaited the restored flagship in the port of New York. She tied up once more in peacetime colors at Pier 88, the scene of her wartime incarceration. The *Queen Elizabeth*, in port across the slip, saluted her with a rhapsodic, whistled concert.

For two years, the *Normandie* continued her prewar schedule of Wednesday sailings from both Le Havre and New York. She sailed at first in awkward tandem with the slower *Ile de France*, but when the *Liberté* joined the CGT fleet, the company's express service, now fully competitive with the *Queens*', switched to Friday sailings. There was no further attempt to wrest the Blue Ribband away from Cunard White Star; indeed, that Anglo-French rivalry was laid to academic rest over the summer of 1952 when the *United States* swept the North Atlantic forever.

In the autumn of 1953, the vessel nearly went back to war, when a movement within the National Assembly attempted to charter *Normandie* as a troopship. In essence, the plan was to embark a beefed-up brigade of paratroopers, Legionnaires, and regular infantry onto the hastily reconverted liner for fast passage out to French Indochina in support of beleaguered Dien Bien Phu. However, the lack of a suitable deep-water port as well as a means of transporting reinforcements into the battle zone made the scheme impractical, and it was abandoned.

In truth, the *Normandie* and all North Atlantic tonnage were involved in another war in the Atlantic. Fifties rivalry had become less an intraship competition than a life-and-death struggle with airborne upstarts. Although the French Line had never boasted a faster or more popular fleet, by the late fifties annual revenue was declining alarmingly, especially during winter crossings. Planners at 6 Rue Auber, the company's Parisian headquarters, proposed countermeasures.

It was decided that cruising would be profitable; as a result, the *Normandie* spent much of the winter of 1958 back at St.-Nazaire, undergoing renovation for the last time. The vessel was entirely air-conditioned. One naval architect suggested that a pool be installed between the second and third funnels, reducing, perforce, the height of the Grand Salon below it. Wiser heads prevailed, though, and instead, workers fashioned a pool at the afterend of Promenade Deck, surrounded by an expansive lido. The crew would become sole proprietors of the original outdoor pool farther aft. Several Promenade Deck cabins on the vessel's starboard side had to be sacrificed in order to create access to the new outdoor facility.

Thereafter, the *Normandie* regularly spent winter months on fortnightly Caribbean cruises out of New York. It was in one sense a new life for the beloved liner, but in another, a recall of her prewar Rio voyages. Among the most popular destinations were Martinique and Guadeloupe: "See Caribbean France on a French ship" urged a persuasive campaign. The *Normandie*, newly renovated, proved a popular draw, carrying larger passenger loads than during summer crossings of the North Atlantic.

Emboldened by that resurgent demand, the company organized longer warm-weather excursions. A program of Mediterranean cruises was scheduled for the spring and fall of 1962. The *Normandie* embarked the bulk of her cruising passengers in New York, then raced eastbound for Gibraltar, picking up additional French clients at Cannes. These were virgin waters for the flagship: Throughout the war, she had never entered the Mediterranean. French and Italian port authorities outdid themselves mounting elaborate welcoming ceremonies.

But a proposed world cruise over the winter of 1964 was aborted; about to enter her fourth decade, *Normandie* was feeling her age. Over the summer, cumulative breakdowns disrupted the vessel's regime. Plumbing failures proliferated: A saltwater feed pipe amidships on Main Deck ruptured suddenly, cascading gallons of water down through successive decks below. Portside private dining rooms were inundated, and an unsightly stain disfigured the dining room's ceiling for the rest of the ship's life. There were electrical troubles as well, innumerable, baffling short circuits, including two that scorched paneling in the Smoking Room, luckily when the ship was tied up at Pier 88 during turnaround.

For a year, the *Normandie* limped gallantly on. But a new champion was taking shape at Penhoët, a third *France* scheduled to displace her as the company's flagship in 1966. So it happened that, during the mid-sixties, there was an abrupt, almost brutal attrition of prewar tonnage. The *Liberté* went first, cut up at La Spezia. Japanese scrap merchants snapped up the *Ile de France*; and although those two vessels vanished with relatively little comment from the press, there was a public outcry when the *Normandie* was finally withdrawn in 1966; the brand-new *France*, inbound from St.-Nazaire, saluted her great predecessor as the two vessels met for the first time.

For months, as the *Normandie* rusted in a Havrois backwater, proponents all over the world debated her future. The Syndicats d'Initiatifs of three French ports, Le Havre, Bordeaux and Cherbourg, offered schemes to preserve the old liner as a floating resort and museum, to be moored permanently along their respective waterfronts. From the other side of the Atlantic, queries came from both Philadelphia and New York about the possibility of obtaining the French vessel; additional informal offers were submitted to the French Line. Though the *Mary* would not reach Long Beach for another two years, popular sentiment urged the preservation, at any cost, of such a vast transatlantic icon as *Normandie*.

But in the end, nothing happened; none of the competing municipalities had a realistic economic proposal, and the preservationists' outcry was stilled. The *Normandie* was finally cut up for scrap at Dunkirk, just down-Channel from Le Havre. A handful of Parisian reporters and photographers were on board for the final tow, and squares of her red funnel casing still turn up as souvenirs all along the Channel coast. Some of her china and cutlery was transferred to the *France*, but her fittings and furniture sold briskly at auction in Paris. *Normandie* was gone.

One thing I realize from this exercise in wish fulfillment is that a curiously comforting moral can be drawn from the *Normandie*'s early demise. Lost at a tragically early age, she never suffered the ravages of old or even middle age and knew neither disenchantment nor despair. Taken from us swiftly, if calamitously, while new, she remains in the mind's eye forever young, sporting, as in *Hamlet*, "a very riband in the cap of youth."

Early on in this chapter, I posed the question: Why our consuming preoccupation with *Normandie?* Perhaps we have discovered the answer: because she neither aged nor was discarded but was only lamented. Perhaps it is appropriate, in this regard, that our next chapter should dwell exclusively on maritime newborns.

Chapter 6

*But the restriction on the emigration movement has so
reduced the volume of travel that, coupled with high building
and operating costs, the building of further steamships of the
monster type in the near future is rendered problematical.*
   —*Harold Sanderson, chairman, White Star Line, 1924*

The QE2 *is the most famous cruise ship in the world. . . .
The* Crystal Harmony *will be superior to the* QE2. *It will be
superior to the* Royal Viking Sun.
   —*President Minoru Okabe of Crystal Cruises, quoted in
      the* New York Times, *June 8, 1990*

*Personally, I would RUN miles to avoid being involved with a
boatload of Japanese revelers who have no idea of the social
mores which attend civilized behavior and couldn't care less.*
   —*An English expatriate after twenty-one years in Japan*

Special Deliveries

T here used to be a purser on board an RCCL vessel who should
obviously remain unnamed. I say "used to be" because I can
only guess that he no longer works there or, indeed, on board any
cruise ship anywhere.

This man's obsession was an overwhelming distaste for passengers, the phobic equivalent, if you will, of a butcher who cannot
stand beef or a dentist repelled by teeth. Such was his loathing that
he tried to avoid even seeing, let alone addressing, any passengers
throughout their week on board. He went so far as to rearrange
the furniture in his office so that, in the event he inadvertently
glanced up from his desk, he saw a blank wall rather than a passenger. Somehow he managed to avoid both captain's receptions, remaining in self-imposed purdah until disembarkation, when he
rejoiced in a few hours of carefree peace before the next passenger
load engulfed him.

This misanthropic episode underscores the darker side of seven-day passenger-crew symbiosis. Though I touched on matters of this kind in "Backstage," chapter 7 of *Liners to the Sun*, perhaps it deserves a chapter of its own someday. Patently, that unhappy purser was in the wrong business, and I can only assume that he managed to find more suitable employment ashore.

Having said that, as a marine historian rather than a purser, I must confess that I, too, secretly relish a deserted vessel. Evaluating newbuilding is easier without passenger clutter: A sweep of pool and Sun Deck, first impression of public rooms in repose, a deserted embarkation lobby—all seem somehow easier to absorb and comprehend unused. So I rejoice in the pristine look of what is called in the shipping industry newbuilding, any vessel fresh from the yard. The first of any new class is always the most special, but even the successors have their own individual appeal.

It is a curious fact that maritime younger sisters occasionally overshadow their predecessors. A classic case in point involves the second of the White Star Line's *Olympic*-class vessels: The RMS *Titanic* sailed on her maiden voyage a year later than the *Olympic*, and because of that iceberg, her four-day career has been scrutinized far more exhaustively than her older sister's quarter century. Conversely, second-of-the-class *Queen Elizabeth* never aroused the same loving passenger response as did the *Queen Mary*. Though unquestionably the more modern and daring of the pair, she never achieved *Queen Mary*'s legendary appeal; moreover, according to her crew, she was never as happy a ship, either.

The tenor of a delivery crossing is unique. All is not only new; it is also scarcely unpacked. One can see precisely what owner and designer intend. Each passing sea day, the ship, its decor, and its systems come more alive. There is a compelling deadline, of course, to have everything ready, not only for the U.S. Coast Guard's rigorous inspection of lifesaving systems but also for hordes of travel agents and the travel press, who, long before the ship was handed over at the yard, were invited for an overnight cruise or at least a reception and dinner, as well as a chance to examine cabins and public rooms.

Over the past decade, I have been fortunate enough to have sailed on a variety of new ships as they were delivered from the yard of their birth to their first passenger port. In this chapter, I propose documenting four of these special deliveries: the *Sovereign of the Seas*, the *Royal Viking Sun*, the *Crystal Harmony*, and the

Crown Princess. Three crossed the North Atlantic and one the Pacific, or at least the Pacific as far as Hawaii. Two carried selected passenger loads, one traveled at full capacity, and one traveled with only two passengers—myself and my wife, Mary.

Because the *Sovereign of the Seas* was touted as the world's largest cruise ship (about which more in a moment), let us deal with her first. She was a prototype, the first 74,000-ton megaship for Royal Caribbean Cruise Line. Laid down in the French yard called Chantiers de l'Atlantique at St.-Nazaire in June 1986, she was the company's fifth hull, three times the size of the first. Having started business with an identical 18,500-ton trio in the early 1970s, ten years later they ordered the 37,000-ton *Song of America*, an experimental bridge ship uniting modest *Song of Norway* with leviathan *Sovereign of the Seas* to come.

The *Sovereign of the Seas* was a giant step beyond anything the company had ever undertaken before and the first company newbuilding not ordered from Wärtsilä, the historic Finnish builder.

Overwhelming economic considerations mandated the change from Finland to France. The *Sovereign* cost Royal Caribbean Cruise Line $200 million, but a large additional cost was underwritten by the French government. Garnering the *Sovereign*-class, three-ship contract was a lucrative coup for the French yard. Director General Alain Grill told me that to maintain optimum industrial health, his yard should ideally launch one passenger newbuilding each year. And over the eighties and into the nineties, he has managed to do nearly that. The Chantiers de l'Atlantique's recent and forthcoming newbuilding flotilla is impressive: the *Nieuw Amsterdam* (1983), the *Noordam* (1984), the car ferry *Marrakech* (1986), the *Sovereign of the Seas* (1987), the *Star Princess* and the car ferries *Daniele Casanova* and *Bretagne* (1989), the *Nordic Empress* (1990), the *Monarch of the Seas* (1991), the *Majesty of the Seas* and the *Dreamward* (1992), and the *Windward* (1993). (These last two, while still unnamed, were prechristened by wags *Forward* and *Backward*.)

If you go shopping on board both the *Sovereign of the Seas* and NCL's *Norway* today, you can buy company-logoed T-shirts that proclaim each vessel the world's largest. Just as they always did on the North Atlantic, superlatives still sell. At 1,035 feet overall, the *Norway-ex-France* is unquestionably the longest passenger vessel in the world; it is also the widest, exceeding, alas, by only one foot that *ne plus ultra* of the shipbuilding trade known as "Panamax," the largest beam acceptable for transiting Panama's 110-foot-wide locks. French President Charles de Gaulle airily dismissed that serious *France* shortcoming with the breezy assurance that the ship was not too wide, *the canal was too narrow*. In fact, the exigencies of length-to-beam ratio argue that any hull exceeding 1,000 feet is invariably wider that 110 feet. Of the three other 1,000-foot-plus vessels ever built—the *Normandie*, the *Queen Mary*, and the *Queen Elizabeth*—none could negotiate Panama's canal. Cunard's current flagship, *Queen Elizabeth 2*, with a beam of 105 feet 2½ inches, manages to squeeze through.

On New Year's Day, 1988, *Norway*'s passenger capacity—with every bunk filled—was 2,285. That weekend, RCCL's *Sovereign of the Seas* ("The World's Largest Cruise Ship") swept into Miami. Though she was only 880 feet overall and can negotiate the Panama Canal with ease, her owners maintained that at 74,000 gross registered tons, with a maximum passenger capacity of 2,512, *Sovereign* could justifiably usurp *Norway*'s title; capacity and the area of enclosed deck are what really add up. End of round 1.

Round 2 began in the fall of 1990, and *Norway* came out swinging. After a vertical expansion at Bremerhaven, she returned to Florida with 135 new cabins parked up around her twin funnels, which raised both her enclosed deck tally as well as her passenger capacity to above the *Sovereign*'s. Her new maximum passenger load is 2,565.

Round 3? Royal Caribbean Cruise Line returned to the fray with *Monarch of the Seas* in the fall of 1991. Because of various structural amplifications from prototype *Sovereign*—one less passenger cinema and one less crew gymnasium—she boasts a maximum passenger load of 2,766, or 254 more than her sister and 201 more than *Norway*.

And so it goes. Does it matter—does anyone care? Apparently both companies do. No one should ever underestimate the potent marketing lure of "the biggest." This recent NCL/RCCL imbroglio duplicates the post–World War I fracas involving Ballin's Hamburg American trio; new owners of the renamed *Berengaria*, *Leviathan*, and *Majestic* squabbled continually over "the biggest" throughout the twenties.

While the *Sovereign* was under construction, I had visited the shipyard on the Loire six months before my projected December embarkation. Shipyard inspections when a vessel is, as they say, "in steel" are daunting for a variety of reasons. Large interior spaces are filled with scaffolding, cabins are littered and seem distressingly small, and progress everywhere is hampered underfoot by a tangle of wires, cables, hoses, and pipes that the French workers call, with good reason, *le jardin des serpents*. Additionally, vertical ascent before elevators are installed is punishing: clambering from tank top to top-hamper in one go—fourteen decks' worth—demands stamina.

Another confusion about ships in steel is that unless you know what to look for in the way of pipe intrusions, for example, dining room and always-adjacent galley seem sometimes interchangeable; so, too, are lobbies, offices, and small public rooms. Then again, distinguishing passenger from crew areas is difficult, although one invaluable clue is the angle of ascent of their respective staircases. Passenger flights have a conventional, easy slope, whereas back-stage crew stairs are more demanding—steeper, no-nonsense climbs that betray themselves at once.

But however exhausting the ascent to the *Sovereign*'s summit, reward awaited: glimpses of the incomplete top deck that would, alas, never be seen by passengers. The first was construction of a fixture common to all RCCL tonnage, the Viking Crown Lounge, a distinctive, round public room wrapping the single after funnel. Still exposed between interior ceiling and exterior cladding was a fan of radial joists, for all the world like the frame of an open umbrella. Although the joists were aluminum, they exhibited all the simple honesty of Shaker barn framing. Forward, I came across another splendid achievement, the base of the mast. Sheets of glistening aluminum had been cut, shaped, and welded together into a seamless, Brancusi-like whole, workmanship of a high order. It would be covered with white paint, of course, and once the *Sovereign* was in service, passengers would pass it by without a second glance.

Although isolated construction details of this kind have nothing to do with delivery, I record them here in connection with the *Sovereign of the Seas* because they seem symptomatic of the un-sung details of fine shipbuilding. Those almost accidental aesthetics underscore the superb craftsmanship of those St.-Nazairean ship-wrights, their steel-and-aluminum joinery every bit as wondrous as that which their Breton forebears had achieved in wood.

Day visitors to the yard are deprived of those rewarding new-building phenomena, sudden spurts of growth. Unlike unfinished New York skyscrapers, which sometimes seem stalled, a hull

TOP: *The* Sovereign's *Normandie-like stern getting a coat of primer. Midway through construction, the Liberian port of registry was changed from Monrovia to Norway's Oslo; only the two "o"s could be reused.* (Author's collection)

CENTER: *Poised to leave St.-Nazaire forever, the* Sovereign of the Seas *moored in the fitting-out basin at Chantiers de l'Atlantique. Handed over the day previously, she belongs now to RCCL.* (Author's collection)

BOTTOM: *On the bridge for departure: Pilot André Cam, Staff Captain Olav Nyseter (left) and Captain Tor Stangeland.* (Author's collection)

changes overnight. Abruptly, large prefabricated sections of ship materialize from elsewhere in the yard, and once shipfitters have attached them, the profile has changed forever. The soaring line of a stem, for example, is complete only after final bow sections have been welded in place.

When I came back in December for the *Sovereign*'s official handing over, I no longer knew her. Though she still lay within the limpid waters of the shipyard's fitting-out basin, her gray-primed hull was no more: *Sovereign of the Seas* was bridal white. Splashes of color enlivened the profile: Decorative blue-green racing stripes outlined some public-room windows, a palisade of green glass surrounded her upper decks, and orange-topped lifeboats festooned each flank. Both anchors, legacy of some recent test following her regular sea trials, hung clear of the hawsepipe down near the water. Two busy cranes atop the fitting-out pier to starboard swung final loads on board for the crossing to Florida.

Inside Centrum, the five-deck atrium through which one would board in Miami, the scaffolding had vanished. Brass trim glowed along the walls and also the sweeping margins of staircases bisecting the void, what Norwegian designer Njål Eide has called "parade staircases." Since every square foot of lobby and stair was newly carpeted, cautionary signs, taped everywhere, reminded shipyard workers to walk in stockinged feet; this they did, shoes suspended around their necks by tied laces, for all the world like bathers coming home from the beach.

The day of the handing over was unseasonably balmy. A special train from Paris brought 300 shipyard guests down to St.-Nazaire, and we gathered in rare, springlike warmth atop the vessel. After some brief speeches (there would be longer ones at lunch), the tricolor atop the mast came down to the strains of "La Marseillaise." Moments later, Captain Tor Stangeland commanded: "Hoist the Norwegian flag!" The band struck up Norway's national anthem, "Ja, vi elsker detter landet" ("Yes, we love this land of ours"). Once Norway's postal banner was fluttering proudly aloft, RCCL's company flag, bearing the crown-and-anchor logo, joined it at the hoist. It was that simple—the yard no longer owned the vessel; it now belonged to Royal Caribbean Cruise Line.

The vessel was ostensibly complete. Yet although it was certainly navigable, large areas within, around, and atop the vessel, as well as behind the scenes, required additional work. More than 200 shipyard workers would sail with us to Miami to help the crew sort things out. This was in no way unusual. The vessel is never finished, neither "finished" in the sense of passenger-ready nor "finished" in the sense of patina. That is why passengers are seldom invited on deliveries; no one on board has time for them.

Conversely, delivering a vessel with a reduced passenger load does serve one invaluable purpose. As we shall see on board both the *Royal Viking Sun* and the *Crystal Harmony*, they are embarked as guinea pigs and, during the crossing to follow, will help break in stewards, galleys, indeed, the full gamut of passenger expectations: shops, photographers, gymnasia, sauna, cinema, etc. When the *Queen Elizabeth 2* embarked her first passengers in 1969, they were company personnel, "rewarded" with a free cruise but in reality to work the operational kinks out of Cunard's new flagship without company embarrassment.

Two days later, we prepared to sail. I have never departed any port less formally. Customs and immigration officials were tracked to their lair in a nondescript, harbor-front entry of the Port Autonome. There an indifferent *douanier* cleared some Paris Christmas purchases, stamping our passports almost reluctantly.

We boarded that afternoon, quitting our hotel with regret. The Hotel du Berry is a Chantiers de l'Atlantique institution, scrupulously and comfortably run by the Raymond family. So many technical people and cruise-line personnel put up there that it has become almost a quasi-official extension of the yard. In the summer of 1990, a prospective RCCL pastry chef flew from his native Austria to join the *Nordic Empress*. On arrival in Paris, he discovered that he had forgotten his passport. Since, it being Sunday, the yard was closed and no bona fides could be provided, he suggested to Orly's immigration officials in desperation that they telephone Madame Andrée Raymond at the hotel. She vouched for him at once, and he entered France forthwith.

We boarded that afternoon, and a distracted purser's assistant in civilian clothes assigned us a cabin up on Deck 9, just below the top of the line. We manhandled our luggage up there and, at Tor Stangeland's request, repaired to the bridge for departure. At 4:15 P.M. sharp, the *Sovereign's* whistle bellowed, and shepherded by tugs, she backed out of the fitting-out basin for the last time.

As we turned downstream, one fellow passenger, naval architect Odd Martin Hallen, stood with me on the port bridge wing, tearful with joy. "It starts with a simple line on a piece of paper," he exulted, "and ends with"—his open-armed gesture encompassed all of the *Sovereign*—"*this!*"

Thousands of St.-Nazaireans had come out in December's overcast to bid "*adieu à notre* Souverain des Mers.*" Every pier, promontory, and mole was black with townspeople. Inhabitants of shipbuilding ports grow understandably proprietary about local newbuilding and are loath to see it depart; the *Sovereign's* huge bulk represented untold millions of man-hours to St.-Nazaire, but—comforting thought—two more of the same class were to follow.

A flotilla of small craft accompanied us downriver almost as far as the pilot station. Our master never strayed far from the bridge's whistle control, returning dozens of salutes with the *Sovereign's* triple, majestic boom. Royal Caribbean's photographer, perched dangerously in the open door of a persistent helicopter, swarmed about the bow, taking first photographs of the company's completed ship at sea.

Half an hour later, after André Cam, St.-Nazaire's chief pilot, had disembarked, the *Sovereign of the Seas* stood out into the Bay of Biscay. Voyage 00001 had begun.

That evening, we found that we were not quite the vessel's only passengers dining in Outward Bound isolation: Half a hundred French, Norwegian, and American technical staff and subcontractors were on board as well. Since our crossing would encompass Christmas and New Year's, many had brought wives and some their children. A broad cross section of shipmates thus gathered that first hesitant evening in one corner of Kismet, one of the ship's two 600-seat dining rooms. Predictably, the various nationalities staked out their own tables from which some of them never moved throughout the voyage to come. I was reminded of Edward Steiner's dining-saloon memoir penned on board an unnamed steamer years earlier:

> Dinner in the first cabin was fashionably quiet; for it was our first evening meal together, and we were measuring and scanning one another after the manner of fashionable folk, trying to decide with whom it was safe to speak.

But in fact there was one conversational icebreaker, to make an irresistible pun: That dinner, which we realized with alarm was the first of a dozen more, was glacially cold, served from atop an inoperative steam table within the dining-room buffet. There was, hissed a distraught French wife with eyes like pebbles, *"une problème avec vapeur"*: Our steam table was patently bereft of steam. That evening's pork chops had congealed, blanketed with *sauce arctique*, so we made do with some admirable *chèvre*. Mercifully, *vapeur* reappeared on the morrow and remained for the balance of the crossing. My notes about those cafeteria dinners in Kismet dining room set the tone:

> kings of the kitchen—Hotel Manager, Cruise Director, Food and Beverage Manager—gather with all the wine they can handle; we passengers, even the French, must make do with water or orange juice. . . .

In fact, the powers that be later relented, and wine was allowed at the low tables as well.

Although one hallmark of any sea voyage is indolence, it was conspicuously absent on board the *Sovereign* over the next week and a half. All outer decks had to be covered—the Sun Deck with acres of green Astroturf and the encircling promenade with a kind of rubberoid decking. This latter was also glued directly on top of the steel. The seams of the pink-and-ocher sections were weighted down as their adhesive dried with Belgian paving blocks that the resourceful staff captain, Olav Nyseter, had remembered to bring from France. Each evening, he jogged around the still-uncompleted deck, skipping nimbly through an obstacle course of paving blocks, demijohns of cement, and rolls of decking.

Indoors, the whine of vacuum cleaners never ceased; regardless, the heels of all of our shoes throughout the crossing were adorned with fluff whiskers, legacy of brand-new carpet. Signage went up, loudspeakers were tested, light levels were set, and kilometers of brass railing were coaxed to a shine. One of the hardest tasks was removing handprints from Centrum's highest brass reaches. Chief Passenger Steward Roderick Smith ("I cannot *stand* a dirty ship!") supervised a team of cleaners roped as though for the Matterhorn. They clambered cautiously atop thirty-five-foot ladders, wielding long-handled mops and squeegees to erase every offending smudge.

Paradoxically, the *Sovereign*-class ships' most successful public room is that huge atrium. Earlier, we discussed its superiority over *Fantasy*'s equivalent space, Grand Spectrum. Rather than Grand Spectrum's excavation, Centrum's void is bisected and bridged by staircases, via which passengers may ascend or descend as well as move forward or aft. Unlike department-store escalator flights that are interconnected top and bottom, successive Centrum stairs are not contiguous but are removed from each other; one is obliged to remain on each level momentarily, walking around the edge to continue one's vertical progression. Hence, one *lingers* in Centrum by design.

And with reason, for there is always something to see. Centrum is a vertical and horizontal crossroads, accommodating intriguing passenger and crew traffic on any of its several levels throughout the day. In fact, I found during the maiden voyage that passengers spent as much time hanging over Centrum's railings as they did over the railings lining Promenade Deck. This is a significant design achievement and should suggest to cruise-ship planners that sun, sea, and scenery are not necessarily their vessel's only currency.

There was one irresistible Centrum goof that came to light along the purser's marble desk. Although a handsome mail slot had been cut and beveled through the counter, I noticed one day that it had been taped over. It turned out that an unnamed St.-Nazairean carpenter had thought of everything but a means of emptying it: No supplementary door had been provided to retrieve letters.

One overwhelming demand of *Sovereign*-sized tonnage is that there must be at least one public room on board to accommodate one sitting; in other words, half the ship's capacity passenger load. Hence, the huge 1,200-seat auditorium, Follies, which dominates the afterend of what is called, alas, Showtime Deck. (Oh, owners, pray stick with generic and avoid fanciful deck names!) Follies was designed by the Danish designer Mogens Hammer, who was our shipmate for the crossing. He had cut his show-lounge teeth, if you will, with the *Song of America*'s Can-Can Lounge five years earlier. Follies is a handsome space with admirable sight lines, made better by the providential removal of four steel columns that were redundant, it turned out during the *Sovereign*'s vibration-free trials.

One amusing inaccuracy, still in place, mars the starboard enterclose. En route into Follies, photographs line the walls, captioned, presumably, by someone (Mogens?) whose first language is certainly not English. One photograph—taken, I would guess, at Paris's Crazy Horse Saloon—shows a line of bare-breasted chorus

TOP: *One of the hanging stair-cases that so pleasingly bifurcates Centrum. Few other shipboard atria work as well.* (Author's collection)

Crown Lounge genesis: CENTER: *A model of the proposed, clearly inadequate original treatment for the* Song of Norway's *"funnel pavilion."* BOTTOM: *Seating over 250, the ultimate Viking Crown Lounge on the* Sovereign of the Seas, *with its neon-fired, indigo-spilling logo just below.* (Author's collection)

girls wearing, for some pornochoreographic conceit, American football shoulder pads. The caption proclaims that "to please American tourists, nipples peep coyly from beneath beautifully abbreviated *baseball* uniforms" (italics mine). I was going to alert Mogens but decided not to—it seemed nit-picking. To my knowledge, the spurious caption is still in place, and I am only surprised that passenger jocks have not objected; maybe the girls cloud the mind.

Throughout the crossing, Follies echoed to the thunder of tapping feet; the cruise director, Ray Rouse, and his entertainers were deep in rehearsal, readying (yet) another production show for the *Sovereign*'s maiden voyage. It saddens me that within today's enormous seagoing music halls, so little fresh or original work is performed.

My profound apologies to the boys and girls of the chorus and their hardworking choreographers: You and your talented colleagues, at sea all over the world, sing and dance your hearts out, putting in killing hours to such indifferent ends. The fault lies not with you—you are merely doing your job and doing it well—but back at company headquarters, at the top of the entertainment chain. There every company's resident impresarios are hunkered down for a relentless chorus-line war with their rivals, a war that has escalated, Vietnam-like, out of control.

Ammunition for this unwinnable war is restricted to more and more ambitious (and more and more identical) production shows. On board almost every ship of every line, cruise after cruise, numbingly derivative numbers are proudly unveiled, each a forgettable facsimile of dozens more that have gone before. They all seem to be "Salutes": Salute to Broadway, Salute to Hollywood, Salute to Rogers and Hammerstein, Salute to Gershwin, Salute to Cole Porter, Salute to Oscar—salute, ultimately, ad nauseam. The musical lingua franca is whatever will appeal to the lowest common passenger denominator, instantly identifiable standards to send the ship's company whistling on their way, as inoffensively bland and familiar as Muzak.

There must be something more—more riveting, more enterprising, or more interesting—to animate those huge shipboard stages than this repetitive musical pap. As it is, as a chronic passenger who enjoys an evening of cabaret, I almost never go to production shows; moreover, I seldom see passengers leaving them who are not yawning. During the *Seaward*'s delivery crossing, there was some kind of intergalactic nonsense onstage, interrupted at a climactic moment by a breathy "radio" voice intoning over a loud-speaker: "Mission in trouble, mission in trouble," words that might well be the leitmotif of contemporary shipboard entertainment.

With that off my chest, back to the delivery of the *Sovereign of the Seas*. I remarked earlier that the vessel was not finished; however, all of its public rooms were. Though filled with empty chairs and tables, they remained unoccupied by passengers and unmanned by stewards or musicians. The cumulative effect of those brilliantly illuminated, empty spaces was unsettling; in the deserted Schooner Bar, almost imperceptible engine tremors caused empty barstools to revolve eerily, as though just vacated by ghost passengers. The end result was that mealtimes, especially dinners, were cherished, just as they used to be years ago, before bingo, horse racing, casinos, or production shows offered alternatives elsewhere. Our corner of Kismet served as our only, addictive social focus; each evening, no one wanted to relinquish that fragile shipboard community.

Stays at table lengthened, never more than on Christmas and New Year's eves, when Captain Stangeland hosted two banquets to test lounges as well as dining rooms—Gigi for Christmas Eve and Kismet a week later. The entire shipload was invited. What evocative and festive evenings they were! Even the Chinese laundrymen, who have their own galley far below and seldom ascend above it, attended en masse. The dining room was filled, every table crowded for the first time. As at Christmastime on board all Norwegian vessels, cabled greetings arrived throughout the evening from officer friends on other ships; each was read aloud by the master as it was delivered to the dining room.

In between banquets, all the stewards who waited on us sat down to a dinner of their own; the ship's officers and many of us supernumeraries became pro tem stewards for the occasion. Our steward-clients enjoyed themselves hugely and, over postprandial brandy and cigars, blithely presented Captain Stangeland with a generally positive passenger comment card, a Christmas dig at RCCL's reliance on their passenger-rating system.

Among the many subcontractors I met on board the *Sovereign* that crossing was the man in charge of installing and manning many cruise ships' laundries, Karl Woraschk, a white-bearded Brahms look-alike. His firm, headquartered in Bremerhaven, not only designs and selects the equipment for keeping cruise ships' linen and uniforms in trim; it also supplies hardworking Chinese from Hong

Kong to man them, a Sino-Teutonic linkage of which I had never been aware before. In fact, on that crossing, Karl shared a piece of ship's laundry lore that I have observed ever since. Never, he told me, tokenly refold your napkin at the end of a meal; it only means that somewhere far below the following day, a Chinese worker has to *un*fold it before it goes into the washing machine.

Let us complete *Sovereign*'s Christmas celebration with Karl's Yule cabin episode. He was on board with a charming companion, Jutta Johlmann. When they finally left the Christmas Eve dinner, they went below to their cabin on B Deck. There Jutta produced two precious sparklers, brought especially from Germany for the occasion. At midnight, seated solemnly on opposing bunks, Karl and Jutta lit their sparklers, reenacting a traditional custom from both their childhoods.

After the sparklers had gone out, Karl glanced out the porthole and was surprised to see a single red light glowing in the distance. He called Jutta over to look, wondering what mysterious vessel was accompanying them that far out in mid-Atlantic. Jutta pointed out that the little red light was not outside the cabin but a porthole reflection of their ceiling's smoke alarm, reacting to the smoke of their Christmas sparklers.

At that very moment, the telephone rang, a call from the bridge.

"This is the officer of the watch speaking," announced a crisp Norwegian voice. "Do you have a fire down there?"

"No" was Karl's inspired reply, "just some heavy smokers."

As we reached Miami's latitude and turned west, the winter weather relented, and for the first time, Sun Deck pools were flushed of shipyard grime and filled with warmed seawater. A stroll along the Promenade Deck after dinner became a pleasant evening ritual, and I was pleased to discover one of the *Sovereign*'s marvelous accidental aesthetics. Standing amidships at the rail, I noticed that the roiled white water of our passage was tinged violet. The light came from above my head, from the RCCL crown-and-anchor logo at the funnel's base. Too far outboard to be floodlit, as on other company tonnage, the *Sovereign*'s logo is self-illuminated, outlined in neon tubing instead. As a result, an enchanting indigo wash parallels the vessel all night.

Arrival in Florida was stunning. Royal Caribbean Cruise Line had ingeniously contrived to have *Sovereign of the Seas* reach Miami for the first time on Sunday afternoon of New Year's Day weekend. Hence, the ship made her ceremonial entry into the

TOP: *In mid-Atlantic, half of the* Sovereign's *Sun Deck has been surfaced with artificial turf. Deck chairs came aboard in Miami.* (Author's collection)

BOTTOM: *Delivery achieved: Escorted by an armada of pleasure boats, inbound* Sovereign of the Seas *arrives on Miami station.* (Royal Caribbean Cruise Line)

port at 2:00 P.M. We encountered not only an armada of more than a hundred Sunday sailors but a grandstand assembly of Sunday-sailing cruise ships as well, lining Dodge Island's berths along our port side. Escorted by our welcoming yacht flotilla, heralded by tugs sending red, white, and blue water plumes aloft, and buzzed by squadrons of news helicopters, the *Sovereign of the Seas* made her majestic way up Government Cut. Every railing was packed with cheering figures. Our whistle, mute since France, bellowed repeatedly as Stangeland, resplendent in tropical whites now, acknowledged salutes from all sides.

Those triple-blast whistles, ours and theirs, provided a nonstop accompaniment to our port entry. As we glided past each moored vessel, their whistled hail and *Sovereign*'s response lasted exactly as long as our hulls overlapped. The cumulative intensity of those whistled exchanges, the unceasing roar of helicopters, the cheers, and, indeed, our stately progression into the very heart of Miami were no less deafening than moving; one's eyes filled. Nothing that followed, neither christening nor maiden voyage, surpassed the poignancy of *Sovereign*'s first American landfall, completion of a very special delivery.

The *Royal Viking Sun*'s late-1989 delivery seemed more like a regular seasonal positioning crossing, as when Royal Viking vessels forsake summer Mediterranean for winter Caribbean. There were 400 passengers on board, slightly more than half a shipload, who had been recruited in two successive waves. First, the company offered free passage to anyone who had already booked the *Royal Viking Sun*'s entire circle-Pacific cruise to come. However, since this delivery involved a December Atlantic crossing from Greenwich to Miami, very few accepted the offer. So Royal Viking broadened its appeal, selling the crossing (at a favorably reduced per diem) to any former Royal Viking passenger who chose to come. Both groups sailed subject to an iron-clad, two-word company caveat: "No complaints."

As an inveterate delivery-crossing aficionado, I asked if I could come as well and was driven through a late-November evening downpour from London to Greenwich. Security that sodden evening was tight because the Princess Royal was coming on board for a Save the Children benefit. The *Sun* was anchored out in the Thames, and we rode one of her modernistic tenders to embark. Embarking with us were four Household Cavalry trumpeters in mufti, carrying their instruments as well as glistening, thigh-high boots wrapped in plastic.

On board, a London constable stood sentry in the vessel's lower lobby. At the purser's office, we found we had been given a splendid cabin, number 43, on the starboard side of Discovery Deck. It was very large and comfortable, complete with (our first) terraced balcony, which would prove both a delight and a hazard during the crossing to follow. The beds, we discovered late that evening, after Her Royal Highness had disembarked, were the most comfortable we had ever encountered on board any ship—a kind of Swedish mark called Dux, I believe, with a suspiciously thin mattress atop an extraordinarily thick box spring. The cabin contained three sliding doors in all, one for the balcony, another for a walk-in closet, and a third dividing bathroom and sink from toilet; all, alas, would prove defective, one way or the other, in the days to come.

The great unspoken advantage of a private balcony is that it means, in effect, one has an openable porthole. This is a luxury aboard today's air-conditioned ships. Leaving our door slightly ajar overnight infused the cabin with the haunting aroma and sound of the sea.

That first night at anchor, peering over the edge of our balcony in the Thames drizzle, I was surprised that the ring of lifeboats surrounding the *Royal Viking Sun* was well out of sight, hanging two decks farther down. This was a change from previous Royal Viking tonnage, where occupants of high-priced balcony suites often found their view was blocked by lifeboats. Clearly, on this fourth and radically revamped Royal Viking vessel, lifeboats had been banished from all upper decks adorned with balconies; but, as I would find out once daylight broke, at unfortunate cost to almost every public room.

Before one can properly evaluate the *Sun*, a glimpse of the earliest Royal Viking predecessors is revealing. Let us contrast this fourth Royal Viking vessel with the first, *Royal Viking Star*, which entered service back in 1972. Her original design included no balconies whatsoever, though a few were added later, top-deck dressing built into the vessel when she was stretched in the early eighties.

I have always felt that the initial lack of balconies on the *Star* was symptomatic of the company's entire philosophy. Early Royal Viking cruise life was intended to be luxurious but paradoxically simple, a classic, old-fashioned shipboard regime for experienced

TOP: *First sight of the* Royal Viking Sun *anchored off Greenwich in December 1989. Decks are stacked the full width of the vessel, promising capacious interiors.* (Author's collection)

BOTTOM: *The seating area on the stern seems curiously bleak, isolated from the rest of the* Sun's *shipboard life.* (Author's collection)

passengers. From the beginning, the line booked older and richer passengers than sailed on board other cruise ships; their tastes and expectations had been shaped by years on board ocean liners as well as the *Kungsholm* and the *Gripsholm* of the Swedish-American Line. On board Royal Viking ships, they found elegant service, generous if traditional cabins, and public rooms of the old school. There was significantly little glitz. However, one fundamental design limitation resulted from founder Warren Titus's insistence that the single-sitting dining room (a Royal Viking hallmark) abut the Bergen Lounge on the same deck. This meant that a galley occupied the forward part of Main Deck, denying passengers a forward, semicircular lounge, as on, for instance, rivals *Sagafjord* and *Vistafjord*.

But there was splendid forward-looking compensation high above, sited atop the bridge. The *Star's* Stella Polaris Lounge, a horseshoe-shaped aerie walled with plate glass, overlooked the bow and both forward flanks. Extraordinarily comfortable chairs furnished this ideal arena for sightseeing, reading, dozing, tea, or cocktails, a room for all hours with hypnotic views that, for comfort and visibility, has never been equaled—certainly not on board the *Royal Viking Sun.*

But the most subtle and ingenious aspect of that original Royal Viking design manifested itself out of doors, at the confluence of several open decks aft. There, just outside the cheerful Dolphin Bar, was a sheltered veranda overlooking the swimming pool. Umbrellaed tables and chairs along it gave way, on either side, to deck chairs lining afterpromenades that extended toward the stern to form an open, U-shaped balcony enclosing the pool on three sides.

Passengers trudging around Promenade Deck had, periodically, to pass through that veranda, underscoring its designation as the *Royal Viking Star's* bustling crossroads, the same role that Centrum fulfills indoors on board the *Sovereign of the Seas.* During every late morning at sea, sedentary needlepointers or readers sitting in the veranda's shade mingled with Bloody Mary drinkers spilling out from the Dolphin Bar; ranks of deck-chaired sun worshipers to port and starboard lay within hailing distance of swimmers at the pool. After their final laps, walkers would join friends already enjoying a cocktail and awaiting lunch, most often an al fresco alternative offered nearby.

(All morning, cooks and stewards had been setting up an elaborate outdoor spread. That informal but lavish buffet was dished up at a location that the vessel's Finnish designers had obviously never anticipated; I suspect that it was an expedient dreamed up by an early Royal Viking hotel manager. Though an arduous daily chore, that deck luncheon became an integral part of Royal Viking's indulgent formula, and no passenger, to my knowledge, ever objected to squealing galley racks of platters being manhandled back and forth over the Bergen Lounge's carpet, the only major artery from the galley aft.)

I have purposely re-created a typical sea day on the *Star* because it illustrates cruising's great socioarchitectural truth, to wit: Rewarding passenger life is inevitably contingent on sound naval architecture. However disparately occupied, the *Star*'s passengers basked in splendid *adjacency*—not crowded but within congenial reach of one another, whether swimmers, sunners, walkers, sitters, drinkers, needlepointers, dreamers, sleepers, or readers.

Deck configurations on the *Sun*, alas, have subverted that traditional Royal Viking communality. And the villain of the piece is the large number of private balconies—145 spread over three decks—flanking the superstructure. Herein lies the *Royal Viking Sun's* disappointingly retrograde design.

Incorporating unobstructed views for so many balconies meant lowering the lifeboat ring from its position high up on the *Star* to the lowest public-room deck on the *Sun*. To be fair, lifeboats and their placement are a perennial naval architectural conundrum; although essential to safety, lifeboats are often antithetical to efficient or pleasing design; like uninvited guests, they must be grudgingly accommodated somewhere.

So, on the *Sun*, hanging above the Promenade Deck encircling the dining room, are all the vessel's lifeboats. They obscure every public-room window. Elitism colors this design decision: Passengers with balconies have no lifeboats blocking their view; those *without* balconies, using the public rooms, cannot avoid them. Did nobody at Wärtsilä or Royal Viking headquarters stop to think what was happening? Apparently not.

And what happens to walkers using this low Promenade Deck? Their after crossover expands into a sitting area, a pallid equivalent, if you will, of the *Star*'s sociable little veranda. There is neither adjacent bar nor adjacent pool; in fact, there is precious little adjacency anywhere on board the *Sun*. Though it carries the same number of passengers—750—as did the *Star*, it is far bigger and hence spread out. Those walkers, needlepointers, and readers are

TOP: *Almost every public-room window the length of Norway Deck has its view obscured by a lifeboat.* (Author's collection)

CENTER: *The handsome interior of the Sun's Stella Polaris lookout does not compensate for the flawed exterior view.* BOTTOM: *Moral for owners: If you cannot see the prow, the lookout does not work.* (Author's collection)

isolated on their afterdecks, out of touch with fellow passengers dispersed higher up throughout the vessel.

Some are doubtless swimming. Of the three pools on board, one forward is for the crew; passengers swim in two alternatives farther aft. The first is a rectangular pool in a narrow cul-de-sac between gym and spa at the afterend of Scandinavia Deck, a bleak exercise facility, for fitness rather than fun. The second pool is two decks higher still, in the midst of a sun bowl atop the vessel. Strange anomaly, that upper pool's afterend boasts what is called a "swim-up bar," a disconcerting crescent of underwater barstools. This seems wow-the-rubes gimmickry for seven-day tonnage rather than for Royal Viking's flagship.

In sum, on the *Sun*, the *Star*'s admirable passenger focus is diffused. Dispersed over too many ample decks, passengers have no congenial crossroads anywhere. By day, they are irreparably fragmented, yesterday's enviable Royal Viking symbiosis a thing of the past.

One final design shortcoming awaits high up and forward in the lookout bar, still nostalgically called Stella Polaris. This is less horseshoe than semicircle, with more front-row seats than on the *Star, from none of which can the bow be seen.* For directly outside Stella Polaris's windowed facade lies an encircling apron of teak, a throwaway deck without access. It cannot be used, and worse, it cuts off the lower half of the view as ruthlessly as a ruffled Elizabethan collar.

When I asked why that intrusive (and useless) extension existed, Captain Ola Harsheim advised me that its purpose was "to preserve the forward profile slope of the ship." Something is very wrong when ship stylists care more about their vessel's appearance from afar than perquisites for its (paying) passengers on board.

One sensed immediately from several characteristics of the *Royal Viking Sun* that the company was anxious to break away from its ancient constituents. These days, cruise lines that once catered largely to widows or the elderly have their corporate hearts set on attracting younger passengers. Ever since I first started sailing with the line in 1981, that quest has continued relentlessly.

What they seek—indeed, what *all* cruise lines seek—are elusive dream passengers: rich, bronzed, ageless and chic sportifs, the kind of flawless godlike mannequins adorning every cruise line rendering, those familiar "active relaxers" from Holland America.

I always wonder: How many active relaxers are really out there? Are there enough to go around?

Royal Viking obviously thinks so. Too much of the *Sun* has been wrought specifically to accommodate them: a heavy preoccupation with sports (there is even a miniature croquet course to port of the funnel), an elaborate, Nautilus-equipped gymnasium, a sauna-spa, a lap pool, provision of a larger (and louder) show lounge, generally gaudier decor, that little swim-up bar, and, perhaps the most blatant widow-discouragement of all, not one single cabin anywhere on board. At least there is no discotheque, although my suspicion is that for the most part the discotheque has peaked.

For the delivery crossing, I was delighted that Karl and Jutta, our German shipmates from the *Sovereign of the Seas*, were on board for the *Sun*'s delivery as well. We four sat together throughout the crossing and chose a table in one of the vessel's trio of dining rooms. When the first three Royal Viking ships were lengthened, the dining rooms became long, imposing marathon tray runs for stewards stationed at the dining rooms' afterend. On the *Sun*, the dining area is kidney-shaped, wrapped around a portside galley and, like Gaul, divided into three parts: Two larger sections amidships and aft are connected by a smaller, narrow third. The aftermost is presumably the most coveted, incorporating the captain's table as well as greenhouse views over the stern. Ceiling domes over many tables are irritating acoustical traps, however, and alcoves for some of the largest round tables are too tight for easy steward access.

We preferred what I call the corridor dining room, the space connecting aft and forward chambers. Admittedly, it was sometimes choked with traffic, passengers en route to and from their tables aft as well as sommeliers queued up at their *cave*. Nevertheless, I liked its view of the sea, its central location, and even its bustle.

Then, too, that narrow dining room boasted its own private escape, a mirrored semicircular staircase leading one deck up to my favorite room on board, the paneled, Muzak-free Oak Room, an evening snuggery for fifteen lucky passengers sited between the barren Cardroom and the conventional Casino. The U.S. Coast Guard as well as company prudence vetoed its working fireplace despite exhaustive fire-protection provisions worked into its original specifications. Facsimile electric coals glow comfortingly instead. I noticed a smoke smudge on the otherwise pristine firebrick, and a Wärtsilä chum confessed that he and some colleagues had actually roasted some sausages there at the yard, incontrovertible proof that cruising's first working fireplace actually could work.

That Oak Room is a sheer delight, the kind of public room that is becoming increasingly rare on contemporary ships, despite the classic, uncomplicated ambience it provides: somewhere quiet for passengers to sit and talk. The Oak Room is as serene as it is convivial; one only wishes that lamps were on the tables, provision of which would do much to domesticate the space a little more.

Throughout the delivery crossing, we ate every meal in the dining room, as though in the old days. In fact, no other dining room was complete. Once the vessel entered proper service, *Royal Viking Sun* passengers would have two catering alternatives high atop the afterend of the ship. By day, lunch would be served to starboard in an elegant cafeteria called the Garden Café, indoor equivalent of the company's former outdoor luncheons. At night, passengers could also use the Royal Grill to port. That Grill is extra-tariff: In other words, for a supplementary charge of forty-five dollars per person, passengers book dinner with friends of their choice during evenings at sea.

Extra-tariff restaurants on board ships date back from earlier days on the North Atlantic. The first one ever established was on board the *Deutschland* in 1903. Perhaps the finest were the *Normandie's* Café-Grill and the famous Veranda grills atop both *Queens*. Interestingly enough, the only three extra-tariff restaurants on board contemporary vessels exist on board Kloster Cruises tonnage: the *Seaward's* Palm Restaurant, Le Rendezvous on board the *Norway*, and the *Sun's* above-mentioned Royal Grill.

Since the first two are located on board seven-day ships in the Caribbean, I had been convinced in advance that most *Seaward* or *Norway* passengers would have neither the money nor the inclination to pay extra for a meal during their week-long cruise. On the other hand, on board the upscale *Sun*, I had anticipated that passengers sailing for several weeks at a time would flock to book a table in a supplementary restaurant, regardless of price.

How wrong I was! The very reverse has proved true. Whereas both Palm and Le Rendezvous flourish, the poor Royal Grill has gone out of business, save for occasional in-port lunches. Not surprisingly, Royal Viking regulars would have none of it: Conditioned to high catering standards down in the regular dining room, they saw no reason to pay heavily for a "better" meal elsewhere. Wrote a disillusioned French waiter-friend working in the Grill near the end:

> Royal Viking's cuisine is based on a Germano-Austrian organization, for us poor French located on Deck 11 at the Royal Grill, we are not given a good reputation, due to the charges which are asked for the passengers to eat in the Grill. . . . It is still very difficult to learn the French way to the American clientele which is mostly afraid to miss the last show instead of the last chocolate soufflé.

So much for marketing surveys: Royal Viking passengers, young and old alike, intransigent to the end, could not be gulled away from free meals in their regular dining room, regardless that many of them in the old days probably did just that on board the *Queens*.

Let us return to the sliding doors in our cabin. Astonishingly, the closet doors had not been equipped with a catch, so that once we entered the Bay of Biscay, the doors opened and closed randomly; I had, finally, to lash them in place with a spare belt overnight. The sliding door within the bathroom, genteel partition between loo and tub, came adrift inside its pocket, and I can only guess that others like it must give trouble all over the ship.

One night, I decided to endure a production show to see how the Norway Lounge, Royal Viking's first deep-dish performing amphitheater, worked out. On the *Star*, the *Sea*, and the *Sky*, the line made do for years with old-fashioned, flat-floored lounges, perfectly adequate for dancing or cabaret but inadequate for increasingly ambitious spectaculars. "For years," deadpanned cruise director Ray Avon by way of introduction that evening, "you thought our performers had no legs." To be honest, I was less worried in the Norway Lounge about the dancers' legs than the legs of some of our more fragile shipmates negotiating the auditorium's precipitous slopes. So steep is the descent that, especially when the Atlantic misbehaved, stewards on permanent *Alpenjäger* duty conducted hesitant clients to their seats.

Mary had retired early that night, and once the show was over, I went up to bed, too. But since she had taken our only "key," a white plastic card with coded holes punched through one end, I was locked out. I knocked on our cabin door, to no response; I knocked harder—still no response. I found a telephone and called, but it chirped unanswered. Concluding that Mary had changed her mind about going to bed early and was still up somewhere on board, I searched the public rooms. Perhaps at the movies? No, the night's film had long since ended, and the cinema was deserted. She was nowhere to be found, not even at our favorite roulette wheel.

So I stopped at the purser's desk and had a duplicate key punched out on a machine kept there specifically for that purpose, then climbed back up to Discovery Deck and opened the door to Cabin 43.

It was empty. So was its adjoining bathroom. But out on the balcony, I saw a crumpled white form that turned out to be Mary, curled up in a corner and wearing, fortunately, a warm nightgown. She had lain down, she told me subsequently, because she had bare feet and the deck underfoot was cold.

Now, on her feet again and obviously fit, Mary signaled in urgent pantomime to her vastly relieved husband to open the sliding balcony door from the inside. I tried but found it completely jammed, as though locked. After pulling, tugging, and wrenching at it to no avail, I called the purser's desk and explained our predicament. Help was dispatched.

Within five minutes, a wonderfully burly Filipino night watchman appeared in the cabin. After I had explained the problem, he tackled the recalcitrant door with the same fruitless results. He soon gave up, and while poor Mary waited arms akimbo, he telephoned the purser's desk and summoned a carpenter. I presumed that he would bring the maritime equivalent of the jaws of life, that lifesaving pneumatic tool that extricates trapped passengers from their crumpled automobiles.

While we waited, I examined the door closely. It seemed racked out of the vertical, with a slightly wider gap between it and the frame at the bottom than at the top. I had a sudden brainstorm. Unlimbering my Swiss Army Knife—without which I *never* travel—I opened its largest screwdriver, inserted it between the door and its jamb, high up near the top, and twisted the knife through ninety degrees. As though I had turned a skeleton key, the door slid magically open and a thoroughly chilled but grateful Mary was finally sprung.

She told me later that she had gone outside for a breath of air before retiring. A gentle pitch of the *Sun* had sent the door sliding forward; it shut and jammed behind her. Fortunately, the night was dry and not unbearably cold, although she found her predicament increasingly uncomfortable.

Thank heaven Mary was relatively warmly dressed; thank heaven, too, she had a husband. If a widow or, indeed, anyone traveling alone had found herself similarly outcarcerated, she might well have spent the night in the open. There is no way to attract anyone's attention that high above the Promenade Deck, especially since it is largely deserted after dark. An agile prisoner might have clambered atop the rail and around the partition onto an adjacent balcony for assistance, but that was patently not a solution for acrophobic Mary. She was not the only balcony prisoner, it turned out: The following day, a stewardess setting up deck chairs and tables along her passengers' balconies was similarly jammed out. One can only assume those sliding doors have since been fixed.

Our arrival in Miami was curiously low-keyed. In fact, the *Sun* was the first Royal Viking vessel to enter the port; customarily, they call at tonier Port Everglades up the coast. So a showy maiden arrival had been laid on.

Landfall was made on December 11, 1989, a Monday; although several cruise ships were in port, we passed nowhere near them. *Royal Viking Sun* was scheduled to tie up at Berth 12, Dodge Island's newest pier, located on the *south* side of the island. Once inside the breakwaters and starting up Government Cut, we veered to port, completely bypassing every cruise ship moored along Miami's conventional entry.

There were fireworks at the pier, of course, although in bright sunlight they tend to be noisy rather than picturesque. Just off the berth, a tug was on station, not to push us into the pier but to serve as a waterborne support for a broad red banner strung across our path, its other end attached to a forklift ashore. The theory was that the *Sun*'s bow would, like a sprinter at the finish line, sunder the tape.

But whoever had selected that broad banner had woefully underestimated its strength. Our raked and rounded bow touched it but did not cut it. We continued inexorably forward, pulling the stubbornly intact banner with us. For a perilous moment, it seemed that either the tug might be capsized or the forklift toppled into Biscayne Bay. The ribbon was finally let go at one end, and to the accompaniment of a brass band and thunderous pyrotechnical salutes, the *Royal Viking Sun* concluded its delivery crossing.

Even before the passengers had disembarked, hundreds of NBC personnel rushed on board, together with florists' assistants carrying what seemed like every poinsettia in South Florida. Bob Hope taped his Christmas special on board the following night, an enviable public relations coup for Royal Viking Line's new vessel.

One difficulty facing Royal Viking was to reconcile the new design of their ship with the expectations of their regular passengers. For years, legions of Royal Viking's clients had known and loved three identical Royal Viking vessels. Many disliked the new ship, some quite articulately. Herewith an extract from a Royal Viking regular with whom we have sailed many times. He wrote from the *Sun* in the midst of the Indian Ocean:

> Dear John and Mary:
>   Getting down to basics: I am not enamored of this new ship. Stupid design flaws (the theatre, for example: too small and a flat floor). GLITZY. And all those myriad tiny, *uncomfortable* barrel-shaped armchairs upholstered in plush which are in the public rooms should be tossed overboard. And the Norway Lounge is a disaster—too many chairs, too many tables, and *no* aisles. Getting either in or out are major endeavors.

Then the tone of his letter brightened, leading me to believe that perhaps there is some hope for the new *Sun* with the old guard.

> They did upgrade my cabin. I now have a private verandah. I never thought I would use it but I do and love it. In fact, I'm out there now sitting in a comfy deck chair.
>   But, Mary, I'm *very* careful and don't quite close the sliding door.

Now fly with me across the Pacific to the port of Yokohama for our third delivery crossing. On a brilliant July day in 1990, we boarded Crystal Cruises' gleaming *Crystal Harmony*, the largest and most ambitious modern cruise ship to be built by Japan's premier Pacific passenger shipping line, NYK, the abbreviation for Nippon Yusem Kaisha, or Japanese Mail Line. Together with 500 Japanese fellow passengers, we were bound for Hawaii, seven calendar days away; because our course lay across the International Date Line, we would profit from an extra sea day, a repeat of July 9 in addition to the regular one.

The *Crystal Harmony* was built at Japan's Mitsubishi yard in Nagasaki. Painted around the white mast base are two horizontal red stripes, subliminal reproduction of NYK's traditional funnel livery of three white and two red stripes banding a black funnel. This is the only, discreet adornment betraying the vessel's Japanese origins. Crystal's American management has selected as its logo twin seahorses facing inboard. And almost every decorative element on board, save for one glorious five-deck chinoiserie mural, seems irrevocably American, or at the least in the international style that contemporary cruise lines affect.

I was anxious to see those interiors, because Dennis Lennon, the British inspiration for the *Queen Elizabeth 2*'s interiors, had originally been approached by a delegation from Mitsubishi. Would he consider the job of designing their new vessel? Dennis was intrigued at the prospect of conjuring up a between-the-wars, across-the-Pacific pastiche, but as he warmed to this theme, he was stopped short. Their vessel's look, the Japanese insisted politely, should have no trace of Japanese or even Pacific idiom at all. It was to look like every other cruise ship. Regretfully, Lennon bowed out.

The Japanese almost got their way. Among all its public rooms, only the little Kyoto restaurant was designed by a Japanese. The rest came from the studios of European designers, the Scandinavians predominating. Robert Tillberg, a Swede, produced the majority of the public rooms as well as the outer decks. Mogens Hammer, Denmark's grand old man of ship design, created the Galaxy Show Lounge, a commission he had also executed so well on board the *Sovereign of the Seas*.

Scandinavia predominates among the officer corps as well. Senior bridge and engineering officers are all Norwegian, with only a leavening of Japanese subordinates. The *Crystal Harmony*'s master was Captain Kai Julsen, an old friend I remembered from the *Sagafjord* back in the early eighties, before Cunard's takeover. The company's head of hotel operations, responsible for the tenor of the vessel's passenger procedures, was young, bespectacled Erling Frydenberg, who served with Royal Viking for years; so, too, had his Austrian hotel manager on board, Dietmar Wertanzl.

It is appropriate that this discussion of the *Crystal Harmony* should follow closely in the *Royal Viking Sun*'s wake, for the two are very similar. Royal Viking's imprint on board *Crystal Harmony* is as inescapable as it is pervasive. RVL regulars will recognize a

TOP: *The Oak Room is unquestionably the most successful public room on board the* Sun. *Even without its working fireplace, it remains a peerless, peaceful original.* (Author's collection)

CENTER: *Crystal Cruise's logo includes a subliminal environmental frisson: the interstices between sea horses suggest a whale's flukes.* (Author's collection)

BOTTOM: *A cruising first: Kyoto Restaurant by day atop Sun Deck offers alternate dining at no extra charge. Italian Restaurant Prego adjoins farther aft.* (Author's collection)

host of familiar faces and resonances, from deft, courteous service to the daily program layout, from Scandinavian cabin stewardesses to sumptuous international buffets.

In fact, there is only one curious but radical departure from the Royal Viking prototype: *Crystal Harmony*'s passengers are accommodated at *two* dining-room sittings rather than one. If Crystal Cruises wishes to attract upscale passengers, it is doubly surprising that this two-sitting ukase was ever formulated; one might have anticipated it from inexperienced Japanese owners, but certainly not from Crystal's savvy American management in Los Angeles. There, at least, they must have been aware that, on upscale cruise lines, Royal Viking in particular, double sittings are the mark of the maritime beast. Though acceptable for seven-day Caribbean tonnage, they remain a definite no-no among cruising's elite.

Regardless, whoever made the decision, Crystal is stuck with it. Short of massive interior renovation, changing two sittings back to one is extremely difficult. Erling Frydenberg suggests that the decision was made back in 1986, during discussion of general arrangements. General arrangements involve basic, immutable decisions, such as numbers and dimensions of decks, speed and motive power, and, certainly, how passengers are accommodated and fed. Monkeying with the G.A. after the fact is dicey: All manner of interlocking spatial as well as manning ramifications are at stake.

The *Crystal Harmony* can embark a hefty 960-passenger capacity (200 more than the *Royal Viking Sun*). Admittedly, a single sitting for a thousand would have meant a dining room the size of an airplane hangar. So, one wonders, why did they not consider two identical dining rooms fore and aft of the galley? This would have fed the shipload at one sitting comfortably, a solution achieved on many luxurious predecessors, the ancient upscale *Caronia* among them.

But Crystal Cruises opted instead for one dining room half the size that would seat the *Harmony*'s passengers in two consecutive shifts. About five hundred can eat at one time within Tillberg's pleasant Crystal Dining Room, sited on Crystal Deck (just aft of Crystal Plaza, near which you can have a cocktail in—natch—Crystal Cove). On the credit side, if one ignores the overpowering sociomaritime stigma, the company's decision not only saved room; it also saved manpower: Half as many dining-room stewards are required; hence, fewer crew cabins had to be provided below.

Inevitably, that dining-room decision spawned a contingent

show-lounge decision: If you feed half the passengers at a time, you entertain half of them at a time as well. Only five hundred *Crystal Harmony* passengers can be seated in Mogens Hammer's Galaxy Lounge, forward on Tiffany Deck, one deck higher. Again, had the company stuck with one sitting, Hammer's show lounge would have had to accommodate an audience of nearly a thousand, an almost impossible achievement on board a 50,000-ton vessel.

Two more thoughts about this sitting dilemma. I have heard that when the Japanese owners first planned their vessel, they were aiming at a median market, somewhere in that middle brow range between Princess and Holland America Line. As their interiors took shape, ambition soared, and the company raised their sociological sights, drawing a bead on Royal Viking and/or Cunard. By then, it was too late: Irrevocable double sittings were already built in. Finally, several Royal Viking friends have sampled the vessel since our delivery crossing; after debriefing them, I found out that only half disapproved of two sittings.

As though compensating for this anomaly, Crystal Cruises has incorporated stunning dining arrangements elsewhere. There are two additional restaurants up on the afterend of Lido Deck called Prego and Kyoto. Prego offers Italian cuisine, while Kyoto serves Japanese food. Significantly (nay, uniquely!), both restaurants have no extra tariff. One dines there as part of the return on a regular passenger ticket, the only trifling expense a tip for that evening's hardworking steward. This scheme of free, alternative dining has intrigued the cruise industry in prospect for years; pizza parlors adorning Costa, Sitmar, and some Princess Cruises vessels were the closest anyone came to it before. But those dispense essentially fast food for impulse nibbling, whereas one enjoys a genuine dining-room alternative in both of Crystal's no-tariff establishments.

Understandably, Kyoto was enormously popular with the Japanese. Reservations had to be made on a first-come, first-served basis at eight each morning; each successive day, the scene at Kyoto's front desk duplicated the shrill frenzy of a Nikkei futures pit. Even though only two basic menus were offered, numbers of wily Japanese, apparently disenchanted with Crystal Dining Room's (excellent) Western fare, were feeding *au japonais* every evening. In so doing, they deprived their more timid shipmates who had not yet booked a table. Though the maître d'hôtel, Cosmo Constanza—another old friend from *Sagafjord*—began restricting repeaters, he still had to institute three sittings per evening to cope with the phenomenal demand. For the future, offering lunch in those upper-deck restaurants would be a nice bonus: Daytime ocean vistas are superb, and the evening crush might be alleviated.

Prego and Kyoto are clear winners, and there is, in fact, a third eatery on board. Hard by the upper level of the Crystal Plaza is the Bistro, a cheerful little coffee bar where drinks, coffee, espresso, and pastry are available for those who slept through breakfast. Better still, they dish up a tolerably good little lunch as well—cheese, prosciutto, *bundnerfleisch*, and admirably crackly *baguettes* appear on a refrigerated cart at noon. This served as our light midday meal on more than one occasion.

Let us climb up to 11, or Lido, Deck on the after staircase and stray forward. Its outdoor portion embraces two separate swimming pools called Neptune and Seahorse. Neptune, the aftermost, can be sheltered or completely covered by a Magrodome roof at the touch of a button, a wise precaution, especially during the often unpredictable Alaskan weather, which *Crystal Harmony* encounters every summer.

That Neptune pool is less interesting than its Lido, where elaborate luncheon buffets are periodically staged. To lend theatrical verisimilitude to a pasta binge one noontime, a gondola cutout was suspended amusingly above the pool. Then a huge rolled backdrop, of La Scalan dimensions, was hung across the pool area's entire afterwall. Once unrolled, it revealed a Venetian canal scene. Less appealing set pieces included several Italian street peddler's carts festooned with plastic vines, cheeses, and salamis. This was no improvised deck buffet but a boisterous, commedia dell'arte extravaganza.

Neptune and Seahorse pool areas are separated by a deckhouse atop the ship's main staircase. On that staircase an ambitious five-deck mural is located, the work of Jun Yamagishi and a gift from the yard to Crystal Cruises. Ingeniously, the staircase hangs about eighteen inches away from its afterwall, so that vertical progression, from landing to landing, offers tantalizing glimpses of this haunting work. Within 11 Deck's entry, a serene full moon floats above a vista of jagged mountain peaks. As one descends, the mountains relent into heavily foliated, mist-shrouded valleys. Down at the bottom, 6 Deck's staircase landing rests at the painting's water level: A lone, ivory-colored junk drifts past isolated villages along a river's winding course through lush, verdant gorges. It is an

TOP: *The after-pool Italian buffet is enlivened by a gondola cutout, a painted backdrop, and ethnic vendors' carts. If rain threatens, close the roof.* (Author's collection)

CENTER: *Under an expanse of* steel *treillage, a gilded harpist plucks eternally in the Palm Court and Garden Lounge.* (Author's collection)

BOTTOM: *Greenery, wicker, and an elevated ocean view combine to form a perfect shipboard interior.* (Author's collection)

enchanting, no less than inspired, piece of staircase whimsy and, incidentally, ideal encouragement to forgo the *Crystal Harmony's* elevators and climb on foot instead. In addition to the mural, it is worth noting that every tread edge on Crystal staircases is lined with tiny light bulbs, an extravagant decorative touch.

Back up on Lido Deck, only slightly winded but invigorated, we can cross the open forward pool area, with its obligatory Jacuzzis, and venture indoors again, this time through the topmost landing of the *Crystal Harmony's* forward staircase. A double entryway leads into one of cruising's most successful public rooms.

At the time of our delivery crossing, it was called Palm Court and Garden Lounge; current deck plans, I note, use only Palm Court. Readers of chapter 3 will recall that shipboard's first Garden Lounge was created by Arthur Davis on board the *Aquitania* in 1914; additionally, inspiration for much of that Cunarder's look was inspired by the same man's pioneering Palm Court at London's Carlton House Hotel. Whoever named this enchanting room for Crystal knows his transatlantic history. The name seems to be enjoying a contemporary renascence; the dining room on board Princess Cruise's *Regal Princess* is also called the Palm Court.

Occupying the entire width of the vessel, that Palm Court is a tranquil oasis of planting and white wicker. Overhead, recalling another *Aquitania* conceit, an expanse of (steel!) treillage arcs gracefully from starboard to port, separating the room beneath three gentle arches. The outboard arches are pierced by two skylights each. Beneath all four are positioned islands of lavish greenery, around which are clustered sofas and chairs. The pleasing, occasional intrusion of mid-ocean sunlight is a masterful stroke to this otherwise coolly shaded interior. An attractive gilded statue of a lady harpist, half size, nestles in a central garden grotto.

Again, in company brochures, the Palm Court is described as an entertainment lounge, but, I am delighted to report, entertainments here are of a traditional, civilized kind that match the tenor of the room, much of it generated by the passengers themselves. The Palm Court accommodates those who read, those taking tea, those talking, those gazing at the sea, or those enjoying good music. A pianoed alcove—mercifully devoid of electronic amplification— provided perfect teatime settings for a recital one day, a string orchestra the next, followed by a Funny Hat Competition for the Japanese and, an ensuing afternoon, dance lessons across a wide crescent of polished mahogany. The *Crystal Harmony's* Palm Court

TOP: *Insulated from the view forward by a bench and a railed teak crescent, the* Crystal Harmony's Vista Lounge *passengers are relegated to seats in the figurative second balcony.* (Author's collection)

BOTTOM: *Tall, uncurtained windows admit appalling glare for much of the day.* (Author's collection)

is a great success—congenial, elegant, and satisfying use of prime shipboard space.

I only wish I could heap the same unadulterated praise on Lido Deck's forwardmost public room. There yawns the *Crystal Harmony*'s much-vaunted Vista Lounge atop the bridge. I say "yawns" with reason. From outside the vessel, one is instantly aware that the Sun Deck forming Vista Lounge's ceiling has a pronounced upward bend, a subtle and, in this event, acceptable variant from the traditional horizontal deck-line norm. (Another contemporary equivalent appears amidships on board all Wind Star tonnage: The afterroof of the upper-deck restaurant curves up as well, a retroussé eave that adds a pleasing, almost Oriental flair to the profile.)

The upward lift of the *Crystal Harmony*'s Sun Deck heightens the ship's windshield, so to speak, raising the Vista Lounge's sweeping crescent of glass appreciably. But to what end? Intriguing as it may look from an airplane, inside it is troubling. That extravagantly achieved extra height creates a spread of very tall glass panels, subdivided by immensely strong vertical mullions. These mullions polarize the view; from any position but dead ahead, white steel visually displaces glass.

Just in front of those imposing windows, Mitsubishi has repeated Wärtsilä's *Royal Viking Sun*'s goof, impeding Vista Lounge's view with a crescent of deck. Moreover, since this deck is usable, the view from what I am tempted to call the Half-Vista Lounge may well be further obscured by an impenetrable palisade of passenger behinds.

Last of all, those tall glass panels admit fearful glare, against which, curiously, no curtaining or shade has been provided. Even though we were sailing on a southeasterly course, the glare in that involuntary solarium both before lunch and at teatime was distressing. I noted all the way across the Pacific that the space was curiously neglected. Admittedly, the vessel was only half full: Perhaps with a capacity shipload more would have used it. But my sense is that the Vista Lounge's postmeridional glare sent many passengers aft to take their tea gratefully within the Palm Court's tranquil shade. Though a live harpist plays in that forward crescent, cruise director David de Haviland arranged to have her instrument miked, perpetuating, alas, yet another Vista Lounge error.

With only one exception, the other public rooms are successful. I especially liked the out-of-the-way Avenue Saloon, aft on the starboard side of Tiffany Deck. It lies adjacent to a large, restless nightclub called the Club 2100 and far away from the hectic glitz of the Galaxy Lounge. It is removed from both temperamentally as well: Boasting some of the Palm Court's blessed serenity, it remains a pleasant, conversation-friendly rendezvous for drinks before or after dinner. It turned out to be the Norwegian officers' favorite retreat as well, and I always trust their judgment.

The exception? An intrusive casino called Caesar's Palace at Sea, an unlovely Las Vegan import that seems an incongruous decorative addition to such an otherwise harmoniously appointed vessel. Muscling onto Crystal Plaza's upper level, its entrance is framed within dead white Corinthian columns and a bogus plaster bas-relief. Caesar's Palace bar waitresses are kitted out in what are called "signature uniforms," one-shoulder, gold lamé, miniskirted tunics; they project a deadly recapitulation of sixties kitsch. Caesars Palace's Nevada headquarters splits the take with Crystal Cruises in return for handling administrative and manning chores. For the line, though, it seems an ill-advised Faustian bargain with the devil. One can only hope that at contract-renewal time, either that obtrusive "Roman" facade will be replaced or a different operating partner taken on.

I wonder how it impressed our fellow passengers; it was hard for me to gauge their shipboard reaction not only because of a language barrier but also because even the English-fluent maintained a traditional inscrutability. However, from the owner's suite, Minoru Okabe announced to a relieved Erling Frydenberg that "more than 95 percent totally approved."

Japanese passenger dynamics were intriguing. They were clearly an older and very affluent group; many would disembark in Hawaii and be driven to houses or apartments they owned there. Clearly, they enjoyed themselves everywhere on board, even when confronted by sometimes mystifying English-language menus. The company had thoughtfully recruited a corps of hardworking, bilingual Japanese women who circulated during each sitting to offer English translation where required.

All the passengers seemed immensely proud of the fact that this glittering, apparently Western vessel had been produced in their own country. Without exception, they were scrupulously well behaved and, it seemed, anxious to behave as proper Western passengers should. On formal nights, the women donned the most glittering dresses. Gamely, they tried everything. I was struck by their large and enthusiastic turnout for the Palm Court's Funny

Hat Competition, representing as it did the kind of vulnerable, possibly embarrassing exercise in foolishness that might have made them uneasy. But they obviously enjoy dressing up, participating without a trace of reserve.

Never again will they sail in such numbers on board; non-American passengers customarily make up no more than 10 percent. Moreover, how many of them would take the opportunity? Though relentless busloads of Japanese are encountered all over the West, Japan's geographic remoteness, coupled with a strenuous work ethic, discourages a national cruising indulgence. Save for the Chinese mainland or Okinawa, there are few appealing destinations within easy reach of Yokohama, no Caribbean or Alaska at their doorstep. Moreover, for ambitious, upwardly striving executives, departure from Japan for work or play overseas often evokes a palpable corporate frown on their return, unspoken reproof that makes even incentive cruising a challenge. So, in that sense, *Crystal Harmony* is a floating paradox: Designed and built by the Japanese in slavish imitation of a Western cruise ship, apart from our delivery crossing, it will cater to very few of their countrymen.

I thought that Crystal's stewards and stewardesses were particularly well costumed, and I spent an interesting teatime chatting with the man responsible, designer Alan Lurie, who heads his own Chicago firm called Uniforms to You. He dresses the service staffs of most of America's hotel chains, many casinos, and recently, some cruise lines. He created Crystal Cruise Line's entire wardrobe from scratch—"flattering and sophisticated" were his watchwords—and had a team on board fitting every crew member with distinctive day and evening rig. His budget, he reported, was a large one; the results reflected it. During breakfast and lunch, for instance, dining-room stewards are in loosely cut white "harbor" jackets, but instead of a black four-in-hand, they sport a special silk Crystal tie, a "Jackson Pollock/Armani look," suggested Lurie, color-coded with the ship's sea-foam interior decor. This mixture, uniting traditional with unconventional, permeates Lurie's choices.

Each evening, for "turndown" duties, Scandinavian cabin stewardesses don severe but handsome charcoal-gray dresses, topped with formal white aprons and bibs. Conversely, bar waitresses in the Palm Court wear a loose-fitting, patterned floral polyester print called a Beverly because Lurie first designed it for the staff at the Beverly Hills Hotel. Its discreet round cutout at the back of the neck is there, confided Lurie, for a specific reason. Bar waitresses worldwide have discovered that "there is a correlation between the amount of skin shown and the size of tips"; since the *Crystal's* mid-calf, high-neck Beverly reveals almost no skin whatsoever, he included that small token keyhole in compensation. Although the uniforms struck me at first as bizarre, I was quite won over. Those floral dresses not only wear well; they also suit the Palm Court's foliage and wicker to perfection. Additionally—and this is the ultimate test of any uniform—I was told that they are extremely practical and comfortable for the wearer.

The *Crystal Harmony's* cabins, the work of an Italian, Dr. Vittorio Garroni, are pleasantly decorated, though his allotment of bathroom and closet space is inadequate; shades of Sea Goddess crowding for no good reason aboard this 50,000-tonner. Every cabin bathroom on board was prefabricated in Finland, and each one boasts a tub; but most of those tubs are no more than a yard long, allowing scant submersion for all but minors. Never mind that marble trim abounds or that mirrors have been employed to enlarge things. Even the wall across the foot of the tub is mirrored; one showers uneasily à deux with one's reflection until steam mercifully obscures the view.

What can be done about those crowded little bathrooms? One of the problems is the *Crystal Harmony's* corridor design. Company planners have not only made them wider; they have broken up the wall surfaces as well. Every cabin on Penthouse Deck has little inset alcoves surrounding the entry, and down below, Promenade and Crystal Deck cabin corridors are notched. Some of that corridor extravagance might better have been consigned to the cabin interiors. One change made since my crossing is revealing: During the vessel's first dry docking, teams of carpenters worked their way laboriously through the vessel, reversing every bathroom door frame so that doors open out rather than in.

Reversing doors will not help *Crystal Harmony's* meager cabin closets, however. An electronic safe obstructed half of the floor space in ours. This had obviously supplanted a trio of redundant lockable boxes hung on the cabin walls; one might have wished for bookshelves instead.

Although designing a cabin is admittedly complex, I would hazard that one must, especially on such an ambitious vessel, start with rudimentary basics: a decent-sized bathroom for two and a decent-sized closet for two. Both must be carved out of the overall square footage allotted Dr. Garroni by the naval architects. Our cabin—number 9110, aft on the port side of Deck 9—is identified on company deck plans as a "Deluxe Stateroom with Veranda." Its area was 246 square feet, including its veranda. Confronted with all that space, I think the company mistakenly allotted too much to the cabin, boasting, as it does, a sofa between double bed and balcony door. I expect I, as well as countless other passengers who will occupy Cabin 9110 and others like it, would have preferred either a smaller sofa or perhaps even no sofa at all if it meant roomier bathroom and closet. The problem is, once a passenger cabin is complete, companies cannot fudge or fiddle with its cramped bathroom, hoping that mirrors will do the trick. It is there, like two sittings, for all time.

Karl and Jutta were on board with us once again! On the crossing's last evening, they extended what is, aboard every cruise ship, the most coveted invitation, outweighing even a summons from the captain. We were invited to the ship's laundry for a dinner prepared by the Chinese chef.

Since we were sailing late that afternoon from Narwiliwili, our only port of call before Honolulu, we started the evening with a drink on our balcony. A fellow ship lover from Kyoto, Hiroshi Fujiwara, had visited the ship when it called at Kyoto and left a present on board for me, an excellent bottle of amber sake that had been chilling in our cabin icebox for a week. How better to toast both him and the *Crystal Harmony* than with a glass of Japan's national spirit?

At sailing time we gathered on our balcony. For passengers entering or leaving port those balconies are a godsend; for drinks at sunset, they are a delight; and, best of all, for a quiet afternoon at sea, they are incomparable. But for staff captains charged with the vessel's maintenance, balconies are a continual headache. Lining the vessel's flanks, they gulp the vessel's slipstream, accumulating litter, damp, and soot, which is then tracked inside onto cabin carpeting. Moreover, in warm weather, if too many balcony doors are open at once, it raises havoc with the ship's refrigeration output.

That evening, as Narwiliwili's pier receded astern, I discovered the balcony's most insidious spinoff. Since more than half of *Crystal Harmony* passengers have balconies, half the ship's passengers are not on hand for traditional Promenade Deck gatherings during arrivals and, especially, departures. On board every ship at the end of a port day, once the gangway is up, passengers are reunited within their shipboard domain, reaffirming, if you will, their passenger fellowship en masse at the rail. Now, as we slipped out of port, craning over the rail, I could see that every balcony, both forward and above, was occupied by its owners. And it struck me that we had been compartmentalized, locked within our own private decks and detached from our less fortunate shipmates. Regardless of their convenience, luxe, and always, the additional income they generate for the company, in the final analysis, I fear that cruise-ship balconies diminish the shipboard experience, fragmenting and segregating the passenger corpus irrevocably.

After the pilot boat had left us, we toasted each other, Hiroshi, and the ship, captivated by one of those magnificent Pacific sunsets. In fact, we polished off the sake, so I sealed a note and a dollar bill inside the empty bottle and hurled it over the side; if it ever reached Narwiliwili, it has not thus far evoked any response.

Then we descended via crew elevator to the laundry, where Karl introduced us to our host, Lim Khing Yong. Mr. Lim rules the vessel's laundry. After he and Karl had given us a tour of the premises, we were led to an adjoining, plainly furnished dining alcove where an excellent Chinese banquet awaited us. With the ship's housekeeper and crew purser as fellow guests, we sat down to dine.

Mr. Lim told us that he had just come to the *Crystal Harmony* after several years as the *Waschmeister* on board the *Queen Elizabeth 2*, so we discovered that we had a great many Cunard friends in common. Later, the conversation turned to some of the *QE2*'s world-cruise passenger foibles and how careless they often were with valuables: Expensive pins, brooches, and especially, cuff links were habitually left with clothing handed to stewards for laundering. Mr. Lim told us that on one *QE2* Pacific crossing, a dress shirt from a Japanese passenger had turned up with a pair of priceless gold-and-diamond links still impaled through its cuffs. They were returned safely to their owner, of course, but Mr. Lim said he could never understand how passengers could be so careless.

"In fact," he said, rising suddenly from the table, "even you, Mr. Charlie"—all the Chinese call Karl Mr. Charlie—"have left some cuff links in *your* dress shirt." He disappeared from the room and returned a moment later, dropping a pair of gold cuff links on the table. Karl turned beet red above his white beard: The cuff links were *mine*! I had lent them to Karl a week earlier for his

Breaking new ground with crew uniforms: TOP LEFT: *Bar waitresses in their floral print "beverlys," loose-fitting and practical.* TOP RIGHT: *Evening wear for cabin stewardesses is traditional, complete with bib and apron.* (Author's collection)

BOTTOM: *Inbound past the Statue of Liberty in September 1990, dolphin-nosed Crown Princess enters New York on the eve of her christening.* (Princess Cruises)

evening shirt. I do not know whether he or I was more surprised to have them suddenly appear in the midst of that festive Chinese dinner.

We disembarked in Hawaii with regret the following morning. It had been a pleasant crossing on a handsome ship, completion of yet another delivery. Since then, no additional Crystal Cruise ships have been ordered, at least from Japan. Apparently, Mitsubishi's prices are too high even for their countrymen, and there is talk that a European yard will build two additionally projected Crystal hulls; I long to see them.

My westbound voyage aboard the *Crown Princess* scarcely qualifies as a delivery, for the vessel had already spent several weeks in Mediterranean service over the summer of 1990. However, it was her first transatlantic crossing to New York, and once there, she was christened with glorious fanfare by Sophia Loren, about which more later.

Delayed christenings, incidentally, are cruising's new rage, capitalizing on a vessel's finished appearance when unveiling it to the press and public. Since most passengers are American, christenings these days tend to take place just after first arrival in American waters. They serve nowadays as full-blown media events rather than, as originally, symbolic propitiation of worrisome sea gods. Moreover, christening a ship at the moment of first entry into the water no longer makes sense because shipyard launches these days are low-key. Built within dry docks rather than atop sloping ways, hulls are floated off their building blocks merely by flooding the dock; there is no longer a heart-stopping slide down greased ways followed by a dramatic plunge into harbor or river. So, with the shipyard's visual spectacle a thing of the past, the ceremony is delayed until the vessel has been handed over and reached either its home port or, significantly, a communications hub such as New York. There the ship's godmother, the company brass, the brass bands, and the crowds assemble, far from the prosaic yard and long after the hull was first set afloat.

We embarked at Southampton in mid-September of 1990 and made a long southern loop to benefit from smoother seas. We passed alongside the green slopes of the Azores before turning slightly northwest for a calm and uneventful line voyage to New York.

Only two years earlier, Princess Cruises, a subsidiary of Britain's historic Peninsular & Oriental Steam Navigation Company (P&O),

had absorbed Sitmar Cruises, the eminently successful Italian company founded and guided by the late Russian engineer Boris Vlasov. Vlasov was a determined recluse, an immensely busy man who shunned the limelight—indeed, publicity of any sort. His only obscure self-promotion was the simple navy blue "V" adorning the otherwise plain buff funnels of Sitmar tonnage: V for Vlasov. Apart from that depreciatory initial, he remained an éminence grise, a shadowy figure very much in charge but remote from outsiders and subordinates.

I had always hoped to interview Boris Vlasov before he died but was never able to. By splendid coincidence, in August 1991, at P&O's christening dinner on board the *Regal Princess*, the *Crown Princess*'s younger sister, I found myself seated next to his charming widow, Anna Vlasov di Paolis. She told me that her husband had always maintained an inviolate separation between his professional and family lives. Even she had been excluded from the business of the company, sailing only once on the *Fairsky* to Alaska. Sadly, that same familial remoteness would spell Sitmar's doom: After Vlasov died, none of his children was qualified to follow in his footsteps. So Sitmar was sold and absorbed within Princess, an Anglo-Italian liaison that has worked out well.

One Sitmar ship was under construction at St.-Nazaire at the time of the takeover, originally to have been called the *Fair Majesty*. She emerged from the yard with Princess's logo across a surprisingly blank bridge screen (concealing the theater).

The *Star Princess* was followed by a dazzling pair of sister ships, the *Crown Princess* and, subsequently, the *Regal Princess*, displacing 70,000 tons apiece. They were the first Princess Cruise vessels built in Italy, at Fincantieri's yard near Trieste. Charged with their exterior look was Italian designer Renzo Piano, the Genoese architect responsible for Paris's Pompidou Center. Two of his design elements atop the ship are striking, one curiously traditional, the other curiously impractical.

Aft he has placed a perfectly round, paint-pot funnel; apart from some louvered trim, it recalls traditional Atlantic funnels, evocative reminder of Italian liners from the past. Except for the fact that it has no rake whatsoever, Piano's funnel might have sprung intact from the *Conte di Savoia*. It is backed by a lower and thinner galley vent just behind it.

But the profile of the *Crown Princess*'s forward upper deck indicates only too clearly that Signor Piano has never sailed on a crowded cruise ship into eye-filling destinations, such as Venice, Glacier Bay, or Panama's canal. Inexplicably, he rounded the vessel's forward top deck to resemble, the company proudly advises, a dolphin. Though a motif redolent of ecological concern, it drastically reduces the vessel's cruising reward. That dolphin convexity prohibits passengers from the forward margin of the vessel's uppermost deck; one cannot stand atop it any more than one can stand atop a Boeing 747.

With one fanciful stroke of his pencil, Signor Piano denied thousands of future Princess Cruise clients an elevated, forward-facing galleria. When queried about this anomalous design at a Los Angeles press conference, company president Tim Harris prevaricated, suggesting helpfully that even though the *Crown Princess* passengers might not be able to see where they were going, they could certainly see where they had been. To me, it seems faulty design, on a par with the *Royal Viking Sun's* flawed lookout bar. Whom, one wonders, was Signor Piano trying to please with his Disney symbolism, the vessels' occupants or anonymous watchers elsewhere? Urgent note to owners when naval architects or designers submit their earliest renderings: Put yourself in your passengers' shoes and *live* within those deck plans thoroughly before accepting profile exotica. I was on the bridge of the *Crown Princess* when she first entered New York, and a hundred feet aft, passengers craned fitfully and fruitlessly for a look forward. Although there is, admittedly, a crescent of lookout deck below the bridge, it is far too small to accommodate more than a fraction of the ship's 1,600-passenger load.

Piano erred below the dolphin as well. Both of *Crown Princess's* promenade decks are lined with solid bulwark rather than open railing, so that, instead of the sea, deck-chaired passengers face an anonymous expanse of white-painted steel. A view of the horizon from a deck chair is a cherished shipboard perk; to have it eclipsed so thoroughly seems a curious and unnecessary choice.

On the other hand, I was very pleased with the vessel's interiors. The inevitable passenger focus is a modest but pleasing atrium three decks high called the Galleria, which, by its practicality, almost makes up for the missing galleria forward. It is ringed with two surrounding oval balconies. A ceremonial staircase connects the bottom two levels at the afterend; a substantial landing halfway up serves as a splendid rostrum from which the master can welcome passengers at his two cocktail parties. His entire audience remains within easy reach, both on the floor below as well as the railings above.

During those gatherings, the Galleria exudes the same festive intimacy as Venice's Fenice theater, a well-proportioned, balconied forum. By day, the Galleria becomes a piazza, another Venetian parallel. Though it lacks the soaring impact of the *Sovereign's* Centrum, it remains not only a splendid gathering place but also a vital ship's crossroads, incorporating, on its lowest level, the purser's desk and, opposite, a kind of konditorei called La Patisserie. Both upper levels host shop fronts as well as another bar. Because all three Galleria levels serve as connective corridors for the *Crown Princess's* fore and aft, there is constant, casual traffic throughout most of the day. Sufficient comfortable chairs, spread about the lower level or ringing the balconies, promote passenger lingering, always, whether on the *Aquitania* of 1914 or the *Crown Princess* of 1990, an essential requirement of the "compleat" public space.

That atrium, incidentally, permits an interesting cruising refinement. There is no formal receiving line for the captain's reception, no obligatory wait for a photographed handshake, as on board almost every other cruise ship. Instead, the master and his officers roam the atrium's lower level, accessible to all those who wish to shake hands or take pictures themselves. The evening does not begin with an enervating queue but instead comes to talkative life the moment one enters. Our master for the crossing was a charming man, Captain Nicola di Stefano, his purser an old friend from Sitmar's *Fairsky*, Carlo Salsado.

Both the *Star Princess* and the *Crown Princess* have, on the bottom level of their atria, a splendid, if silent, fountain, the work of California sculptor Eric Orr. On the *Star* it was christened "Oceania," a tall bronze column about fourteen inches square, standing in a modest pool. Each face of the column is ridged horizontally. Water pumped silently from the pool up inside the column spills over the top, flowing in sinuous sheets down each side to the bottom. The gentle ridges create what the sculptor describes as "standing waves," which incite random patterns all over the water-covered facades. Remarkably—and the sculptor encourages this—touching that descending sheen causes neither ripple nor splash.

On board the *Crown Princess*, Orr went one better with what he calls "Princess Prime Matter," incorporating a granite wedge next to a similar but triangular column. Its sloping hypotenuse and one vertical side include a raceway, also ridged, that adds another

TOP: *Looking aft on the lowest level of* Crown Princess's *civilized Galleria. Eric Orr's striking sculpture rests at the bottom of the captain's staircase.* (Princess Cruises)

BOTTOM: *In the belly of the beast: Beneath the controversial dome, shutters are closed and ficus foliage has been arranged in clumps rather than hedges.* (Princess Cruises)

dimension of aquatic motion to the piece's trylon-perisphere camaraderie. The same artist is also represented by handsome, mono-
chromatic abstractions that hang to either side of the purser's desk.
Incomprehensibly, the *Regal* has no Eric Orr water sculpture in
its Galleria, and is all the poorer for the lack of it. As shipboard
sculpture goes, I find his work as refreshing as it is enchanting.

The Galleria's top level is Deck 7, a handsome, double-height
succession of corridors and rooms that run from the huge show
Lounge forward to the Dining Room aft, through the Galleria and
past two pleasant double-height midship lounges en route. This is
the artery of the vessel's indoor life, just as the conventional Lido
Deck atop the vessel occupies daytime passengers.

A less successful venue lies forward, directly beneath the infamous dolphin's snout. Though passengers may be barred from
standing atop it, they are encouraged to gather inside it, within a
zoomorphic domed enclosure called, sensibly, The Dome. The
space gave me the impression that I had strayed onto the juvenile
floor of a natural-history museum and, Jonah-like, been swallowed
by a whale. The curved ceiling, lined with frank white ribbing,
which Renzo Piano used to conceal ducts and wiring, creates this
compelling illusion.

Any description of The Dome's use must be preceded by some
crucial background. We must go back one ship, to *Star Princess*,
the former *Fair Majesty*. She has a lookout lounge in the same
location, above the bridge. Completely circular, it is called Windows to the World.

In its original form, Windows to the World was an utter disaster:
no more than a handful of its occupants could see outside because
designers had inexplicably surrounded the room's circumference
with a raised rim. Only those seated atop that encircling ledge had
panoramic views; the rest of the room's occupants saw nothing. It
pleases me to report that a year after the *Star Princess*'s maiden
voyage, Windows to the World was renovated, sensibly, if expensively, raising the room's center so that all can share the view.

Nevertheless—and herewith its bearing on choices made for The
Dome—for an entire year, in-house personnel described Windows
to the World sotto voce as "the room no one ever uses." So, quite
naturally, on board *Crown Princess*, to guarantee passenger attendance in the equivalent top-deck space, the company located the
ship's casino—a sure come-on—in its central section. Aft, there
is an adjacent dance floor and bar. Forward, separated from the

gamblers by a palisade of ficus trees, lies a crescent of tables and chairs that, by daytime, command a view of the surrounding sea, similar to that from the Stella Polaris Lounge on the *Royal Viking Sun*.

Unfortunately, the noise of contemporary casinos these days is not confined to the civilized shuffle of twenty-one decks, the roulette ball's skittering dance, or even the occasional boisterousness of the crap table. Nowadays, casinos generate a cheeping, ringing, chiming chorus, the nonstop cacophony of state-of-the-art slot machines. So a daytime drink overlooking the sea beneath The Dome comes complete with inescapable electronic chatter seeping through the foliage. In addition to that grating irritant, there is no nighttime view because stewards shutter all The Dome's windows at dusk, preventing light spill that might spoil night vision on the bridge. In sum, that mix in The Dome is problematic, and the interior space ends up as impractical as the dolphin's snout it supports.

By contrast, the Fountain Court dining room down on Promenade Deck pleased me, profiting from 7 Deck's tall ceilings. All shipboard dining rooms, I have decided, require height for success, and none, incidentally, has succeeded better in this regard than the *Nordic Empress*, Royal Caribbean Cruise Line's three- and four-day ship, delivered earlier that summer of 1990 to Miami. Her dining room not only occupies the stern, as does the *Crown Princess*'s, but has the advantage as well of an encircling, horseshoe-shaped balcony, which endows the room with a unique, spacious festivity. Beautifully designed by Njål Eide, it is a veritable Hollywood dining room: What movie designers produce in fantasy RCCL has captured in glittering reality. To my mind, it remains cruising's aesthetic benchmark, against which all rival dining rooms must be measured.

Dining on the *Crown Princess* is exhilarating, although the same room on board the *Regal Princess* has been improved: Painted garden vistas enliven the walls, while glass shields to either side of every waiter's dummy have been enlarged and decorated with flowering vines; they not only warm the space, they also serve to break up large expanses of tables into congenial clusters.

Princess's food and service are exemplary, and I have come to the conclusion, after more than half a century afloat, that Italians probably make the most indefatigably charming dining-room stewards. Working within their ethos, they and their concerned superi-

ors cast a comforting, catering spell. Perhaps it has to do with the
national unity one remembered fondly in yesterday's North Atlantic
dining saloons: Almost everyone in the *Crown Princess*'s Fountain
Court, save for the British *sommelieuses*, is Italian, giving every
meal a contagious Neapolitan flair. Lunches and dinners are taken
in company with droll but dependable Rossiniesque factota, clowns
and jugglers, a bubbling commedia dell'arte pastiche that never
flags.

One endearing Sitmar institution has been transferred intact and
con brio to Princess: an irresistible offering of pasta twice daily.
Mary and I gorged on pasta nonstop across the Atlantic. Moreover,
there were other stalwart Italianate touches—crisp, packaged *gris-
sini* from Turin, espresso and/or cappuccino on demand, and at
the captain's dinner especially, an array of unforgettable Roman
desserts.

Captain di Stefano kindly included us at dinner one night, and
it interested me that he had chosen as his table not the central one
facing over the stern but another at the starboard aftercorner of the
dining room. From there he can see both forward and athwartship.
Before dinner, we met for drinks in a handsome interior space
forward in officer country that, on both the *Crown* and the *Regal*,
serves as a pleasant, smaller reception room for the master's cocktail
or dinner guests.

I would be remiss in not dwelling on the splendid celebrations
that P&O's chief, Lord Stirling of Plaistow, lays on for christening
his latest vessels. Christenings have become the natural culmination of deliveries, and no one achieves them with more flourish
than this company. Over the past three years, I have attended
three Princess christenings. In 1988, Audrey Hepburn named the
Star Princess in Fort Lauderdale. (Miss Hepburn's brimmed hat
had a mind of its own that windy afternoon, and she spent the
entire day with one hand holding it atop her head.) The next two
took place in New York. In September 1990, Sophia Loren served
as godmother to the *Crown Princess*, and the year following, Mar-
garet Thatcher christened the *Regal Princess*. Mrs. Thatcher's hat
had an even larger brim but, fortunately, there was no wind at all;
Miss Loren christened hatless.

In this instance, three impressive ships were christened by three
impressive women. It is a delicate business, finding just the right
godmother. They are, incidentally, largely godmothers and not
godfathers. Although the Kaiser christened the *Imperator* and Mr.

and Mrs. Jimmy Stewart both christened the *Royal Viking Sun*, by and large it is an honor almost exclusively conferred on women. But whom to choose? Obviously, someone who is both available and interested but also someone free of controversy. American political figures run the risk of alienating half their constituency, and film stars touched by scandal must be avoided at all cost. Always, newsworthiness as opposed to notoriety is the watchword.

When I received the invitation for the *Crown Princess*'s christening, I thought the handsome, gilt-edged card bore a typographical error in advising me that the ceremony would take place at Pier 8. I called Princess Cruises at once. Surely they meant Pier 88 at New York's Passenger Ship Terminal, where all Manhattan-bound passenger vessels tie up? No, I was advised, Brooklyn's Pier 8 was correct. Choice of that unconventional but enviable site ensured that the *Crown Princess*'s bow would be juxtaposed not against meaningless concrete but a breathtaking segment of the Manhattan skyline. Someone at P&O had done his homework well.

For music, the band and pipers of Britain's First Battalion, Scots Guards, had been lofted transatlantic at presumably vast expense. Their presence throughout the vessel's New York visit, either playing on the pier or marching and countermarching atop a moored barge, produced both rich spectacle and flawless music. Miss Loren's first appearance elicited polite applause from the adjacent VIP barge, a flurry of shutter clicks from the press bleachers, and a shout of greeting from the *Crown Princess*'s Italian crew, festooned along every portside deck.

Speeches at christenings are mercifully brief. Once they had been completed, godmother Sophia released the cutting blade that severed a silk-wrapped line, breaking a bottle of champagne against the vessel's port hawsepipe. The crowd clapped, the crew roared, the *Crown Princess*'s whistle bellowed, the band struck up "Rule Britannia," and an evocative P&O touch, bells pealed from a specially erected tower on the pier as guests and band and press tramped back around the head of the slip and reboarded the *Crown Princess*. There was an al fresco lunch on the vessel's top deck as we cruised slowly back from Brooklyn to Manhattan. Sophia Loren and her husband, Carlo Ponti, took lunch in their suite on board. Carlo Salsado told me later that he had led a delegation of no less than five breathless senior hotel staff up to Aloha Deck forward merely to take the Pontis' order.

There will, I trust, be more special deliveries to come. As I

Chapter 7

C'est en 1953 que le Parlement vote la résolution de
maintenir le pavillon français sur l'Atlantique Nord.
  —Revue de la Compagnie Générale Transatlantique

*The best age for a gondola is seven years. Then she is like a
woman of thirty-five years, polished, well curved, and settled
into herself.*
  —Nevis Tramontin, Venetian boat builder

*The time has come when needless noise must be classified as
common plagues, like flies, mosquitos, rats and dirt.*
  —Professor James Putnam, Boston, 1912

Closing the Circle:

France/Norway

Two chapters ago, I lavished so many superlatives on the *Normandie* that readers may well wonder what can be left for the
France. Was she a suitable successor to the thirties ship? Did she
inherit the *Normandie*'s mantle of distinction? Should the *France*
be accorded the same panegyric?

It is hard to answer any of the above in the unqualified affirma-
tive. The *Normandie* achieved a historic pinnacle that the *France*
never really sought. Although no Blue Ribband winner, there
was, in her aspect from across the water, a similar hauteur and
sense of classic proportion. The *France*'s pair of distinctive winged
funnels—about which more in a moment—did not require a third;
the hull resembled the *Normandie*'s, although with not quite the
same delicate entry forward or the earlier vessel's curious
athwartship paunch when in dry dock. The *France*, both in dry
dock and at sea, seemed a leaner, tauter creation, terminating in

245

a stern that, though incorporating an anchor, did not share the *Normandie*'s (and the *Sovereign* class's) knuckled counter.

As I write these words, I find it less difficult to choose comparatives than tenses. Syntactical confusion in this regard is understandable, for against all odds, *France* still exists; for once, we are not talking about the dead but the living. Unlike other major North Atlantic liners discussed in this volume, the *France* has the incomparable advantage of remaining in service, a blessed dividend for marine historians.

Nowadays, giant gilt letters on the vessel's royal blue bow and stern proclaim *Norway*. (In certain light, one can just discern ghostly outlines of the original letters spelling *France*.) How glorious that she has survived, what a miracle that, almost any Saturday of the year, you can still board her in Miami. And after prowling around on board, you will find that, beneath inevitable layers of cruising adiposity, her stout Penhoët heart still beats as strong as ever.

As this book leaves the presses, the *Norway-ex-France* will be embarking on her fourth decade, an awesome chronological hurdle for every ocean liner. But I think it safe to say that in terms of extending her longevity, the *France/Norway* has done it right. She retired from the North Atlantic fast track after a dozen bruising years before enduring an almost equally damaging period of neglect, five lost years tied up at Le Havre's Quai de l'Oubli. Then came a last-minute reprieve: In 1979, the liner *France* was transformed into the cruise ship *Norway*. After undergoing a rigorous conversion, she retired benignly to Florida, navigating at two-thirds speed through tranquil waters, spared any further punishing Atlantic exposure.

Like my previous *Normandie* chapter, this one will also be divided in half, one about the vessel's French debut, the other about her contemporary cruising life. As of 1992, the two periods will be equal: 1962–74 on the Atlantic as *France*, 1980–92 in the Caribbean as *Norway*. This is not to say that during their separate lives the two did not stray within the other's bailiwick. In fact, I first encountered the *France* in the Caribbean over Christmas and New Year's of 1968, sailing from New York for a frenetic but memorable fortnight down to the Caribbean and back. And, conversely, what a pleasure it was, over the summer of 1984, to sail transatlantic twice, eastbound and westbound, on board the *Norway* as she complemented a Blohm & Voss dry-docking visit with two passenger-carrying crossings as well as some memorable cruising along the Norwegian coast.

As the *France* on the North Atlantic she was utterly anachronistic, of course, launched well after it was apparent that the jets would win. Like any aristocrat bound for the guillotine, though, she endured the prospect of economic failure with a combined de Gaullean flair and stoic shrug, steaming defiantly in the face of airborne adversity. Like the *Normandie* before her, the *France* never aged on the Atlantic; at the time she was withdrawn from service in 1974, she had reached only early middle age.

The French have always loved her but love her even more fervently in retrospect. Her first master, Commandant Georges Croisile, died only recently; for many of his passengers, the *France* lives on as a heartfelt memory. Whereas the derelict *Normandie's* loss was a wartime tragedy, geographically remote from occupied France, the *France* was sailing out of Le Havre right up to her 1974 withdrawal. These days, the first of what I assume will become a torrent of glossy books and magazines compel the French to recall the *France*, to cherish in Kodachrome what they neglected in actuality. Where, one wonders, was that adoring public in the early 1970s, when the *France* was in such desperate need of support?

How hard it is to preserve specific shipboard experiences. Once on board the *Rotterdam* in mid-Pacific, Captain Cornelius Honderdos invited a group of us to dine with him. Stewards had transformed the vessel's private dining room into an exotic hothouse. The stewards themselves were clad in brilliant Indonesian tunics.

After the captain's toast, I responded, thanking the master for his hospitality and then urging my fellow passengers to cherish this *Rotterdam* moment. "Years from now," I suggested, "we will try to conjure up this special evening and wonder how we could ever have let it pass."

Of course, it did pass, as, too, did all those imperishable crossings on board the *France*. Let me try to summon up aspects of some of them, to recall to life that incomparable vessel not only for readers who enjoyed it, as I did, but for those who wish they had.

Foremost about the *France* was her relentless Frenchness. At a time when contemporary cruise ships, even the prestigious *Queen Elizabeth 2*, are selling short their national identity to please their largely American clientele, French Line passengers were engulfed within an indubitably Gallic regime. All of those hundreds of well-trained crewmen and -women were French. Again and again, one felt an almost palpable pride in tradition, a sense of timeworn CGT routine extending back to the company's mid-nineteenth-century origins. The mood was never dispelled. And, as in any first-class hotel in the world, on every level of the vessel's well-defined hierarchy, a patina of concern and courtesy prevailed, from the master down to the humblest mousse.

They still had mousses, of course, clad in the same vivid *Normandie* livery. And that particular scarlet flair seems historically symptomatic of the Compagnie Générale Transatlantique. What were the ramifications of that particular Transat rubric? The company's love affair with red stems, I am sure, from their house flag. The line had begun life as the Compagnie Générale Maritime, by curious coincidence the same name as the French Line's present cargo-carrying residue. Atop the mainmast of those first vessels, the full name was spelled out on the flag, huge, eye-catching red letters filling a white field. But when the Compagnie Générale Transatlantique came into being in 1861, a new house flag was mandated. Not for the French an imperial eagle or shield or lion but an unadorned red circle. Later on, the company's name would be added to the red disc on the flag, two of its three words abbreviated: Cie. Gle. Transatlantique. Although the original choice of this design is lost to us, it is not unreasonable to presume that the founding Péreire brothers, Isaac and Emile, were cunningly imitating America's famous and successful Black Ball Line, in full flower by mid-century. Whereas Black Ball liners sported a large black ball across their foresails, the French never did; their red ball appeared only on the house flag itself.

Though the actual symbol was confined to masthead or poster, flashes of red always permeated everything on board French Line ships, from funnels atop the vessel to details of decor and uniform below. On the *France*, red accents were endemic, as arbitrary as a broad Dubuffet brush stroke. Red colored not only the uniforms of the mousses but also the vessel's brochure cover, the deck of the embarkation lobby, the wood of the deck chairs as well as their black-and-red webbing and their mattresses, the surprising red leather pews in the chapel, and near voyage's end, carmine sugar bows adorning baskets of pastry confections on gala night.

Until 1957, renderings of the *France*'s projected funnels showed ordinary, slightly tapered cylinders, somewhat on the order of the *Liberté*'s. Even closer to launch, when an intricate scale model scooted by remote control back and forth across the testing tank of the Marine Nationale, the identical stacks remained. But after the May 1960 launch, the actual funnels that emerged from St.-Nazaire workshops had revolutionary wings thrusting twenty feet out to either side. The design change was apparently so precipitous that several of the vessel's suppliers who used the new profile in their advertisements near maiden-voyage time included all manner of aberrations: Petrofrance's, for example, showed the famous wings drooping downward as though melting. In fact, the opposite is true. Though perfectly horizontal—Mary and I have stood atop the number 1 funnel wings—they conveyed an illusion of jaunty uplift. But from dead ahead in their traditional Transat colors—tapering red shaft with black tops—the *France* sometimes seemed adorned with funnels that each wore a homburg.

Those unique funnels had been designed to divert stack gas efficiently to one side of the vessel or the other. Within each wing's terminal opening, remotely controlled vents could be closed on command by duty engineers, depending on the wind's direction. But, in truth, the *France*'s funnel wings were not completely successful. When a stiff breeze blew directly abeam, funnel smoke inevitably came back on board and all over the decks. Among the *France* seating that did *not* sport the company red were two dozen armchairs lining the open veranda just outside the Smoking Room. They were upholstered in quilted black leather, with good reason, I found: It would not surprise me that the French Line chose that color to mask from sight inevitable deposits of funnel smut. Several of my white trousers suffered as a result.

But, to my mind, the secret of those funnels was their distinctive chic. Worldwide, wherever she sailed, the *France* was instantly recognizable. They were the ship's signature; although they may have lacked the majesty of the *Normandie*'s trio, they did offer a jazzy, eye-catching sixties summit to an otherwise conventional profile. Moreover, they were lavishly finished. Most steel funnels suffer what the late Cecil Ridgley-Nevitt, a naval architect, used to call "starved-horse syndrome." Over the years, steel plating inevitably droops, following the contours of its supporting framework; the ribs begin to show, most pointedly at the beginning or end of the Caribbean day, when the sun's flat rays can throw any of a ship's steel planes into embarrassing relief. Those *Norway* funnels are immune because, during construction at St.-Nazaire, their steel was overlaid with a substantial coating of mastic that keeps them smooth and unblemished. One of my most precious

TOP: *The line's name in English, in French, and as flown from the mast via the company flag, complete with its distinctive red ball.* (Author's collection)

The France's *funnels, two differing views, both taken on the 1972 world cruise.* CENTER: *At anchor, with shore tenders clustered beneath her counter.* BOTTOM: *Tied up at Singapore; seen from abeam, the funnel wings seem to vanish.* (William Archibald)

France relics is a fragment of that mastic, retrieved after some *Norway* renovations, which reveals the funnels' original red. I think I never saw those funnels better used than when the *Norway* first entered New York harbor in the spring of 1980; half a dozen crewmen were seated in the starboard (Manhattan-side) vent of the number 1 moribund funnel, for all the world as though in a balcony box enjoying a Hippodrome spectacle.

The hull was a marvel as well. Today, on board the *Norway*, Norwegian engineering and navigating officers alike cannot contain their enthusiasm for the wonders of the vessel that carries them through the Caribbean. With each passing year, it becomes more extraordinary because nothing like it will ever be wrought again. All along that graceful blue expanse of plating, there is just the right amount of tumble home, that paradoxical inward sweep of plating as it rises from the water, as well as wondrous sheer and shape. The cumulative lines of that ultimate Penhoët hull are bewitching. Stand alongside any contemporary newbuilding at Miami or Fort Lauderdale and glance along the length of the hull: Though the plating may swoop inboard for a dramatic prow or taper toward the stern, the side in between is a perfectly vertical slab. But stand between Miami's Berth 1 and Berth 2 on any Saturday and try to decipher the glorious subtleties of the *Norway*'s flank; by contrast, it is a paradigm of naval architectural grace and sophistication.

So much for the exterior; let us race to a cabin. Most of the *France*'s original cabins remain more or less as they were on board the *Norway*. Each year, however, more and more are renovated, so it is worth recalling the originals. They were built for strenuous service by both passengers and the elements. An attractive glazed steel bureau separated twin beds. Every drawer could be opened by a central, indestructible pull; a friction point in each suspension track kept all drawers firmly closed no matter what motion ensued. Atop the highest drawer was a flat pullout panel that, cantilevered beyond the bureau's front, served as a convenient desk.

It was the cabin's only writing surface, for the bureau top was surrounded by a substantial rim to keep articles in place. A triangular glass lamp stood immovably at one end of the bureau, bolted in place and topped by a flat parchment shade that never stirred. (During the *Norway*'s delivery crossing, a brisk souvenir trade in those discarded cabin lamps was discouraged by the fact that they had no conventional base for home use.) The black cabin telephones had a patented spring clip to hold the receiver firmly in place.

Everything, in sum, was securely adapted to withstand the worst the Atlantic could offer.

I should not dismiss the beds, for I remember them as superbly comfortable and pillowed with abandon. The linen was just that, linen of a very superior quality, so deluxe that NCL decided that it could not serve for the *Norway*'s passengers; the ship's laundry would not be able to cope. Four complete sets of linen had been ordered for the *France*, two always on the vessel and one each at New York and Le Havre. It represented an enormous logistic investment; the number of table napkins alone exceeded half a million. They, together with sheets, tablecloths, towels, and steward's jackets, had to be laundered and ironed ashore, either in New York or Le Havre. The company preferred French laundresses, as did one of New York's great expatriate cooks: Roger Fessaguet, chef and later owner of La Caravelle restaurant in the 1960s, regularly dispatched a dozen soiled toques for proper washing, starching, and pressing by the expert sisters of a Havrois convent. They came back two months later, a dozen at a time, stacked one inside the other, via a friend on the *France*, sous-chef Serge Primaut.

When the vessel sailed on her two world cruises, Commandant Christian Pettré made an aerial reconnaisance of the itinerary, not only to check piers and harbors but also to find suitable laundries along the way that could handle *France*'s linen requirements during brief stopovers. During early planning sessions, the French Line debated chartering a laundry support vessel that would carry the ship's linen back to Le Havre, but the elapsed sailing time made the scheme unworkable. The vessel had only a very small laundry on board, as on most liners: Passengers had little need of it during a five-day crossing. My congenial fellow passenger and laundry impresario Karl Woraschk installed the *Norway*'s present-day laundry in 1980. He recalls finding only two very small industrial washers and dryers on the ship when he boarded in 1979 for the Bremerhaven refit.

Directly across from the cabin bureau, an extremely well designed dressing table had been provided for lady passengers. Behind it hung an almost full-length oval mirror suspended within a reflective cyclorama; for close-up work, flanking smaller mirrors swung on hinges. The table surface had lockable jewelry compartments below it and incorporated as well a panel with three ivory push buttons. Two bore a pictographic clue, a violin for classical music, a saxophone for something more modern. The third turned the music off.

Two ample closets (they dovetailed with those in the adjoining cabin) bracketed the dressing table. Their doors could remain closed, open, or anywhere in between, thanks to a spring-loaded drag on the sliding bracket at the top. The French Line solved the problem of purloined coat hangers by making their hanging rods—steel, coated with black fluted plastic—extremely thin. The ivory-colored plastic hangers would disappoint souvenir-hungry Americans: The hooks were too small to hang on American rods.

In the bathroom, there was an ingenious cupboard above the sink with hinged doors to either side that would, like the cabin closets, remain fixed in any open position, serving thus as a capital three-way mirror. An ashtray was incorporated within the base of the cabinet—everyone seemed to smoke in the 1960s—as well as a slot for disposing of used razor blades, an early-twentieth-century convenience that seems quaint nowadays. A supplementary long spout above the glistening bathroom faucets delivered iced drinking water on demand; it could be swung off to the side when not in use.

In most of the *Norway*'s cabins today, many of those original French features remain but no longer work. Every cabin has television now—the *Norway* was the first ship to offer that convenience, incidentally—so although the little ivory buttons on the dressing table can still be depressed, music comes exclusively from television channels. The *France*'s steward and stewardess call buttons were different from the *Normandie*'s: red for *garçon de cabin* and green for *femme du chambre*. When pressed, a pair of color-coded translucent fixtures outside in the corridor would turn on. Though inoperative these days on board the *Norway*, they remain in place.

Successful cabin layout, incidentally, is an intricate business, one that land-based designers should approach cautiously. The late Angelo Donghia, a brilliant New York designer who splendidly adapted *Norway*'s interiors for cruising, fared less well in those cabins he created along Pool Deck. These were handsome cabins, wrought out of the *France*'s tourist-class promenade. In an effort to make them luxurious, Donghia furnished them too lavishly: sofa, floor lamp, armchair, coffee table, and television set on a floor pedestal. As a result, the cabin is too crowded, immensely difficult to move about in.

By contrast, navigating throughout one of the *France's* ordinaries was easy. In any confined space, furniture selection and size are crucial. Standard equipment for every cabin included a low steel table, supported on those spiked legs fashionable in the late fifties. NCL replaced that table with a round, glass-topped model that also served as a writing table; the slide-out French desks from the top drawer were either neglected or brutalized by the *Norway* passengers. But the change in dimension—perhaps only two additional square feet—made that larger table an awkward intrusion, as did a television set bulking in one corner. Again, those negligible additions to the *Norway* cabins created obtrusive clutter undreamed of during the simpler *France* regime.

It was Craig Claiborne, the *New York Times's* cerebral food critic, who headlined his story about *France's* first-class dining room: "The Finest French Restaurant in the World." It was, in one sense, an extraordinary claim, for no transatlantic commissariat, dependent on freezer or extended cold storage, can rival a restaurant with daily fresh provisions. But I suspect that what may have influenced Claiborne was the bravura ritual of every meal within the *France's* Restaurant Chambord.

From the moment the two mousses on duty swung open the dining room's glass doors, ushering one down that splendid staircase, everything was deadly serious. Dining-room captain Max Lucas, in whose section I invariably sat, led the way to the table, a tight smile beneath his toothbrush mustache. During the exquisite meal that followed, the noise level was civilized, the stewards deft and knowledgeable, and their supervisors impassive but all-seeing. A sense of ordered tranquility suffused the domed room. Though it lacked the *Normandie's* architectural distinction, an identical mood of purposeful intensity prevailed; and like the *Normandie's* salle à manger, it had no portholes, even though the walls coincided with the side of the hull, as though no view should distract from the business at hand. As in every successful commercial dining room, what seemed effortless ambience to diners was, I am sure, belied by discreet angst beyond the green baize door.

The *France's* table knives were extremely large, with heavy handles. When clearing plates, stewards placed the handle of the knife in the center of the plate, its blade projecting over the edge; this small detail made great sense, avoiding imbalanced spills. When clearing after breakfast, stewards would collect spoons in the Limoges coffee cups, a cheerful ring of cutlery against crockery that

TOP: *Shipshape cabin design of the* France *on the* Pont Embarcations, *or Boat Deck. Bed frames and bureaus are steel, lighting is largely fluorescent, and the lamp is bolted to the bureau top.* (Author's collection)

BOTTOM: *View over the stern: The* France *at sea on a calm day. A haze of funnel smoke hovers over the distinctively broad wake produced by quadruple screws. Beyond the veranda, a glass roof covers tourist class's pool.* (William Archibald)

stays with me still from the Chambord days. And it is worth remembering that never was there any attempt to stage "theme nights." On board too many contemporary cruise ships, Royal Viking's included, during certain preselected evenings, dining rooms are festooned with temporary decorations, and waiters sport aprons and French berets or *gondolieri* straws. I cannot help but feel that it is as demeaning for them as for the room. Designers have spent too much time and effort creating a dining room's decoration to have it periodically "improved" with crepe-paper kitsch. There was only one theme every night on board the *France*—exquisite food.

Except for once, I never endured a bad or badly served meal in that dining room throughout a dozen passages. The sole exception, understandably, was one indifferent breakfast as we sailed into New York at the end of August 1974; it marked the end of the *France*'s last westbound crossing and, by ominous extension, the end of French Line passenger service as well. The night before, word had come via cable from Paris that the ship would be withdrawn.

That grim morning, a woman near me complained petulantly about a stained tablecloth; though within her rights, of course, she had no idea that the world of the anguished steward who replaced it was about to collapse. Many of his colleagues were in tears. Whereas their deck and engineering shipmates might transfer to cargo vessels or tankers, employment for stewards depends on the carriage of passengers.

And of all those incredible meals in the Restaurant Chambord, none was more extravagant than that offered a handful of lucky passengers twice each crossing at the captain's table. We would gather for cocktails in the Salon Debussy, just off the Main Staircase on Promenade Deck. It was a small room, so dominated by a huge piano that as couples entered and were introduced, they were seated in armchairs hugging the walls, as though ensconced in a doctor's waiting room.

That initial arrangement of couples was the first of three rigidly assigned seating plans mandated for the evening. The second would be down at dinner, at which time the youngest and most attractive passenger wives were routinely placed at the extreme outer ends of the table, if not quite below the salt, at least well removed from the master at the center. Their turn would come. After dinner, back up at cabaret in the Salon Fontainebleau, a third and final pecking order was established. The two dining-room outriggers would be reassigned inboard, to either side of the captain. This unvarying and ingenious plan guaranteed the commandant mature conversation during dinner as well as ravishing dancing partners afterward.

In the *France* days, the captain's table in the Restaurant Chambord stood against the forward wall, out from under that echoing dome. Nowadays, on board the *Norway*, NCL has moved it aft, into the hectic middle of the room, which, crowded with more tables, has turned into an acoustic trap. And whereas during the *Norway* captain's dinners, one merely orders from the ship's menu, on board the *France*, a special banquet had always been prepared. Successive courses were paraded with almost medieval pomp, first at one end of the table and then the other, before stewards whisked portions to the diners. The company's best wines and food made up those elaborate dinners. I am dismayed to find that I retained not one of those imperishable menus, inside the cover of which every guest's name had been printed.

A courtier once confided to a man about to be knighted at Buckingham Palace that things ran so smoothly at court because a superfluity of senior staff left nothing to chance. The same overmanning worked beautifully on board the *France*, especially during those captain's dinners. Either Paul Ermel himself, the *France*'s urbane *commissaire principal*, or one of his equally sophisticated subordinates served as majordomo throughout cocktails. Their ease of manner in both French and English was remarkable; every introduction was accomplished with ambassadorial precision.

After exactly half an hour, a tall figure in flawless tailcoat entered the room: Maître d'Hôtel Principal Louis Pellegrin's bow to the master indicated that dinner was ready. We rose to our feet at once and were ushered into specially reserved elevators that carried us down to the Embarkation Lobby. There, with consummate skill, Pellegrin assigned every lady to the correct gentleman's arm—her dinner partner—and led the parade down that *grande descente*. Once on the far side of the room at the captain's table, we would sit and pose for the photographer. (An eight-by-ten in color would be slipped under each guest's cabin door first thing in the morning.) Pellegrin would not permit the shutter to be released before he had removed every disfiguring white napkin from every passenger lap. Throughout the meal he hovered; nothing escaped him. My clearest memory of all those dinners is neither Commandant Pettré nor Commandant Nadal presiding at the head of the table, but the intent preoccupation of Pellegrin, always within reach and controlling half a dozen subordinates with no more than a twitch of one eyebrow.

I sense that this may have been the aura that bewitched Craig Claiborne. One always felt, on board *France*, extremely well looked after; the dedication and finesse, especially of that senior hotel staff, was overwhelming. Yet again, it was probably nothing more than the traditional concern that the CGT had always extended toward its passengers for decades. Everywhere on board, we were cosseted within a sense of pleasing shipboard ritual.

Before we move on to the events of 1979 and conversion of the vessel into the *Norway*, it is worth recalling some amusing *France* stories, typical, really, of shipboard dynamics anywhere. Monsieur Ermel told me once that a passenger showed up at the bureau, reporting that he had mislaid his gold eyeglass case somewhere in the Cardroom after a bridge tournament. A notice was posted and an announcement put in the daily program. Nothing happened. Then Ermel had an inspiration: He inserted a new notice to the effect that a "gold-*colored*" eyeglass case was missing. It was turned in within an hour.

The man in charge of the ship's orchestra had the unlikely name of René Moos. One of his musicians, a saxophonist called Pedro, played in the front row. Bright stage lights were always kept on during dancing each evening, and I noticed that Pedro wore dark glasses every time he played. I once suggested to him during a break that the lights must hurt his eyes and he responded quite cheerfully that yes, they did hurt his eyes, but he liked them nevertheless; he could always tell at a glance which lady passengers had neglected to wear a slip.

During the second world cruise in 1974, the *France* was approaching New Guinea in the Far East. She would remain there long enough to accommodate passengers who wished to fly inland and see the famous stone-age tribes up in the Western Highlands. Thomas Cook's shore excursion department did a fine sales job: Hundreds of world-cruise passengers—mostly Americans—signed up for the tour. Bill Archibald, Cook's man on board, cabled Cook's agent ashore to reserve seats on flights into the interior, so many that every DC-3 in the territory had to be commandeered for the *France* invasion.

But at the airport, as plane after plane loaded, the numbers did not work out. Only then did Bill discover that the rows of dimpled benches facing inboard along every DC-3 fuselage were engineered for island rather than American posteriors. Each aircraft's rated capacity had to be curtailed due to this Western anatomic disparity; several dozen fuming passengers cooled their heels in Port Moresby's sea-level humidity while awaiting the return of empty planes from the interior.

For a final glimpse into the workings of the vessel's *comme il faut* regime, a story that took place when the *France* was empty, dead-loading between New York and Boston. Jean-Claude Potier, director of the French Line's North American office, was the only quondam passenger aboard. The night of the New York departure, M. Pellegrin inquired of Potier if he would prefer breakfast in his cabin or in the dining room; Potier said he would come down to the dining room. The next morning, as he descended the staircase into the deserted Restaurant Chambord, he discovered, to his horror, that no less than five men—a maitre d'hôtel, a captain, two chefs de rang, and a *commis de rang*—had been routed out of bed to attend to Monsieur le Directeur.

It is impossible to discuss the conversion of the *France* into the *Norway* without a preliminary glimpse of the man responsible— the genius behind Norwegian Caribbean Line (now Norwegian Cruise Line), Knut Utstein Kloster, head of Oslo's Klosters Rederei, one of Norway's largest and most successful family-owned shipping companies. A tall, dark-haired, and dedicated man, Knut Kloster is as accessible as he is congenial, with seawater in his veins and a ready smile on his face. As devoid of pretension as most Norwegians, he moves easily throughout his vessels, confidant to all the crew.

In 1979 his phenomenally successful cruise line desperately needed additional berthing capacity. Shipowners intent on expansion have four options: build, stretch, buy, or convert. Building a fifth NCL vessel from scratch would have taken at least three years; stretching the existing four hulls, besides removing them from profitable service one at a time, would have added only 500 more cabins; buying a ship from a rival is difficult when the cruise market is bullish. Kloster's final expedient was to find an existing hull that, though out of service, might profitably be converted to company use.

An Oslo ship broker submitted a list of twenty laid-up hulls. One by one, each potential candidate was crossed off until only one remained: the SS *France*, then enduring its fifth dreary year of layup at Le Havre. A preliminary inspection team flew to France and reported back favorably to Kloster. Following that initial reconnaissance a sixty-strong NCL group—engineers as well as operations and marketing personnel—conducted a full-scale evaluation and feasibility study. They confirmed to Kloster that, subject to some radical rebuilding, the vessel would make an admirable and, at that time, uniquely large cruise ship for the Caribbean.

Kloster bought the vessel and, long before she was renamed the *Norway*, boarded an advance party of engineers and electricians to start deciphering the French systems. The Norwegians were overtly snubbed by residual French hands still on board. Tor Johansen, who would serve as the *Norway*'s chief electrical officer for years, remembers that during his early weeks on board, his French opposite number never once asked him to lunch in the officers' mess; Tor made do instead with a sandwich out on deck. Although, in retrospect, one cannot condone that inhospitable behavior, perhaps it was understandable that the French were bitterly aggrieved that those doughty Norwegians were resurrecting the vessel that their government as well as their unions could not keep in service.

France was rechristened *Norway* at Le Havre just before departure. Armed French soldiers lined the François Premier Lock as she passed through. Captain Torbjorn Hauge had been assigned four bodyguards in anticipation of trouble, but there was, as it turned out, no open defiance from Havrois dockers. The pride of France's merchant marine slipped out of her home port for the last time without incident and departed under tow for Bremerhaven. There she would undergo an ambitious, winter-long refit, thanks to the guiding wizardry of Danish naval architect Tage Wandborg. With dozens of newbuilding and/or conversions to his credit, owlish, silver-thatched Wandborg is, to my mind, as inextricably attached to the *Norway* as is Kloster. He oversaw her initial debut into service and has been charged with every subsequent renovation since.

Janet Olczak, a nurse who organized the *Norway*'s medical facilities, remembers that a ghostly *Mary Celeste*–like aura suffused the *France*'s hospital on the starboard side of what is now called Viking Deck. Pencils, pens, syringes, instruments, and even clothes were in place, as though just deserted the day before rather than five years previously. During that winter's arduous conversion, she requested a small icebox in which to keep certain medications, such as insulin. Hartvig von Harling, the staff captain, arranged delivery instead of a sizable pantry refrigerator, so vast that it had to be accommodated across the hall in a separate cabin, the doors and walls of which were removed to permit entry. Finally plugged in, the compressor churned out so much heat that a special ventilation trunk had to be added one deck higher. In the end, Janet found a small icebox for the insulin; that huge "hospital" refrigerator was used only to keep soft drinks cold for the nursing staff.

The two outboard propellers were removed, and five more were added, bow and stern thrusters that, working in tandem, pirouette the *Norway* gracefully in Miami's turning basin each arrival morning. The *France's* semi-indoor tourist-class pool aft was replaced with a larger open-air one, and another was added between the funnels. The afterwall of the Salon Riviera, *France's* first-class Smoking Room, was closed up because an outdoor restaurant would obliterate its outer veranda, the one on which funnel soot used to rain down. Donghia transformed that Smoking Room into the Club Internationale, a handsome, double-height public room that remains among the most successful afloat.

The following spring of 1980, the *Norway* emerged from Bremerhaven's HAPAG-Lloyd yard with a royal blue hull, new funnel livery, an expanse of open decks aft, and two giant tenders mounted on the foredeck below the bridge. Mary and I boarded her in Kristiansand, on Norway's south coast, for what I can only describe as the ultimate delivery crossing. The *Norway* was not really ready for even the modest half-passenger load she embarked for the transatlantic journey: approaching the vessel via tender, I could see, stacked hastily beneath the afterdeck overhang, rolls of carpeting and cardboard boxes, a sure sign that things below were incomplete.

Before she sailed for New York, the *Norway* made a majestic entry up the Oslo Fjord to the capital; Knut Kloster was determined to show off his giant ship to his king and countrymen before surrendering her to the Caribbean. In hot spring weather, we steamed ceremonially toward Oslo, surrounded by a flotilla of small craft, everything that floated in Norway, it seemed. A cousin of mine, Charlotte Ferner, was among them, and we had agreed that for ease of identification I would wear a bright yellow slicker on deck; conversely, she and her husband, Finn, agreed to drape a navy blue sail cover across the boom so that I could pick out their vessel. To no avail: It was so hot that my slicker was intolerable, and nearly

ABOVE: *Knut Utstein Kloster, the Norwegian shipping genius who rescued* France *from certain oblivion in 1979 and wrought her into* Norway. (Norwegian Cruise Line)

LEFT: *The* Norway's *funnels in their new NCL colors: white, dark blue, and cornflower blue. The swooping vertical stripe on the forward curve visually reduces the funnel's height.* (Nelson Arnstein, M.D., collection)

all of the hundreds of yachts at my feet had navy blue sail covers across their booms; the Ferners and I met later on the pier.

During the final approach to the famous Akershus ramparts, one of my favorite Klosterisms surfaced. Both of the *Norway*'s open-air pools had been netted, crammed in readiness with blue and white helium balloons. Just before the vessel tied up, they were released in an inverse shower of stunning color. As thousands of balloons lofted into the sunlight and began drifting gently eastward, Knut Kloster, on the bridge and in the midst of having wrought the *Norway*'s maritime miracle, confided to a friend that he felt awful about polluting Sweden in this way.

After three days of celebration, the *Norway* set sail for Southampton and New York. Life on board was irresistible, if occasionally bizarre. Plumbing troubles predominated. Once the *Norway*'s water had been turned back on in Bremerhaven, pipes had fractured all over the vessel; as a result, many cabins were still without water. Mary and I changed cabins several times, finally ending up in an inside, what had been Cabin 63 on the *France*'s Pont Principal but was now Cabin 101 on Norway Deck. Whether or not it had a porthole was of less importance than whether it had running water, which it did in abundance, filling the largest bathtub I have ever seen on board any ship anywhere.

Because of the shortage of working cabins, dozens of dilatory and opportunistic passengers continually relocated themselves around the vessel. Like restless birds of passage, they migrated as working faucets dictated. No one knew where anyone was, least of all poor Walter Perkins, late of U.S. Lines and chief purser for the crossing. He tried his best to keep track of hundreds of passengers, who, day by day, co-opted renovated accommodations as soon as they were finished.

One company shipmate made a valiant effort not only to find out who was living where but also to document every cabin failing. The charming wife of company president Helge Naarstad, Nini—born on September 9 and so nicknamed forever with the Norwegian for "9/9"—organized many of us into scouting parties that roamed the ship, knocking on cabin doors, identifying and enumerating occupants, and checking out lighting, furnishing, or plumbing inadequacies.

One of our table companions was Angelo Donghia's man on board for the crossing, Peter Duke. One afternoon, he had just stepped out of his shower when he heard a peremptory knock at the door.

"Who is in this cabin?" demanded an authoritative voice from the corridor, one of Nini's inspection teams.

"Duke, of Donghia," Peter shouted hastily groping for a towel.

There was a long pause. "Sorry to have disturbed you, Your Grace," responded the nonplussed scouting party, and continued along the corridor, wondering how an Italian nobleman had suddenly surfaced on board.

Matters were gradually sorted out, and with each passing day, conditions improved. Sometimes there were exterior diversions. One day, a rubber life raft appeared on the horizon; as we approached it, the canvas shelter above it caught the wind, and it capsized. Maneuvering with his new bow thrusters, Captain Hauge brought the *Norway* deftly alongside, and crewmen down at a B Deck port managed to haul it on board. The raft had obviously fallen overboard—its parent vessel was the *Rosedale*—but it carried no occupants at all. Rest assured that Oslo newspapers the following afternoon advised their readers that the raft's castaways were being well cared for on board the largest cruise ship in the world; that year, wherever she was, the *Norway* remained news.

The ship's floating population made it easy for a stowaway. More than one passenger, among them the late Jimmy Kirkwood of *A Chorus Line* fame, reported that a shadowy figure, carrying a glass, would sometimes knock on their cabin door. It always happened late at night, long after Nini's census takers had retired. If the cabin was occupied, the intruder would apologize in broken English and disappear. Enough identical sightings alerted Purser Perkins that a probable stowaway was on board, looking for a suitable bolt hole. He alerted security, and somewhere in mid-ocean, the man was finally apprehended.

He was an Oslovian of indeterminate middle age, chronically tipsy, who had wandered on board in Norway and decided to see New York. He was locked up in the brig forward on Biscayne Deck, but the night before our arrival in New York, a sympathetic passenger or crewman set him free again, and he went to ground somewhere in the roiling passenger body. As a result, the *Norway* endured an interminable disembarkation ordeal tied up at Pier 88 while the ship's security team, goaded by U.S. Immigration inspectors, flushed the stowaway out a second time. He surrendered meekly and was led away to Kennedy Airport for a flight home. He was in a hurry, he argued boisterously, because it was

May 17, Norway's Constitution Day, and they were expecting him at a party back home in Oslo.

The vessel arrived on Miami station in June 1980 and began the weekly Caribbean cruise program for which she had been so expensively and successfully converted. At the start of the eighties, the *Norway* was unique, a latter-day *Great Eastern*, if you will, a giant ahead of her time. No other cruise ship in the world came close to carrying 2,000 passengers. RCCL's intermediate *Song of America* would not reach Miami for two years, and their subsequent *Sovereign of the Seas* was undreamed of. Carnival's *Tropicale*, that company's first modest newbuilding, was still under construction in Denmark, while the *Jubilee*-class megaships were no more than a gleam in Ted Arison's eye. *Norway* had the megaship field completely to herself, and she dwarfed the competition strung out along Dodge Island every weekend.

That same royal blue bulk offered marketing clout as well. Thousands of passengers, most of them new to cruising, flocked on board week after week; the *Norway* offered more of everything to impressionable neophytes as well as their starry-eyed travel agents who remembered the *France*. Of course, there were occasional technological glitches—fires, blackouts, and floods, all those systemic breakdowns endemic to older vessels—and patient Norwegian engineers had their jobs cut out for them. In fact, the *Norway*, it was deadpanned ashore in NCL's operations department, "devoured second engineers." In truth, however, second engineers on board the vessel had a marvelous superior, Chief Engineer Egil Fossen, the vastly competent man who had embarked in Bremerhaven to supervise the conversion and remained in charge of everything that moved on board. A gentle, endearing soul, he forged a first-rate team to cope with every crisis, at the same time remaining in perpetual thrall to their beloved, if occasionally obstreperous, charge.

Knut Kloster had correctly perceived that, to make the proper impact, passenger life aboard his giant revived liner had to offer more than could be found on the competition, even more than was offered on board his own white ships, the *Norway*'s quartet of sold-out, smaller consorts. And more there was: Strolling mimes haunted the promenade decks, sometimes antagonizing passengers with caricatures of their walks; violinists prowled the dining rooms, playing schmaltzy favorites tableside at dinner; an extraordinary performer on a unicycle was forever darting in and out of elevators; Eddie Cotts, an accomplished magician, performed table magic in the Club Internationale each evening, producing full goldfish bowls from beneath a trilby.

But the *Norway* offered more than Renaissance street fair. The *France's* cinema, known in former days as the *salle de spectacle*, had been transformed into a venue for ambitious live entertainment, the first of cruising's multimedia music halls. For a long time, the *Norway* was the only cruise ship in the world that provided its passengers with slightly diminished Broadway musicals. And if what was now called Windward Dining Room lacked the catering polish of the Restaurant Chambord, there was good reason to conclude that many of NCL's down-home clientele would have been overwhelmed by Louis Pellegrin's fierce dedication. Out on deck, whereas passengers on rival tonnage might participate in deck games, on board the *Norway*, they entered the only shipboard Olympics in the world.

The *Norway* provided lavish music as well. Bandmaster Chip Hoehler presided over two dozen musicians, what long-gone union chief James Petrillo might have termed a complete Local by itself. A band on deck serenaded each Miami departure; that was as it should be, for Norway the country boasts more brass bands per capita than any other. Those same musicians doubled in indoor brass, convening each evening in the North Cape Lounge as a genuine big band. They also played en masse for the weekly name entertainers who filled the theater twice nightly—Vic Damone, Diahann Carroll, Rita Moreno, Jack Jones, Phyllis Diller, the Smothers Brothers, and Allen & Rossi, an eminent talent roster that raised the *Norway's* entertainment sights well above the cruising competition.

Of course, it was the vessel's huge capacity that provided such a substantial entertainment handle. So it was the *Norway* that first implemented the advantages of economy of scale. Her example sparked the resurgence of larger and larger cruise ships that today rival their North Atlantic predecessors. Every present-day megaship owes a debt to Knut Kloster's pioneering vision in resuscitating and popularizing this classic vessel. Everything about the *Norway* was big—her hull, her tenders, her passenger load, her entertainment, and significantly, her band. Big ship, big band—it seems an appropriate moment to dwell not only on what is called the big-band sound but on shipboard sound as well: The benevolent ghost of one leads to the frightening actuality of the other.

A dozen years ago, one could only hear a genuine big band on board the *Norway*, part of the maritime bigness for which Kloster so rightly strove. Judging from the number of cruise lines that still promise that "big-band sound," it is clear that most of prerock, adult America sees the big band and its sound as a cherished part of its vanished past. Nostalgic middle-aged passengers pleasurably recall the large dance orchestras of their youth, complete with dinner-jacketed woodwind and brass sections that rose on cue for certain choruses or an emphatic finale, sometimes swaying their instruments in hypnotic unison. The big band still powerfully evokes the dances, nightclubs, and shows they enjoyed while growing up.

What has happened to *Norway*'s big band? It has fallen victim on two counts, not only to its high per-musician cost but to the deluge of sound produced by fewer sidemen armed with unlimited amplification. From the very first days on board the *Norway*, as Chip Hoehler's sixteen-man big band delivered a Glenn Miller retrospective in the North Cape Lounge, forward in the orchestra pit of the Saga Theatre, a mere handful of his musicians could generate an equivalent musical volume. The seeds of the big band's destruction were sown by first use of what has become pandemic throughout today's cruise ships, the dread click track.

Why dread? Read on. The click track is nothing more than a taped electronic metronome heard in the earphones of musicians seated on show-lounge stages. That tempo-driving click is only one track of dozens more musical or effects tracks that broadcast accompanying orchestral and choral sound cunningly synchronized to the (live) musicians and performers onstage. Every visible performer must adhere to the beat of unseen, prerecorded colleagues, driven by the track's remorseless click. So much of the "live" show that passengers hear is not live at all but was played and recorded months earlier and thousands of miles away.

In fact, music for these shows is amplified in two senses, made fuller as well as broadcast electronically. And here's the ingenious part: Since the ship's live musicians are also miked, no one can really tell who is actually onstage and who is absent. The show's sound is all contained within the same rich, indistinguishable torrent pouring from show-lounge speakers.

The economic advantages for the cruise lines are obvious: A dozen or more salaries are saved, as is considerable cabin space. Moreover, the argument runs, the click-track prerecordings fulfill an aesthetic function. Contemporary audiences are so conditioned to rich televised or filmed orchestrations that "live" entertainment in huge show lounges must be buttressed to meet their expectations. Finally, the cruise lines suggest, use of a click track guarantees a consistent show, locking in weekly performances to tempi originally devised in the studio.

If the cruise lines really want lavish sound and unshakable showbiz consistency, why not just film the entire show? To my mind, semirecorded performances masquerading as "live" entertainment are essentially dishonest, the shoddy equivalent of television laugh tracks. The cruise lines christen their click-track trickery "augmentation"; but by augmenting their sound, pursuing this Pirandellian conceit—*Six Dancers in Search of an Orchestra*?—they encourage further deceit. Tapping feet and singing voices can just as easily be prerecorded so that hardworking boys and girls out onstage are often only going through the motions and mouthing. Does no one else object to this maritime Milli Vanilli-ism? Only you, the passenger-audience, can put a stop to it. The moment your shipboard musicians don earphones, you should object.

Of course, we are all to blame. Late-twentieth-century America suffers two irresistible and unrelated indulgences—ceaseless litigation and chronic overamplification. The microphone and its attendant amplifier and speaker rule every phase of present-day entertainment. Broadway theaters that for generations offered unadorned actors' voices have all succumbed to footlight or radio microphones, and to meet the demands of the rock generation, increasingly ambitious amplifiers have aggrandized every musical performer from tyro to tyrant.

The entire world is drowning in overamplification. When Washington's Union Station was recently restored into a kind of station-mall, there was an opening celebration complete with amplified musicians. As an avalanche of sound thundered cruelly between those unyielding marble walls, conversation anywhere was impossible. Senator Daniel Patrick Moynihan (ironically, one of the legislators whose efforts had sparked the renovation) futilely requested to have the sound turned down and then, defeated, went home instead.

Across the Atlantic, Woody Hochswender covered the March

1991 opening of Oscar de la Renta's spring collection for the *New York Times*. "In Paris, Ghastly Music and Frye Boots" ran the headline; one section of his account was subtitled "Sonic Disaster."

> The music on the runway this season got the really ghastly reviews. At Mr. de la Renta's show, the driving disco soundtrack was extra loud, perhaps to make a big impression. It simply pounded the jet-lag headaches in deeper and deeper, each jeweled jacket merging with the percussive blasts to ignite a new throb of pain.
>
> Annette de la Renta, the designer's wife, began to cry. Carolyne Roehm asked an usher to lower the volume *but nothing was done* [italics mine].

Who, one wonders, is in charge? Apparently neither Senator Moynihan nor Mr. de la Renta, only their unrelenting musical specialists. An orgy of amplification has not only engulfed us, it offers hearing loss for teenagers and stress for their elders. Dr. Alice Suter, an audiologist at Washington's National Institute for Occupational Safety and Health, laments that stressful "noise seems to be accepted by our society these days as a necessary evil."

Nowhere has this amplified onslaught wrought more havoc than on board today's cruise ships. Look up at the ceiling of almost any lounge and you will see, sited every few yards, perforations indicating a loudspeaker. Although ensuring efficient sound distribution to every corner of the room, that speaker grid also ensures that no passenger can escape it. In the old days, one sat either near the orchestra or far from it, distancing oneself from the music for conversation. But speaker overkill assaults every square foot of every lounge.

The sound merchants descend on bewildered owners and sell them enormous and unnecessary systems. For instance, the *Sea Goddess I*'s passenger lounge cannot measure more than thirty by forty feet. But when the vessel entered service, its tiny little stage was encumbered with enough huge—and ugly—amplifier boxes to deafen Central Park. And sure enough, when the vessel's three-piece orchestra plays for dancing, conversation is out; one microphone has been lowered inside the upright piano just to make sure.

Overloud music remains an abusive problem on board every cruise ship. I have already referred to sound excesses in the *Sovereign of the Seas*' Schooner Bar and the *Fantasy*'s otherwise enchanting Cleopatra's Bar. Herewith, two more appalling sound bytes.

On board the *Rotterdam*, once in mid-Pacific, I was in the balcony of the Ritz-Carlton Lounge while a rather good but brutally amplified orchestra played for dancers below. The man with whom I was talking turned to his companion and asked if "something could be done about the loud music."

"I've asked them again and again" was the response, "but they keep turning the volume back up."

A perfectly normal—alas—shipboard exchange these days, save for the fact that the first speaker was Nico van der Vorm, then chairman of Holland America, and his companion was Dirk Zeller, the ship's hotel manager. That neither of these eminences could prevail over their stubborn musician-employees only momentarily surprised me.

Dissolve to the *Royal Viking Star* in the same waters some years later. I was one of about a hundred passengers dining atop the vessel in the Venus Lounge. We ate as though in a nightclub, all the tables hard by a small but powerful orchestra. A saxophonist, standing no more than four feet away from me, had parked a microphone within the flaring bell of his instrument.

Inevitably, several passengers complained to the maître d'hôtel that his "background" music was intolerable. He dutifully went to the control booth and instructed the technician on duty to lower the gain. This so enraged the saxophonist that he left the bandstand in mid-gig, stalked back to the booth, and turned the gain up higher still; and there it stayed. Once again, who *is* in charge and who should be indulged, temperamental musicians or their (paying) audience? Some courageous cruise lines should decide.

In the summer of 1984, the *Norway* was due in Hamburg for dry-docking. The owner decided to sell both crossings to passengers; he also arranged some cruises up the coast of Norway. Pulling the *Norway* off her Caribbean station for any period of time was understandably resisted by NCL's Miami management, largely because of a curious booking phenomenon. Whenever the vessel leaves Miami for dry-docking, bookings are below par for a long, damaging interval following her return. Travel agents and passengers alike seem somehow unwilling to book on the *Norway* until well after her return; the longer the absence, the longer the lean booking period to follow.

In fact, it has always been a sadness, both to me and to many of the *Norway*'s crew, that this great and gallant vessel remains locked within a pedestrian, seven-day treadmill. I have always felt that she somehow deserved a more challenging itinerary than that weekly carousel between St. Thomas, St. Maarten, the Bahamas, and Miami. By the same token, though, only by sustaining that circuit can her cabins continue to fill. Unvarying routine is the hallmark of the Caribbean's seven-day grind. An established cruise regime, both itinerarial as well as logistic, pulses at the heart of Miami's cruise market. Change is anathema: Just as lifeboat drill must be conducted before Miami departure, just as Wednesday is always St. Thomas, just as "Country Theme Night" is always that evening, so week after week, the daily cycle, in the words of Cole Porter, "repeats and repeats and repeats." Thus positioned and marketed, *Norway* and her Caribbean rivals are on perennial, uncomplicated call for passenger throngs. That constant Dodge Island presence, no less than the smooth inevitability of routine, greases cruising's marketing wheels.

So the prospect of the *Norway*'s escape back to the North Atlantic and Norwegian coast offered compelling reason to book over the summer of 1984. Sadly, not enough did. She carried no more than a thousand passengers eastbound (half full) and fourteen hundred westbound to Miami, with a bonus call at Bermuda en route. Might she have been better patronized with a New York rather than Philadelphia departure and Miami return? We shall never know. The Norwegian coastal cruises in between, however, were sellouts.

Despite the disappointing response, both crossings were fabulous; eastbound especially, I have never known such brilliant North Atlantic weather, as though the gods were smiling on this cruising expatriate from the south. Before the July departure, it amused me that NCL's entertainment department was uneasy at the prospect of passengers being "confined" to the *Norway* for eight days. Conditioned to restless Caribbean clients deposited ashore every other day, they were astonished to find that there was a large northeastern passenger constituency for whom a week exclusively at sea proved an unalloyed pleasure. Nevertheless, determined to dispel possible mid-ocean ennui, in addition to the *Norway*'s regular activities, they laid on a plethora of top-grade entertainment, including two legendary Frenchmen—Michel LeGrand and Stéphane Grappelli—as well as the American jazz pianist Teddy Wilson. What a delight to enjoy their afternoon recitals in the packed Club Internationale, to have on board such distinguished performers—no click tracks they—at their best! Alas, because of those disappointing passenger totals, the *Norway* has never again carried passengers transatlantic; the inescapable Miami syndrome won out.

Just after the *Norway*'s summer vacation of 1984, Knut Kloster made a bold, acquisitive move. He bought the three vessels of the ailing Royal Viking Line, bringing them safely under NCL's corporate umbrella and, at that time, continued Norwegian registry. In fact, Kloster snared the company at the last moment, out from under another potential buyer, who already had advance parties on board the *Royal Viking Star*, devising new proprietary arrangements with the crew. Once news of Kloster's momentous buyout arrived from San Francisco and Oslo, they packed up and went home.

In the first flush of consolidation between Caribbean NCL and worldwide Royal Viking, there was brave talk of allying the two disparate fleets. Through rose-colored glasses at Miami headquarters, it was presumed that Royal Viking passengers might well be lured to the Caribbean, if not to the downscale white fleet, at least to the *Norway*. Conversely, the company hypothesized that *Norway* passengers anxious to move upmarket would graduate from a weekly to a fortnightly or even longer Royal Viking experience.

But it turned out almost at once that cross-pollination of this kind between two disparate companies is fruitless. It is a cruise-marketing truism that clients of one sociological class are not inclined to experiment with ships of another. After some in-house finger wagging and recriminations citing apples and oranges, newly named Kloster Cruises sensibly opted to maintain NCL and RVL fleets on their own separate courses.

At the same time that he so dramatically enlarged his company, Knut Kloster renounced its day-to-day management. He withdrew to concentrate full-time on his *idée fixe* for nearly a decade: another big ship, of course, a bigger ship, a giant ship that will more than triple the *Norway*'s passenger capacity. The 250,000-ton *Phoenix*, a gargantuan vessel to eclipse all others, will accommodate 5,600 passengers within three ziggurats towering above a 1,200-foot tankerlike hull. Concealed within the *Phoenix*'s catamaran stern will be a fleet of four air-conditioned day sailers that can, as self-contained cruising satellites, whisk 400 passengers at a time ashore or to neighboring islands. But islands, it has always seemed to me, would be almost unnecessary attractions to passengers on board the *Phoenix*; her vast self should prove the most exotic destination of all.

For half a dozen years, Knut Kloster, Tage Wandborg, and ex-*Norway* master Captain Aage Hodavik, specifically seconded to the project from NCL, have plotted and planned in the *Phoenix*'s Oslo headquarters. I last sailed with Tage Wandborg on board the *Norway* in late 1990 while he was reconnoitering her new top-deck renovations. We dined together with a large party of officers down in the Chinese laundry, a hilarious and festive banquet during which Tage nevertheless found time to impart a reassuring *Phoenix* fix. Certainly, the technology is all in place: The *Phoenix*'s interminable gestation has ensured unsurpassed and scrupulous plans. It has also created a coterie of enthusiasts, rather like the stubborn airship fraternity that still exists around Lakehurst, New Jersey, site of the tragic *Hindenburg* crash in the thirties. Worldwide, the concept and image of the *Phoenix* have cast their mythic spell. I have been intrigued since the beginning; as a confirmed big-ship devotee, I long to see this ultimate big ship in service, and my faith in Kloster's as well as Wandborg's vision is unshakable.

But there are others who remain less sanguine. Marketing men, as already articulated by Bob Dickinson, dismiss the *Phoenix* as an unworkable white elephant, an imprudent commitment of too many newbuilding dollars into one behemoth. Olav Eftedal, one of the naval architects responsible for RCCL's trio of *Sovereign*-class vessels and the *Nordic Empress*, suggested in a recent note from St.-Nazaire:

> We [Royal Caribbean Cruise Line] will then have received over a period of five years, four ships of a total of about 260,000 gross registered tons* with a capacity of more than 10,000 passengers.

Below was his irresistible footnote:

> *Same GRT as for *Phoenix*, same cost as for *Phoenix*, twice as many passengers as for *Phoenix*.

Naval architects are not alone in their distrust. Most passengers shudder at the prospect of sharing a vessel, however vast, with over five thousand of their fellows. Bridge officers, divided on aesthetic grounds, are unanimously uneasy at the thought of maneuvering the *Phoenix*'s 252-foot beam in and out of port in a crosswind.

The vessel already has, incidentally, been assigned to Port Canaveral. The company has also taken an option on the last hundred acres of available real estate surrounding the *Phoenix*'s projected dock. Here they plan to erect a mammoth support complex, as intricately novel as the vessel it will accommodate. Disembarking and embarking in excess of ten thousand passengers and their luggage in one day, as well as reprovisioning and bunkering the giant ship, will be challenging.

It is symptomatic of the controversial *Phoenix* that, even unbuilt, she arouses as many advocates as opponents. But despite having her port, her profile, and her personality, she has, as yet, no firm building contract from a yard. Years ago, Wärtsilä was interested, followed by a consortium of four German yards. A surge in other newbuilding contracts voided that North Sea possibility, however, so Kloster's most recent and most surprising negotiations have been with the shipping division of New Orleans's Avondale Industries. As presently anticipated, the *Phoenix* would become an American-built and American-flagged vessel, her construction undertaken by what Kloster's New York representative, John Rogers, terms "a national shipyard" or American shipbuilding consortium. Under this scheme, Rogers suggests, floating modules of the *Phoenix* may be built at various American yards, then towed to and assembled at Newport News.

Assembling that hull would only be the beginning. It concerns me that fitting the *Phoenix* out might be beyond the technological clout of American yards, none of which has produced passenger newbuilding for decades. Although much of the necessary technology as well as innumerable prefabricated components would normally come from Europe, Kloster's plan calls for American industry to come up with home-grown alternatives.

If indeed the *Phoenix* is American flagged, she will have an American master, which disqualifies Norwegian master Aage Hodavik. American flagging also means a predominately American crew, and I wonder if an untried cadre of American stewards will be able to service the ship. Since time immemorial, Americans have made consistently dissatisfied stewards, to the degree that even on board American-owned North Atlantic tonnage, those waiting on table and keeping cabins shipshape were largely recruited in Europe. Admittedly, there are splendid U.S.-flag compensations, among them the evasion of Jones Act restrictions. Already, Oslo dreams of a *Phoenix II* for the West Coast that would sail up and down California, calling consecutively at San Francisco, Los Angeles, and San Diego or, courtesy of those comfortable day sailers, at points in between, such as San Simeon or Carmel. Then again, an American flag atop *Phoenix* would permit tax-deductible participation by America's burgeoning incentive-travel market. Finally, in terms of sheer cubic capacity, the *Phoenix* is large enough to accommodate almost any corporate extravagance.

(Those of my readers who framed the dust-jacket chart from *Liners to the Sun* will note that an earlier, four-towered *Phoenix* appears on it, as does the *United States*, two hoped-for probabilities in 1985 that, thus far, have not materialized. Hence, neither is on the chart wrapping this volume. I wish, especially, that the *Phoenix* were, if for no other reason than to fulfill Knut Kloster's long-cherished dream.)

But nothing concrete can or will happen until the financing is assured: The *Phoenix* has become a more than billion-dollar proposition, and in the troubled nineties, despite the cheap dollar, is this grandiose ship a mere pipe dream? I wish Kloster and his colleagues luck in finding financial backing in America, for I sense that until his dream ship sails, he will be unable to turn his talented hand to anything else. To Kloster, the *Phoenix* is more than a cruise ship, more than the world's largest passenger vessel, more than a money-making investment; in his eyes, she assumes allegorical proportions, becomes a floating haven for peace and international cooperation. Just as it was Kloster who, back in 1980, arranged to fly the flag of the United Nations from the *Norway's* truck, so her giant progeny is to serve as yet another vehicle of international understanding. He has even amplified the vessel's name to that noble end, calling her the *Phoenix World City*, clear indication of his vision.

The *Phoenix* preoccupation is pivotal in our story, for since Knut Kloster devoted his full attention to her, he has been sorely missed at the helm of the Florida operation bearing his family's name. Over the last few years, both divisions of Kloster Cruises have encountered rough seas: first a recession, then the *Achille Lauro* scare (although it had minimal impact in the Caribbean), the arrival of competitive big ships in Miami, and throughout the company, a rash of corporate changes and successions.

Nowhere has this malaise impacted more noticeably than on

board the *Norway,* and an inevitable pattern of compromise and retrenchment has set in. It started, ominously, with the banishment of sommeliers from the dining rooms. Ever since, overworked waiters have also had to cope with wine orders during their harried evenings; this makes for a thirstier and frustrated clientele. Then both big-band and big-name entertainers clambered into the tumbrels; no longer would Chip Hoehler and his musicians play for dancing or for Vegas-style backup in the theater. To no one's surprise, the "big" concept moved along Dodge Island to its easternmost tip, what I call RCCL corner. Surely, it was no coincidence that their big ship, the *Sovereign of the Seas,* should have instituted its own big-band and big-name entertainment almost simultaneously. Has the "big ship" torch inadvertently passed from NCL to RCCL?

Shipboard musicians were not the only Kloster casualties: The company ruthlessly pruned shore staffs as well. Significantly, a sinister new corporate post was created at Coral Gables headquarters and given the express responsibility of improving "yield management" throughout the fleet. Such aggressive new yields include a two-dollar surcharge on every cabin-service order as well as shipwide installation of lotto machines.

Whatever additional revenue is realized by subterfuge of this kind is outweighed by diminution of the formerly magical quality of the *Norway*'s appeal. Apart from an optional tip, cabin service has always been free, one of shipboard's traditional perks, and should never be confused with land-based room service. Though a hotel may charge for delivering a tray, they also charge for the food that's on it; shipboard meals have always come with the ticket, and so, it seems to me, should their delivery. As for the lamentable lotto, shipboard gambling, to my mind, should remain in the casinos; cluttering up staircases and lobbies with tacky electronic tote boards seems a mistake.

One interesting *Norway* episode in the late eighties brought *France* back to momentary life. Two Frenchmen, writer Bernard Planche and architect François Jeantet, dreamed up the idea of temporarily restoring *Norway* to her French origins for a giddy experimental week. Together with travel agent Marc Braillon, they organized a charter of the entire vessel in early December 1989. It was marketed as *France "La Croisière"* to a shipload of almost exclusively French passengers.

The emphasis of *France "La Croisière"* was centered naturally around French food and wine. Paul Bocuse dragooned thirty-five of his gastronomic colleagues from all over France to join him aboard the former French Line flagship and provide their passenger-countrymen with a week of sumptuous gluttony. The porcelain factory at Limoges was persuaded to produce an entire new china service of 12,000 plates, cups, and saucers especially for the charter, classic white decorated with a rectangular seal incorporating the *France* and the *Norway* surrounding a bow view. (The new dishes not only proved too delicate for the ship's dishwashers; they also proved to be irresistible souvenirs, snapped up by passengers and crewmen alike.) Commandant Georges Croisile, the *France*'s first master, was summoned out of his Paris retirement as guest of honor, but, regrettably, ill health prevented him from attending.

NCL made a great fuss of *La Croisière*'s departure. A formal rechristening ceremony took place on the pier beneath the *Norway*'s graceful flank as she lay at her Dodge Island berth. Huge plywood cutout letters spelling FRANCE were unveiled, erected, for that week only, up between the funnels. Those six letters were retained, stored inside number 1 funnel for a less ambitious *La Croisière* repeated a year later.

Once their vessel had been renamed, French passengers and Norwegian officers embarked, the ship sailed, and for the next seven days, Louis Pellegrin himself would have been delighted with the achievements inside both Windward and Leeward dining rooms and, more important, inside the intervening galley. I'm told that the food was incredibly good, rivaling the old days. One of the very few Americans on board was retired dean of food critics Craig Claiborne of the *New York Times*, the man who, in the *France* days, had awarded the vessel his unreserved imprimatur. *La Croisière*'s cuisine, Claiborne reports, was incomparable, "some of the greatest food I have ever had." In fact, he confessed, he gained ten pounds over that week, which, two years later, he was still trying to lose.

Another American passenger was Richard Holman, publisher of New York's *Wall Street Transcript*. He, too, found the food incredible, although he recalled that the service was patchy. The continuing absence of trained sommeliers on board the *Norway* meant that the elementary ritual of having a passenger taste the wine was neglected. But after the steward had absorbed that lesson, he then filled every glass and decamped, leaving the original taster's empty. In general, though, the dining-room stewards rose to the occasion, having been drilled the previous week by hotel manager Bjorn-Erik Julseth to relinquish their customary "Hey, mon" patois greeting in favor of a more formal *"Bonjour, Monsieur et Madame."* They were also issued white gloves for dining-room wear every evening.

Although the vessel followed its customary seven-day on-board schedule, officers and staff discovered that the week's most popular attraction was, inevitably, eating. While regular cabaret, *Barnum*, and multimedia *Sea Legs* drew indifferent crowds, the dining room remained the center of attention, packed with preoccupied, diligent gourmands each night until midnight. The French passengers did not indulge in as many T-shirts and ship souvenirs as the *Norway*'s customary passengers, but they did buy a great many Havana cigars and bottles of spirits. Another abnormality, which did not distress the crew at all, was the French lady passengers' custom of doffing their bathing-suit tops around the pools.

The second *La Croisière* a year later ended on a note of discord. On Friday night before the vessel's return to Miami, the French stayed up till all hours, en masse; none bothered to place their luggage outside their cabin doors before retiring, as requested. The following day, disembarkation morning, most of the ship's luggage was still on board. Miami's hard-pressed detachment of U.S. Customs agents left the *Norway/France* temporarily uncleared, departing instead to cope with neighboring tonnage until all luggage had been brought down to the pier.

So unhappy were the French at this delay—for which they were largely responsible—that a large contingent stormed the bridge, holding Captain Geir Lokoen hostage until customs agents returned to the pier. When they finally did, the master was released, the off-loaded baggage was inspected, and the French departed for the airport. But their troubles were not over. Either because of their lateness or because of equipment failure, there had to be substitution of several aircraft, all with different seating configurations. The Paris-bound French, unhappy at being deprived of their previously reserved seat assignments, rioted in the terminal. One wonders whether *la grande bouffe flottante* will ever be repeated.

In the fall of 1990, the *Norway* steamed empty to Bremerhaven (her fourth European renovation since 1980) for a massive upper-deck expansion. It is not uncommon for cruise ships to expand horizontally with a new floating section added amidships. The *Norway*, however, was expanded vertically. One hundred and thirty-five cabins were added up around the funnels, two decks' worth

TOP: *Before and after a vertical expansion, achieved at Bremerhaven's Lloydwerft yard in the fall of 1990. The new double cabin rows add substance above the bridge.* (Nelson Arnstein, M.D., collection and Michael Maxtone-Graham)

BOTTOM: *The price of progress: The underside of the vast top-deck additions, looking rather like the bottom of a bathtub.* (Author's collection)

around the forward one and a single layer around the second. When Tage Wandborg was on board planning the renovation, he told me that, in fact, the ship's number 1 funnel was four meters higher than the second, allowing him the double layer forward. He also advised me that once the additions were complete atop the vessel, her freeboard would diminish by an almost imperceptible twenty-five centimeters.

The company had long envisioned another Bremerhaven addition belowdecks. The after Lido Bar on Pool Deck became Le Rendezvous, an extremely attractive and timely extra-tariff restaurant with its own galley slightly forward on the starboard side. By day, it is unused, remaining a passageway from the North Cape Lounge forward out to the swimming pool aft, traffic that ceases after sunset. Installation of this facility—one of only three in existence—did much to restore *Norway's* diminished grandeur, and I can only hope that more of the *Norway's* clients will book tables there than did passengers on board the *Royal Viking Sun*.

All of us who cherished the *Norway* were distressed at the prospect of tampering with her profile. Raising the level of her upper decks around the funnels would have the effect of making them seem shorter. Cruise staff on board began referring to the *Norway's* "Smurf funnels," after the comic strip's blue-and-white abbreviated figures. Fortunately, I was relieved at the result. Those funnels, perhaps the most famous in the world, still have their clout and have receded only slightly into the surrounding superstructure. Curiously, the most damaged view is from the bridge, which appears to be located under one end of a huge bathtub; neither funnel can be seen.

It is imperative that we *France/Norway* buffs take the long view. The rationale of those new decks was not merely raising the passenger count but creating, for the ex-liner *Norway*, some fashionable cabin rows symptomatic of all present-day cruise ships. Significantly, while 1988's *Sovereign of the Seas* had no balconies, three years later, her younger sister, the *Monarch of the Seas*, does. Clearly, upscale balconied cabins are here to stay.

They were rare in the old days. Although the *Normandie* boasted some modified balconies aft on Promenade Deck as well as a pair of huge terraced suites facing aft, neither the *Queen Mary* nor the *Queen Elizabeth* had any. The balcony emerged largely as a warm-weather cruising perquisite. On board North Atlantic liners, the very best cabins were always sited amidships in the hull. The *France's* most lavish suites, called Normandie and Ile de France, were purposely located on Upper Deck, far from the weather and deep in the hull. Even by the late 1950s, with cruising already a reality, naval architects were loath to risk balconied cabins atop the ship. Since then, Cunard has added two supplementary decks of luxury cabins between funnel and bridge on the *Queen Elizabeth 2*, with, admittedly, balconies and splendid views. However, during rough weather on the North Atlantic, I far prefer to be housed comfortably amidships down on 1 or 2 Deck, in the *Queen's* original top-drawer accommodations.

In the Caribbean, balconies are de rigueur. Like all high-priced options ashore or afloat, whether orchestra seats or suites, they book the most briskly. So, if adding those cabins makes the *Norway* more competitive as well as NCL more profitable, then it is churlish to carp at what turned out to be a negligible change in profile. Occupants of those new cabins facing aft do have a perpetual one-on-one basketball game below their balconies, but their marble bathrooms and spacious quarters presumably outweigh that disadvantage. The partitions dividing the *Norway's* new balconies are made of transparent Lexan, lighter and tougher than glass; whereas I would have thought transparent partitions would have cut down on privacy, one senior NCL hand suggests that it doubtless improves sociability!

Since we shared some *France* stories, it seems only fair to pass on a few more about life on board the *Norway*. Hotel Manager Kjell Jorkjen occupies the same office off the original embarkation lobby that Commissaire Principal Ermel once used. It has been redecorated since the *France* days; the entire forward wall is paneled with mirrors. Those mirrors have been put to good use on more than one occasion when disgruntled passengers come calling. On Kjell's first cruise, an irate man stormed uninvited into his office, sat down on the opposite side of the desk, and began a tirade. Wisely, Kjell only nodded and let him continue. After a few minutes, he was fascinated to note that the man kept turning and venting much of his spleen *at his own mirrored reflection*. Obviously, the effect was beneficial. After a few more minutes, the man calmed down completely, apologized profusely to the hotel manager for taking his time, and left.

"I never said a word," Kjell reported later. "The mirror did it all." He immediately rearranged his office slightly so that incoming visitors could not avoid their reflection and has staunchly advocated looking-glass therapy many times since.

A stone's throw away from that mirrored office is the ceremonial staircase entry into the Windward Dining Room. Retained by the Norwegians, that *grande descente* was a perennial feature of all French Line vessels, designed so that lady passengers dressed in their best could participate in dazzling evening entries. One night at a *Norway* first sitting, however, a poor demented woman entered dressed in her least: In full view of an astonished dining room, wearing nothing but a life preserver, she strolled languidly down to dine. A quick-witted steward wrapped her in a tablecloth, and the maître d'hôtel conducted her down to the doctor. I always wondered how she managed to get as far as the dining room.

In port or at anchor, the *Norway's* officers communicate with each other via walkie-talkie radios. One day at St. Thomas, Captain Ragnar Nilsen, an exacting master, spoke to his security officer from his office behind the bridge and asked him where he was. "I'm down on B Deck at the port gangway," replied the security officer, whom I shall call Sven. In fact, Sven had just awakened and was speaking from his cabin. Moments later, the captain strolled onto the bridge to find Sven slouched in the fog chair, sipping a mug of coffee, several decks and at least a hundred yards from where he had just reported he was. Moral for delinquent officers: Walkie-talkies are as incriminating as they are convenient.

And finally, another stowaway story, this one about a twelve-year-old boy from Miami called Jerome. Somehow Jerome managed to sneak on board the *Norway* undetected (he never confessed how) and remained incognito for two sea days until St. Maarten. History does not relate where Jerome slept, but he had an ingenious means of getting fed. Breakfast and lunch were easy, crowded among anonymous throngs at the cafeteria serving tables at the Great Outdoor Restaurant. In the evenings, he found a foolproof way of dining in the Windward Dining Room. He marched down the staircase—still in shorts, tank top, and cap—and told the dining-room manager a plaintive tale: He did not know his cabin number, his parents were asleep, and he was awfully hungry. Jerome was immediately ushered to an empty table, where he ate his fill. He managed this trick twice in succession, once in each dining room.

But Jerome gave himself away when he made a foolish—and

fatal—error: He stole a fellow passenger's camera. Since it was rather a good one, security was summoned, and Jerome, who was carrying it around openly on deck, was restrained, questioned, and unmasked. He was flown back to Miami escorted by Arne Jorgensen, at that time the ship's staff captain and about to go on leave.

Arne told me that Jerome was as congenial as he was unrepentant. "My friends do this all the time," he announced cheerfully as they drove to the airport. "We go cruising on lots of ships." How many Jeromes, I wonder, enjoy themselves each week on board Miami's seven-day fleet?

With or without them, the *Norway* continues on her customary circuit, calling on alternate weeks in San Juan so as to give passengers and especially crew a fortnightly evening ashore. Her new upper-deck suites book uncommonly well, and it is, as always, a pleasure to know that this historic vessel still attracts a loyal and enthusiastic clientele. It is doubly miraculous that crossing *France* is still with us as cruising *Norway*, inspiration for every economy-of-scale hull that sails in her wake.

How long will she last? I hope NCL will cherish her forever. She remains an imperishable, crossing/cruising link with our North Atlantic past, and the Caribbean would be a sadder place without her.

Chapter 8

*Whatever you do, whatever folly you commit, never, never
be tempted to take a sea voyage. It is quite the nastiest thing
you can take—I have had three days of it now, so I know.*
  —Anna Buchan, writing home from the Scotia, date
    unknown

To travel hopefully is a better thing than to arrive.
  —Robert Louis Stevenson, 1891

*My passion for travel cools when I consider that it consists
entirely of departures and arrivals.*
  —Marquis de Custine, 1839

*A ship is an island . . . inhabited yet mysteriously
unexplored, self-centered, secretive, wonderful, unique.
Situated against a sunset horizon or towering white-topped
above a quayside, ablaze with lights or gay with flags, it
seems cut off in time as well as space—a presence whose
scale is impossible to grasp, and whose indifference to
admiration is as maddening as a cat's.*
  —Sir Hugh Casson, 1969

Landfall

Our voyage is nearly over, and shoreside angst infects us all.
This chapter is the literary equivalent of a final sea day,
when empty suitcases reappear for packing, when addresses are
exchanged and tips dispensed, and when all crewmen, formerly
relaxed and loquacious, gird themselves against embarkation of yet
another passenger load.

I hope readers have enjoyed their passage, that information and
opinions imparted herein have informed or amused. I wonder,
guiltily, whether *Crossing & Cruising* really qualifies as history,
with one chapter segueing chronologically into another; it is, rather,
an anthology of essays, historical and critical, offering vicarious
berths aboard present-day or vanished vessels. "What was it like
on board?" I hope these pages have lived up to the self-imposed
mandate of the introduction.

One great reward of my maritime career has been repeated

encounters with so many inhabitants of what is, as I have already suggested, a very small world. Owners and employees of cruise lines, shipyard and shore personnel, officers, crew, and staff of countless ships, fellow historians and colleagues, and a dedicated corps of repeat passengers remain a congenial, close-knit fraternity; I come across them all over the world in the course of my work. Just as the ships of my introduction materialize unexpectedly over the horizon, so shipping friends and shipmates continually reappear in my world as well.

A nice case in point: When I embarked on the *Crown Princess* for her first transatlantic crossing in 1990, the dance team on board was that incomparably graceful and talented pair James and Jackie McVicar. I had first encountered them during several *France* crossings in the early seventies; although we had exchanged occasional visits in both England and New York, I had not sailed with them for two decades. Needless to say, we picked up as though parted for no more than a week; good shipboard friends never really say good-bye.

The shipping world has changed over the past two decades, no more so than recently. The nineties ushered in as harsh an era for the cruise lines as it did for most of us. As we, conscience-stricken, renounce the extravagances of the preceding decade, the cruise industry uneasily does so, too. Whereas only seventeen newbuildings were launched in the seventies, thirty-four saw life in the eighties. Can enough recession-plagued passengers, new or old, fill them? Retrenchment and consolidation have inevitably taken a toll.

Indeed, today's shipping companies seem engrossed in an adult replay of the Monopoly games of our childhood, those deadly serious sessions that consumed entire rainy days. As suppertime approached, the game's pace intensified: Acquisitive owners of Boardwalk, Park Place, and those expensive red properties began absorbing their vulnerable, cash-starved opponents.

The same ruthless attrition typifies recent cruise-line strife. As we have already discussed, Holland America Line absorbed both Home Line and Wind Star Sail Cruises, only to be digested in turn by Carnival Cruise Lines, which, unsated, nibbles at Seabourn; Sitmar was swallowed whole by Princess Cruises; Kloster Cruises, having snapped up Royal Viking in the mid-eighties, has since disgorged most of it, sharing one hull with their recently ingested Royal Cruise Lines and two more with NCL; Royal Caribbean

Cruise Line has gulped down Admiral Cruises; Commodore Cruise Lines devoured Bermuda Star Line and is shadowing Crown Cruise Line.

Faced with the spectacle of this feeding frenzy, of big fish gobbling up little fish, independent new companies—Seabourn, Renaissance, Star Clipper, Radisson among them—must swim with care, avoiding predators until they grow sufficiently strong and agile, proving to owners and accountants alike that they can navigate the perilous nineties with impunity. I wish every new company well, for it is largely among bold new boys at the school of cruising that innovation flourishes.

Mary and I continue to spend about a quarter of our year at sea. I am sometimes asked if such extensive sea time cloys; in a word, never. Someone once said about passage on one of Cunard's *Queens* (I think it was I) that there was never anything to do but never enough time to do it all. I find all my sea days chockablock, even though I am at pains to avoid the sun and seldom do the same things that most passengers do.

What do I do on board? During a *Norway* week three years ago, I kept an abbreviated diary:

Saturday: Pick up galleys and embark.

Sunday: 0530–0830: Write letters.
0930–1200: Proofread galleys.
1200–1330: Start cleaning *France* exhibition.
1330: Lunch.
1400: Finish cleaning *France* exhibition.
1500: Nap during Superbowl broadcast.
2030: Dinner w/Mai Britt & Robin Rhinehart.

Monday: 0930–1230: More galley proofing.
1230: Walked and took photographs.
1330: Lunch.
1400–1530: Final galley corrections.
1600: Tea, followed by nap.
1900: Drinks with chief radio officer Jarl Nygaard.
2030: Captain's dinner.

Tuesday: 0600–0830: Write letters.
0930–1200: Organize lecture slides.
1230: Walk on deck.

1330: Lunch.
1400–1530: Organize more lecture slides.
1600: Tea, followed by nap.
1930: Lecture for passengers.
2030: Dinner.
2400: Lecture for crew.

Wednesday: 0900–1230: Letters.
1230: Climb atop funnel with chief engineer Harald Vaagnes.
1300: Ashore to St. Thomas for *New York Times* and post office errands.
1430: Tape new voice-over for *France* film.
1600: Tea, followed by nap.
1900: Drinks with the Morrises.
2030: Hotel director for dinner.

Thursday: 0900–1330: Sign books in drugstore.
1330: Lunch.
1400: Organize lecture slides.
1600: Tea.
1700: Lecture for passengers.
2030: Chief purser for dinner.

Friday: 0900–1330: Letters.
1330: Lunch.
1400: Televised interview with cruise director.
1600: Visit engineer's museum.
1945–2030: *Tales for Travelers* performance with Mary for passengers.
2200: Pack slides, return slide trays, sign more books.

Saturday: Disembark and deliver corrected ms.

Mary and I embark with an inordinate amount of what my father called clobber—boxes of lecture slides and reams of paper, including several months' worth of letters long overdue for response as well as manuscripts or galleys in the process of completion or revision. During the *Norway* week itemized above, I think the galleys in question were for a Royal Caribbean Cruise Line history due at cruise's end.

We disembark, incidentally, with even more paper, for it is my habit to collect and file scrupulously everything delivered to the cabin—daily programs, invitations, notes, letters, photographs, etc., cruising's ephemera that, years from now, I hope another historian may find invaluable.

The *France* exhibition mentioned above is one that I arranged nearly a decade ago. Mounted in a wall case outside the ship's drugstore, it shows the *France's* construction and public rooms, together with some of her signs, brochures, and memorabilia, a primer for *Norway* passengers about their vessel's past. It is mounted, alas, in a glass case never designed for long-term display; each time I board, I have to brush off a film of dust and clean the glass doors' interiors.

Much of my passenger time is spent on administrative chores that could just as easily be accomplished in an office ashore. But, by the same token, there is invaluable return on those hours spent on board. Long sessions at a table in the *Norway's* International Deck's library for instance, are enriched by shipboard traffic; officers, passengers, and staff are forever passing by, providing an interruptive input that I enjoy. Isolated work in the cabin is inevitably discommoded by a mirror—desks are also dressing tables these days, and working *en face* with my reflection is almost as unsettling as showering in one of those mirrored tubs on board the *Crystal Harmony*.

More complex than how my time passes at sea is exactly what role I fulfill on board: part historian, part entertainer, part snoop, and most devotedly, part keeper of the passenger flame. Though in one sense sedentary—never sweating in the racket-ball court or loping about the deck or struggling ashore with golf clubs, and seldom in the swimming pool or lazing in the sun—I am never idle; and though Muzak appalls and I eschew production shows, I try hard to keep an open mind; as Le Corbusier once remarked, "*J'ai une haute curiosité.*"

Is such an unconventional passenger really qualified to evaluate present-day cruising? I believe so, for I doubt that anyone sails as regularly on as wide a variety of old and new ships. Moreover, the shipboard I cherish is the shipboard of tradition, of passenger basics that never have and never will change, whether Atlantic or Caribbean. The euphoria of departure, of sailing, of new faces and new conversation, of cabins, of reading, reflection, and celebration—those are the recurring rituals enjoyed at both ends of this century, seagoing constants and timeworn pleasures of the voyage.

They are not, incidentally, listed in any of the top-heavy daily programs devised to divert us. I am always struck by how hard cruise lines work to amuse their clientele. But I also wonder, is not shipboard itself diversion enough? I contend that today's passengers need far less hand-holding than companies seem desperate to provide. If I disembark having persuaded even one Newpassenger couple to see through cruising's forest for shipboard trees, then I feel I have earned my keep.

The ship has been cleared now, and we can go ashore. Every time Mary and I disembark onto Manhattan's piers, we invariably meet smiling Frank Scaramell, the man in charge of security at the Passenger Ship Terminal. Much as we love ships and the sea, we also love having Frank greet us at the foot of the gangway, welcoming us home to our New York.

I don't think this marine historian could live anywhere else, despite the decline of our passenger shipping. For too much of the year, Manhattan's terminal is moribund: From the January departure of world cruise ships until the Bermuda boats start sailing in April, the piers play host exclusively to flower shows and flea markets.

But New York still exerts a powerful pull. Crowding the banks of what old-timers still call the North River, the city has been witness to so much ocean-liner history. Here, on the threshold of this great city-port, most of America's immigrants were greeted by the verdigris benevolence of Bartholdi's statue before submitting to the ordeal of Ellis Island. Here, too, *Aquitania, Normandie*, and *France* were saluted as they first steamed upharbor and here, at the very pier where Mary and I so often disembark, poor *Lafayette* came to such a tragic end.

Walter Lord has said it so well: What the riverboat was to New Orleans, the ocean liner is to New York. Although Cunard's *Queen Elizabeth 2* is the world's only surviving ocean liner, New York has become an increasingly busy cruise port. In addition to the aforementioned Bermuda trade, many companies have started offering round-trips up to New England and Canada, fall foliage cruises that are increasingly well booked. Additionally, cruise ships that are being seasonally repositioned between North American and European markets often sail in or out of the port. And always, when a cruise line wants to show off an important new vessel, New York is invariably scheduled as maiden U.S. call.

For whether liner or cruise ship, whether crossing or cruising,

Officer Frank Scaramell, perpetually on duty, it seems, at Pier 88, welcomes Mary Maxtone-Graham home to New York from Southampton. (Author's collection)

it makes little difference; shipboard, I trust readers will now agree, is still blessedly shipboard.

> *For a rolled, uncreased copy of the jacket's cruise-ship chart suitable for framing, send $10.00 payable to the author at 117 West 78th Street, New York, New York 10024; overseas customers should remit an international money order in the amount of U.S. $12.00, or a Sterling check for £7.50.*

Bibliography

Ardman, Harvey. *"Normandie," Her Life and Times*. New York: Franklin Watts, 1985.

Barbance, Marthe. *Histoire de la Compagnie Générale Transatlantique*. Paris: Arts et Métiers Graphiques, 1955.

Barr, Robert. *In a Steamer Chair*. New York: Frederick A. Stokes, 1892.

de Baudéan, Captain Raoul. *Captain of the Ile*. Translated by Salvatore Attanasio. New York: McGraw-Hill, 1960.

Braynard, Frank O. *Picture History of the "Normandie."* New York: Dover Publications, 1987.

Coleman, Terry. *Passage to America*. Harmondsworth, Middlesex: Penguin Books, 1976.

Foucart, Bruno, Charles Offrey, François Robichon, and Claude Villers. *"Normandie," Queen of the Seas*. New York: Vendome Press, 1985.

Gibson-Martin, W. A. *Ship Furnishing and Decoration*. Liverpool: Journal of Commerce, 1932.

Gonnard, René. *L'Emigration Européenne au XIXème Siècle*. Paris: Librairie Armand Colin, 1906.

Harding, Steven. *Gray Ghost*. Missoula, Mont.: Pictorial Histories, 1982.

Kennedy, Ludovic, ed. *A Book of Sea Journeys*. Bungay, Suffolk: Fontana Collins, 1982.

Konings, Chris. *"Queen Elizabeth" at War*. Wellingborough, Northamptonshire: Patrick Stephens, 1985.

Marin, Pierre-Henri. *Les Paquebots, Ambassadeurs des Mers*. Paris: Gallimard, 1989.

Mencken, August, ed. *First-Class Passenger*. New York: Alfred A. Knopf, 1938.

293

Miller, William H., and David F. Hutchings. *Transatlantic Liners at War*. New York: Arco, 1985.

Mogui, Jean-Pierre. *Le "Normandie," Seigneur de l'Atlantique*. Paris: Editions Denoel, 1985.

Novitski, Joseph. *"Windstar," the Building of a Sailship*. New York: Macmillan, 1987.

Olson, Harvey S. *Aboard and Abroad*. Philadelphia & New York: Lippincott, 1959.

Parlette, Ralph. *A Globegadder's Diary*. Chicago: Parlette-Padget, 1927.

Peillard, Leonce. *Sur les Chemins de l'Océan*. Paris: Librairie Hachette, 1972.

Pettré, Commandant Christian. *Splendeur et Rouille "France."* Paris: Editions du Pen Duick, 1978.

Roberts, Cecil. *The Grand Cruise*. London: Hodder and Stoughton, 1963.

Roberts, Kenneth L. *Why Europe Leaves Home*. New York: Bobbs-Merrill, 1922.

Robinson, Wilfrid C. *Antwerp, An Historical Sketch*. New York: Benziger Bros., 1904.

Russell, W. Clark. *The Emigrant Ship*. New York: Cassell, 1893.

Shaum, John H., Jr., and William H. Flayhart III. *Majesty at Sea*. New York: Norton, 1981.

Schaap, Dick, and Dick Schaap. *A Bridge to the Seven Seas*. New York: Holland American Cruises, 1973.

Steiner, Edward A. *The Immigrant Tide: Its Ebb and Flow*. New York: Fleming H. Revell, 1909.

Turner, Robert D. *The Pacific Empresses*. Victoria, Canada: Sono Nis Press, 1981.

Walker, Mack. *Germany and the Emigration, 1816–1885*. Cambridge, Mass.: Harvard University Press, 1964.

Warren, Mark. *The Quadruple-Screw Turbine-Driven Cunard*

Liner "Aquitania." Wellingborough, Northamptonshire: Patrick Stephens, 1988.

Wilson, George. *"France."* Rennes: Editions Ouest-France, 1989.

Works Projects Administration. *A Maritime History of New York.* Garden City, N.Y.: Doubleday, Doran, 1941.

Index

(Page numbers in **boldface** refer to illustrations.)

About the Author

JOHN MAXTONE-GRAHAM grew up on both sides of the North Atlantic. Son of a Scots father and an American mother, he rejoiced in dual nationality until his eighteenth birthday, before choosing to become an American. Maxtone-Graham made his first crossing—eastbound, on the little *Minnewaska*—at the age of six months in 1930. Since then, he has sailed hundreds of times on both crossings and cruises.

Although Maxtone-Graham was always bewitched by the great liners that carried him to sea, it was not until long after he had established a career as a Broadway stage manager that he put his accumulated knowledge and expertise to good use: *The Only Way to Cross* was published in 1972 (Macmillan) and has remained in print ever since, an instant, evocative classic. Since then, marine historian Maxtone-Graham has produced additional volumes about the sea and is in constant demand as a lecturer both afloat and ashore. When not at sea, he and his second wife, Mary, live in a brownstone in New York City.

ENDPAPERS: Group picture in a costume ball aboard *Conte Biancamarno*, 1928. (Courtesy of Jane T. Zweifler, private collection)